Restrictive Language Policy in Practice

BILINGUAL EDUCATION & BILINGUALISM

Series Editors: Nancy H. Hornberger *(University of Pennsylvania, USA)* and Wayne E. Wright *(Purdue University, USA)*

Bilingual Education and Bilingualism is an international, multidisciplinary series publishing research on the philosophy, politics, policy, provision and practice of language planning, Indigenous and minority language education, multilingualism, multiculturalism, biliteracy, bilingualism and bilingual education. The series aims to mirror current debates and discussions. New proposals for single-authored, multiple-authored, or edited books in the series are warmly welcomed, in any of the following categories or others authors may propose: overview or introductory texts; course readers or general reference texts; focus books on particular multilingual education program types; school-based case studies; national case studies; collected cases with a clear programmatic or conceptual theme; and professional education manuals.

Full details of all the books in this series and of all our other publications can be found on http://www.multilingual-matters.com, or by writing to Multilingual Matters, St Nicholas House, 31-34 High Street, Bristol BS1 2AW, UK.

BILINGUAL EDUCATION & BILINGUALISM: 103

Restrictive Language Policy in Practice

English Learners in Arizona

Amy J. Heineke

MULTILINGUAL MATTERS
Bristol • Buffalo • Toronto

This book is dedicated to Cynthia Laube and John Heineke,
my first and favorite teachers.

Library of Congress Cataloging in Publication Data
A catalog record for this book is available from the Library of Congress.
Names: Heineke, Amy J., author.
Title: Restrictive Language Policy in Practice: English Learners in Arizona/
    Amy J. Heineke.
Description: Bristol; Buffalo: Multilingual Matters, [2016] | Series: Bilingual Education
    & Bilingualism: 103 | Includes bibliographical references and index.
Identifiers: LCCN 2016022812| ISBN 9781783096411 (hbk : alk. paper) | ISBN
    9781783096435 (epub) | ISBN 9781783096442 (kindle)
Subjects: LCSH: Language policy--Arizona. | Education, Bilingual--Arizona. |
    English language--Study and teaching--Arizona--Foreign speakers.
Classification: LCC P119.32.A75 H45 2016 | DDC 306.44/9791--dc23 LC record
    available at https://lccn.loc.gov/2016022812

British Library Cataloguing in Publication Data
A catalogue entry for this book is available from the British Library.

ISBN-13: 978-1-78309-641-1 (hbk)
ISBN-13: 978-1-78309-921-4 (pbk)

Multilingual Matters
UK: St Nicholas House, 31-34 High Street, Bristol BS1 2AW, UK.
USA: UTP, 2250 Military Road, Tonawanda, NY 14150, USA.
Canada: UTP, 5201 Dufferin Street, North York, Ontario M3H 5T8, Canada.

Website: www.multilingual-matters.com
Twitter: Multi_Ling_Mat
Facebook: https://www.facebook.com/multilingualmatters
Blog: www.channelviewpublications.wordpress.com

The policy of Multilingual Matters/Channel View Publications is to use papers that
are natural, renewable and recyclable products, made from wood grown in sustainable
forests. In the manufacturing process of our books, and to further support our policy,
preference is given to printers that have FSC and PEFC Chain of Custody certification.
The FSC and/or PEFC logos will appear on those books where full certification has been
granted to the printer concerned.

Typeset by Deanta Global Publishing Services Limited.
Printed and bound in the UK by the CPI Books Group Ltd.
Printed and bound in the US by Edwards Brothers Malloy, Inc.

Contents

Part 3: Discussion

Part 1

Context

1 Introduction

The face of classrooms and schools across the US is changing with more cultural and linguistic diversity today than ever before (US Department of Education, 2010). The student body in K-12 schools continues to become more linguistically diverse as the number of English learners (ELs)[1] rapidly increases in classrooms in all corners of the nation (Gándara & Hopkins, 2010; Shin & Kominski, 2010). Representing a subgroup of children and adolescents who speak a native language other than English, students labeled as ELs are still in the process of attaining English as measured by standardized tests of language proficiency in speaking, listening, reading and writing (Linquanti & Cook, 2013). In the past decade, the population of ELs enrolled in US public schools has nearly doubled, climbing from 3.5 million to 5.3 million, with approximately 80% of students coming from Spanish-speaking homes and families (Gándara & Hopkins, 2010; National Clearinghouse for English Language Acquisition [NCELA], 2010). If the growth trend continues, one in every three students will be considered an EL by the year 2043 (Crawford & Krashen, 2007). Nevertheless, ELs are often the most underperforming student population in the US (Gándara & Hopkins, 2010).

The *EL achievement gap* (Fry, 2007) denotes the current reality that ELs' academic performance remains substantially lower than their mainstream peers in nearly every measure of achievement (Gándara & Hopkins, 2010; Zamora, 2007). Minority students have long been juxtaposed from the mainstream in schools with the common assumption that diminished social resources outside of school leads to underperformance at school (Murrell, 2007). The historical trend of minority students having poor standardized test scores in comparison with mainstream peers' scores has led to the oft-cited phenomena of the *achievement gap* – inequality of educational outcomes for African Americans, Latinos and Native Americans as compared to European Americans (Meece & Kurtz-Costes, 2001). When analyzing the academic outcomes specifically for those labeled as ELs, the achievement gap widens even further, demonstrating that US schools have not met the unique and diverse needs of this heterogeneous group of students (Fry, 2007; Heineke *et al.*, 2012). For example, in a nationwide assessment of fourth-grade reading, 8% of ELs scored at or above the proficient level as compared to 40% of non-ELs; in eighth grade, only 4% of ELs scored proficient in contrast to 36% of non-ELs (National Center for Education Statistics [NCES], 2015). Further exacerbating the issue of supporting and measuring ELs' learning, standardized tests written for and statistically normed on native English speakers serve as the sole measure of EL student performance and achievement (Adebi & Gándara, 2006).

As educators and other stakeholders across the nation seek to understand and close the academic achievement gaps between native and non-native speakers of English (Fry, 2007), various questions continue to arise: What is the best way to educate ELs? How can educators support the teaching and learning of ELs? The persistence of EL achievement gaps throughout various approaches and models of language education has led national and international educational researchers and practitioners to fix the microscope on the recent shift in EL educational policy and practice in the southwestern state of Arizona (Carpenter *et al.*, 2006; Fry, 2007). Adopting what scholars now deem to be the most restrictive educational context in the US for ELs, Arizona's English Language Development (ELD) approach requires ELs to be separated daily from mainstream, English-speaking peers for four hours of skill-based, English language instruction with discrete blocks of time dedicated to grammar, vocabulary, conversation, reading and writing (Gándara & Hopkins, 2010; Heineke, 2015).

This text investigates this unique context of language policy in practice, honing in on the state of Arizona education for ELs five years after the initial implementation of the ELD approach to teaching and learning. Like peeling layers away from the dense and complex series of processes and policies that directly and indirectly influence EL education, the chapters that follow provide windows into the lived experiences of those engaged in the daily work of language policy. Drawing from the varied perspectives of teachers, leaders, administrators, teacher educators, lawmakers and community activists, the text presents the complex realities of restrictive language policy in practice for educators, stakeholders and readers to consider the definitive impacts on the large and growing population of ELs in the state and nation.

The State of Arizona Education

Situated on land that was Mexican territory prior to the Gadsen Purchase of 1854, Arizona's geography includes a 370-mile border with Mexico; over 25% of the state's land is designated for tribal reservations (Milem *et al.,* 2013). In part because of the rich history of both groups in the Grand Canyon state, Latinos and Native Americans make up greater proportions in the state population than in the US as a whole (see Figure 1.1): twice the nation's proportion of Latinos and four times the proportion of Native Americans live in Arizona (Milem *et al.*, 2013). In Arizona classrooms and schools, the past 15 years have brought dramatic transformation in students' racial and ethnic backgrounds, where students of color are the increasing majority. Latinos now surpass Whites as the largest group enrolled in Arizona K-12 classrooms (Milem *et al.*, 2013). As a whole, Arizona K-12

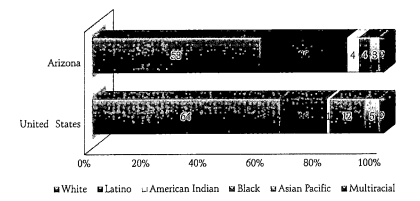

White   Latino   American Indian   Black   Asian Pacific   Multiracial

Figure 1.1 Arizona and US population demographics, 2010

education lags behind national averages and trends of student performance, with multiple data sets in the past decade showing negative gains across all demographic groups and academic subjects (Ushomirsky, 2013).

Challenges faced by ELs in classrooms across the state highlight the shortcomings of Arizona's education system. Similar to the 51% growth nationwide, there was a 48% increase in ELs in Arizona schools in 10 years, with approximately 94% speaking Spanish as a native language (NCELA, 2010). The 166,000 ELs enrolled in Arizona schools in 2007–2008 comprised 15% of the state student population (Jiménez-Castellanos *et al.*, 2013); however, existing policies and programming within the education system in Arizona have yet to make a meaningful dent in successfully supporting ELs' development and achievement. In 2010–2011, 86% of Arizona ELs scored below basic proficiency on Arizona's Instrument to Measure Standards (AIMS), whereas only 36% of non-ELs scored below; more shockingly, 13% of ELs scored at or above basic, in stark contrast to 64% of non-ELs (Haycock, 2011). Additionally, graduation rates vary based on language proficiency, with only 25% of ELs graduating from 4-year Arizona high schools compared to 85% of native English speakers (see Figure 1.2; Center for the Future of Arizona [CFA], 2013). Consistently ranking last nationally in per-pupil spending, scant EL funding has led to two decades of legal battles via the *Flores v. Arizona* case at both state and federal levels (Hogan, 2014; Jiménez-Castellanos *et al.*, 2013). Despite the dismal state of educational opportunities for ELs in Arizona, educational deficiencies take a backseat to other issues concerning language minority populations that receive more national focus, such as immigration.

Arizona is currently the epicenter of the contemporary immigration debate in the US, making national and international headlines in recent years for controversial policies and practices. A growing anti-immigrant sentiment has pervaded Arizona for the past 15 years (Kohut *et al.*, 2006),

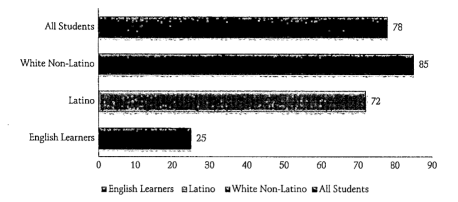

Figure 1.2 Arizona 4-year high-school graduation rates

even as the number of undocumented immigrants soared 300% from 1996 to 2009 to an estimated 460,000 individuals (Sandoval & Tambini, 2014). Negative sentiments provoked anti-immigration movements and legislation, charged by local law enforcement and state lawmakers. What began with infamous Sheriff Joe Arpaio's movement to enforce federal immigration policy at the local level in Maricopa County around the Phoenix metropolitan area (i.e. Section 287g of the Immigration and Nationality Act in 2007) evolved into the controversial 'show-me-your-papers' law in 2010 after the passage of Senate Bill 1070. Critiqued by opponents for its lack of reform to provide paths to legal residence or citizenship, SB 1070 nonetheless achieved proponents' desired purpose of 'attrition through enforcement' (SB 1070, 2010: 1), as approximately 1000 undocumented individuals departed Arizona voluntarily through fear or involuntarily via deportation (Sandoval & Tambini, 2014). In recent years, this crisis has resulted in economic and educational decline as immigrant children and families have left the state, many of them ELs enrolled in Arizona schools (Jiménez-Castellanos et al., 2013; Milem et al., 2013).

Pervasive anti-immigrant sentiments, corresponding to the presumed threat of linguistic diversity, led to widespread public support of educational policies touting English monolingualism (Crawford, 2000). Figure 1.3 summarizes notable language policies in Arizona. Situated between the successful English-only education movements in California (i.e. Proposition 227, 1998) and Massachusetts (i.e. Question 2, 2004), Proposition 203 passed in 2000, declaring English as the official medium of instruction in Arizona public schools and nearly eradicating bilingual education. Since then, Arizona schools have served as primary locales where monolingual and assimilative policies manifest in daily practice with culturally and linguistically diverse children and adolescents. Funded

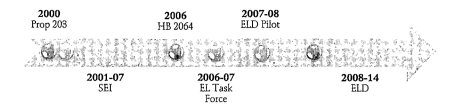

Figure 1.3 Brief history of language policy in Arizona

by millionaire software entrepreneur Ron Unz, the *English for the Children* campaign led voters to pass restrictive language policy by huge margins (Delisario & Dunne, 2000). To avoid submersion, or the sink-or-swim approach of placing ELs in English-only settings, policymakers called for Structured English Immersion (SEI), where ELs learn content and language simultaneously in classrooms with English-proficient peers (Echevarria *et al.*, 2013). ➔Clay elements. Spanish· speaking classes + English only

When SEI did not improve ELs' achievement, perhaps due to the lack of research base in the approach or the widespread implementation across the state, House Bill 2064 called for a more prescriptive, cost-efficient approach developed by the EL Task Force (Combs, 2012; Hogan, 2014; Krashen, 2001, 2004; MacSwan, 2004; Mahoney *et al.*, 2004, 2005; Wright, 2005a). In the resulting ELD model, which went into effect in fall 2008, schools grouped students in classrooms based on language proficiency as determined and classified by the standardized Arizona English Language Learner Assessment (AZELLA). With 4 hours of mandated skill-based language instruction, ELD classrooms excluded typical content areas, such as science or social studies, to instead prioritize the explicit teaching of English-language reading, writing, grammar, vocabulary and conversation (Clark, 2009). Now multiple school years removed from the ELD implementation, this text explores the perspectives and experiences of educational stakeholders engaged in language policy work.

Language Policy Appropriation: Layers and Players

Language policy refers broadly to the management mechanisms, practices and beliefs that influence language use in a community or society (Shohamy, 2006; Spolsky, 2004). Traditionally, the field of language planning and policy emphasized the former, probing how nation-states strategically planned in attempt to resolve particular language problems (Fishman, 1979; Haugen, 1972). In this way, scholarship centered on the political authority's top-down efforts to change daily language use, typically by targeting languages to serve as mediums of communication in public settings such as government, politics, commerce and education (Schmidt, 2000). In the past four decades, the field evolved as researchers captured the dynamism and complexity of language policy in local communities, recognizing the intersection of ideologies, official regulations, unofficial guidelines and practices as situated within unique sociocultural contexts (Johnson, 2013; McCarty, 2011; Ricento, 2000; Ricento & Hornberger, 1996; Shohamy, 2006; Spolsky, 2004). In this way, moving beyond an emphasis on the top-down planning processes of governments and political entities, language policy is understood to be more complex, referred to as 'an integrated and dynamic whole that operates within intersecting planes of local, regional, national, and global influence' (McCarty, 2011: 8). The educational domain exemplifies the complexity of language policy, where formal regulations and informal expectations attempt to manage and influence the language use of participants from varied language backgrounds, beliefs and repertoires within classrooms, schools and communities (Ricento & Hornberger, 1996; Spolsky, 2007).

Drawing from extant definitions and understandings in the field, I conceptualize *language policy in practice* as the 'integrated and dynamic whole' (McCarty, 2011: 6) that merges the interrelated and multidirectional facets of ideologies, paradigms, regulations and practices as situated within unique sociocultural contexts (Johnson, 2013; McCarty, 2011; Pennycook, 2000). *Language ideologies* are cultural systems of ideas, often discussed as beliefs, feelings, attitudes, assumptions and orientations concerning language use in a community (Gee, 2005; Ricento, 2000; Ruiz, 1984). Grounded in ideologies and often inconspicuously driving formal regulations, *policy paradigms* regulate what community members perceive as viable solutions and actions, described by scholars as unofficial, covert or *de facto* policies (Johnson, 2013; Mehta, 2013; Menken, 2008; Shohamy, 2006). Language policies, referred to here as *policy regulations*, are formal attempts to manage and standardize language use through power and politics (Spolsky, 2004). Johnson (2013: 9) describes this facet as 'official regulations often enacted in the form of written documents, intended to effect some change in the form, function, use, or acquisition of language'. *Policy practices* emphasize the daily work of individuals across multiple layers of policy (Johnson, 2013). With daily communication in life and education occurring through language (Gee, 2005), individuals make decisions about how they will communicate with others in and across these settings and in so doing 'express, work out, contest, interpret, and at some level analyze language policies' (Ricento & Hornberger, 1996: 420). When making meaning of language policy in practice, or the daily work across layers and players involved in EL education, the multidirectional interactions and influences of ideologies, paradigms, regulations and practices must be considered (Figure 1.4).

Within the context of the southwestern US, language policy has prioritized the English language, evidenced by explicit regulations and

Sociocultural Context

Figure 1.4 Language policy in practice

implicit expectations for English as the primary language of government, commerce and education (Crawford, 2000; Ricento, 2000; Schmidt, 2000). Grounded in the monolingual ideology that assumes the need to assimilate immigrants (Schmidt, 2000; Valdéz, 2001), restrictive language policies have persisted as the 'highly emotional and volatile political issue in the United States over the past three decades' (Schmidt, 2000: 2). With increased attention to the politics around language, the past 30 years have been marked by top-down attempts to protect the English language while restricting the use of other languages in what Crawford (2000: 1) refers to as the 'social phenomenon of Babel in reverse'. Scholars have long recognized education as the center for public policy, including language policy, with classrooms serving as prime sites to assimilate students who enter school speaking languages other than English (Levinson & Sutton, 2001; Spolksy, 2006; Valdéz, 2000). Whereas bilingual ideologies once prevailed across the US, particularly following the civil rights movement in the 1960s, a national shift from prioritizing bilingualism to English language acquisition in schools has occurred over time. Mirroring the national shift, regional English-only movements have yielded restrictive language education policies in California, Arizona and Massachusetts in the past two decades (Crawford, 2000). Despite official regulations attempting to restrict practice, local educators engage in daily work where they actively make decisions about language policy (Johnson, 2013; Shohamy, 2006).

Particularly when situated in contexts where policies attempt to restrict the language of daily practice, research must capture the complexities of language and language use (Hornberger & Johnson, 2007; McCarty, 2011; Menken & García, 2010). Rather than traditional research focused on the laws and policies themselves or the evaluation of those policies after the assumed top-down and linear policy process, a sociocultural approach to policy research acknowledges the co-construction of educational policy and change (Levinson & Sutton, 2001). Policy relies upon the interplay of structure, culture and agency (Datnow *et al.*, 2002); thus, the sociocultural paradigm highlights agency within structure as actors interpret and negotiate meaning (Levinson & Sutton, 2001; Ricento & Hornberger, 1996). In this framework, there is no divide between policy formation and implementation, but rather the holistic construct of *appropriation* that 'highlights the way creative agents "take in" elements of policy, thereby incorporating these discursive and institutional resources into their own schemes of interest, motivation, and action' (Levinson & Sutton, 2001: 3). With various agents engaged in language policy work, researchers, educators and policymakers must focus on micro-level practice in schools and communities to understand how individuals and groups co-construct policy through active decisions and negotiations of macro-level structures (Ricento & Hornberger, 1996).

Within the field of sociocultural policy analysis, I draw from educational (Datnow *et al.*, 2002; Levinson & Sutton, 2001) and language policy (Hornberger & Johnson, 2007; Menken & García, 2010; Ricento, 2000; Ricento & Hornberger, 1996) researchers to recognize the multilayered nature of language policy in practice. The various layers, which span micro-level (e.g. classroom, school) to macro-level (e.g. state government) contexts, 'affect and interact with each other to varying degrees' (Ricento & Hornberger, 1996: 408). On each layer, various players (e.g. classroom teachers, school leaders, state administrators) interact with and negotiate language ideologies, policy paradigms and policy regulations in their daily practices, exercising their agency and engaging in policy appropriation, whether knowingly or unknowingly (Hornberger & Johnson, 2007; Levinson & Sutton, 2001; Menken & García, 2010; Ricento & Hornberger, 1996). Whereas traditional policy analysis emphasizes the authoritative role of policymakers, Ricento and Hornberger (1996) described the language policy *onion*, comprised of layer upon layer of persons and contexts influencing and influenced by changes in language policy (see Figure 1.5). I will refer to and expand on this onion conceptual imagery throughout this text in an effort to explicate the nature and interplay of the varied and diverse layers – and players – in US language policy.

Within this conceptual framework to study language policy in practice, classroom practitioners are at the center with other policy layers building out and around. In addition to the pertinent agency of the classroom teacher in appropriating language policy in practice, *intermediary actors*, those situated on the layers between the macro level of language policy and the micro level of classroom practice (Hornberger & Johnson, 2007) include school leaders (Datnow *et al.*, 2002; Elfers & Stritikus, 2014), district administrators (Datnow *et al.*, 2002; Hornberger & Johnson, 2007;

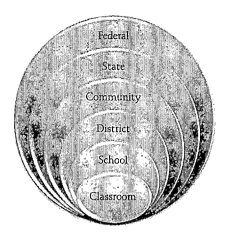

Figure 1.5 Language policy layers

Johnson & Freeman, 2010), state administrators (Datnow et al., 2002) and community leaders. Central to the framework and understanding of language policy appropriation, as policy moves across layers, it is interpreted, negotiated and modified before being carried out in practice (Levinson & Sutton, 2001; Ricento & Hornberger, 1996). Whereas past research has honed in on one particular layer, my study provides a comprehensive approach to the multiple layers and players of language policy in practice in the unique sociocultural context of ELD education in the southwestern state of Arizona.

Background and Organization of the Book

I began teaching in Arizona in 2002, shortly after Proposition 203 passed, which eliminated most bilingual education programs across the state. My first teaching assignment was with kindergarteners, some of whom had immigrated from Mexico only weeks before and were accustomed to speaking Spanish exclusively at home and in their communities. Despite moving to the southwest in hopes of using my bilingualism to teach Mexican immigrant and Mexican American students at a South Phoenix elementary school, I found myself within a monolingual ideological context which mandated English-only formal instruction and informal speech in the classroom. Whereas Proposition 203 called for SEI, the only preparation that I received was adamant pressure from school administrators to speak, read and write in English only. Fear dominated the school environment: we teachers were threatened with dismissal for speaking Spanish anywhere in the school setting, and all Spanish-medium texts and materials were expelled from classrooms. Nevertheless, with little direction to teach ELs under the new policy, and with the cheery faces of 35 five- and six-year-olds greeting me each morning eager to learn, I enacted what worked best for my young students as the teacher in the classroom with them day in and day out: I closed the classroom door and used Spanish language instruction to support early literacy development.

I shifted from classroom practitioner to educational researcher as Arizona state leaders initiated efforts to standardize and stipulate the teaching and learning of ELs. The passage of House Bill 2064 led to the formation of the EL Task Force, which designed the more restrictive ELD model of instruction that was first piloted in 2007–2008 and formally implemented in 2008–2009. I conducted my dissertation research (Heineke, 2009) at a Phoenix metropolitan elementary school in the first semester of policy implementation, working with a study group of ELD classroom teachers and an instructional coach engaged in daily policy work. As the policy pendulum swung in the opposite direction from the nebulous SEI model, practitioners maneuvered and negotiated the restrictive mandates within the skill-based ELD instructional block with ELs segregated from mainstream peers based on language assessment score. That is, whereas previous policy merged ELs with English-proficient peers to learn math, science and social studies, the policy shift now required that ELs be placed in separate classrooms to learn English grammar and other skills. *Compliance* dominated study group conversations, due to top-down pressures from state, district and school administrators to act in accordance with the 4-hour structure, which lacked substance and detail, as well as corresponding materials and training to support teaching and learning, in its first year of implementation.

Despite moving to the Midwest state of Illinois in 2010 to take a faculty position in bilingual education, I remained intrigued by the language policy and educational context in Arizona. Moreover, after my experiences as an Arizona elementary teacher during those tempestuous years of initial language policy implementation, I felt committed to EL students similar to those in my elementary classroom in South Phoenix. Five school years after the official implementation of ELD policy and my original dissertation research in the 2008–2009 school year, I returned to Arizona in the 2013–2014 school year to revisit language policy in practice through the perspectives and experiences of individuals engaged in the policy work. My qualitative study, grounded in sociocultural theory, centered on interviews with 26 stakeholders from the layers of language policy, including ELD teachers, school leaders, district administrators, state administrators, state legislators, language education experts, community advocates and teacher educators. The result of that research, this text explores the complexities of education in Arizona through investigation of the multiple and intricate layers and players engaged in language policy in practice as well as how those layers and players interact and influence each other and the education of ELs.

In Part 1 of the text, the introductory chapters aim to set the context through historical and contemporary lenses on Arizona educational policy and practice, specifically focused on EL education. Chapter 2 outlines the history of EL education in Arizona, organized around the primary legislation that shaped the evolution of Arizona language policy, Proposition 203, which shifted the once bilingual context to a predominantly monolingual state. Following the English for the Children initiative and the passage of Proposition 203 in 2000, state legislation required English-medium instruction for students labeled as ELs. To skirt federal mandates against submersion, Arizona language policy called for schools to implement SEI, an approach that placed ELs in general education classrooms with proficient English-speaking peers for simultaneous content and language instruction. This nebulous approach to the teaching and learning of ELs became more restrictive with the passage of House Bill 2064 in 2006, which created and charged the EL Task Force to design a standardized SEI program model for implementation across Arizona schools. Educators implemented the state-mandated program model, referred to as *ELD*, in the 2008–2009 school year.

Characterized by four hours of skill-based language instruction, ELD is the current approach to the teaching and learning of ELs in the state of Arizona. To provide a holistic understanding of this unique and restrictive language policy, Chapter 3 explores the facets of the current ELD approach, including the role of standardized language assessments, the 4-hour block of language instruction and mandated teacher preparation and training. The ELD model centers around students' scores on standardized tests of language proficiency; if parents indicate a language other than English on the Home Language Survey, then students must take the AZELLA. If their AZELLA scores do not indicate English language proficiency, then students are labeled as ELs and placed in classrooms apart from proficient English-speaking peers for four hours of skill-based language instruction, including designated time blocks for grammar, vocabulary, conversation, reading and writing. To close the chapter and the first part of the text, I describe my 2014 qualitative study of Arizona language policy across classroom, school, district, state and community layers.

The findings of the investigation comprise Part 2 of the text, organized by layers of Arizona language policy: classroom, local school district, state education and state government. Chapters 4 and 5 begin with the local context of language policy in practice. Situated in the diverse suburban community of Greenwood, the narrative explores the multiple layers and players within one elementary school district, including classroom teachers, school leaders and district administrators. Starting with the center of the onion (Ricento & Hornberger, 1996), Chapter 4 begins with an introduction to the local context of Greenwood[2] and then provides thick description of the experiences of three ELD classroom teachers across primary, intermediate and middle-school contexts in the district. Chapter 5 then considers the actions and interactions between and across adjacent policy players of classroom teachers, school leaders, district coaches and district administrators. By building out from the center rather than beginning with the top and working down, the findings chapters delve into interpretations and interactions within and across the layers and players that directly influence language policy in local practice with ELs (Ricento & Hornberger, 1996).

Spanning out from the local educational context, Chapters 6 and 7 explore how state-level layers and players shape language policy in practice with foci on state education and state government. Chapter 6 focuses on the education-specific layers and players in the state of Arizona. Using the perspectives and experiences of Arizona Department of Education (ADE) administrators, EL Task Force members, teacher educators and a charter school leader, the third findings chapter probes the complexities across state educational layers through lenses of position, power and ideology and considers individual, social and historical influences impacting state players' perceptions on overarching issues in the ELD approach. Chapter 7 then moves outward to the broader layers and players within state government, including state and federal educational laws, policies and guidelines and the state legislators and community leaders who use them to politicize and prioritize practices in classrooms, schools and districts. In this tight-knit and powerful network of legislators, lobbyists and advocates at the macro level of state government, findings probe various players' lenses, agendas and agency brought to the policy conversation in the attempt to change practice in Arizona schools.

Part 3 merges and discusses the findings to first probe the holistic, integrated and complex realities of Arizona language policy in practice and then provide recommendations to improve the education of ELs within and beyond the state of Arizona. The discussion of the findings, Chapter 8 melds policy layers and players to explore complexities of the holistic educational landscape of Arizona. Examining language policy in practice across layers, the discussion considers how players engage in daily policy work as influenced by and influencing language ideologies, unofficial policy paradigms and official policy regulations. I explore the alignment, misalignment and dependency resulting from players' policy negotiation and the corresponding outcomes – both intended and unintended. The chapter closes by considering the impact of players' agency on Arizona students, describing the amplification of appropriation when moving to external layers of language policy. Chapter 9 explores implications and recommendations for Arizona stakeholders as they consider directions to improve education for ELs, including comprehensive revisions to language policy and considerations for issues such as teacher preparation. In addition to language policy in the state of Arizona, recommendations expand to policy players in other contexts seeking to understand a holistic approach to policy and practice for diverse students.

Note

(1) While I use the term English learners (ELs) throughout the text, direct quotations from some sources utilize the term English language learners (ELLs). These terms are synonymous.
(2) All location and participant names are pseudonyms.

2 Looking Back: Historical Lens on Arizona Policies and Practices

My study investigates the multiple layers and players influencing the education of English learners (ELs) in the state of Arizona (Hornberger & Johnson, 2007; Levinson & Sutton, 2001; Ricento & Hornberger, 1996). In this chapter, I integrate educational policy and extant literature to thickly describe the history of EL education in Arizona. I first provide context on state and local layers of Arizona education, followed by an exploration of the past century of EL education in Arizona as defined by two major language policies: Proposition 203 (2000) and House Bill 2064 (2006). A third factor driving EL education policy for two decades, the *Flores v. Arizona* court case, is woven throughout the sequential narrative on bilingual, Structured English Immersion (SEI) and English Language Development (ELD) instruction in this southwestern state. In future chapters, I share findings on language policy in practice during the initial five years of ELD through the complex and dynamic interplay of classroom teachers, leaders, administrators, teacher educators, state legislators and community leaders in state government, state education and local education. Even with the contemporary research focus on policy players' perspectives and experiences from 2008 to 2013, a historical lens on Arizona education is pertinent to contextualize the study findings.

The Education System in Arizona: An Introduction

Public education in the state of Arizona

Shifting from Mexican to US territory in the Gadsen Purchase of 1854, Arizona commenced its formal education system in 1871 when the governor appointed a Territorial Board of Education and Superintendent of Public Instruction. When Arizona joined the US as a state in 1912, Arizona leaders continued to draw from its territorial roots to structure education (Pickering, 1966). Adopted upon its statehood, the Arizona Constitution guided the organization of education due to its responsibility for regulating the state's public schools. Demonstrating the influence on education by both executive and legislative branches of state government, the governor, the State Senate and the State House of Representatives led educational policymaking. With legislative representation from across the state, both the Senate and House utilized education committees to spearhead education-related bills and legislation to the Arizona Constitution. Within this broader layer of executive and legislative leaders within state government, Pickering (1966: 26) described the long-standing organization of education: 'The central structure of the Arizona educational system is composed of three entities: the State Board of Education, the State Superintendent of Public Instruction, and the State Department of Public Instruction'.

Termed the Territorial Board prior to 1912, the State Board of Education has remained central to Arizona educational policy (Arizona Revised Statutes [ARS] 15-203). The mission of this entity is 'to aggressively set policies that foster excellence in public education' (Arizona Department of Education [ADE], 2015a: 1). In line with this stated mission, the Board of Education has maintained supervisory and regulatory roles in Arizona's public education system, among other powers and duties. The makeup of the State Board, as well as the specific roles and responsibilities of its members, have evolved across the past century of Arizona's statehood; however, key facets have remained the same since territorial days, such as the role of the governor in appointing members (Pickering, 1966). The State Board consists of 11 appointed members, including the Superintendent of Public Instruction, the president of a state university or college, four lay members, a president or chancellor of a community-college district, an owner or administrator of a charter school, a superintendent of a high-school district, a K-12 classroom teacher and a county school superintendent. Each member, other than the Superintendent of Public Instruction, must be appointed by the governor and confirmed by the Senate for a 4-year term (ADE, 2015a).

The Arizona Constitution shifted the role of State Superintendent of Public Instruction from its originally appointed position as Territorial Superintendent of Public Instruction to a publicly elected position with 2-year terms (ARS 15-251). The state has contended that 'The job of the state superintendent is to "superintend" the K-12 public education system in Arizona through the state department of education' including 'kindergarten schools, common schools, high schools and normal schools' (ADE, 2015b: 1). In this state-level leadership role, the superintendent has espoused an executive role with responsibilities to distribute funding and carry out state and federal educational laws and Board of Education policies. To accomplish these tasks, the superintendent must lead the State Department of Public Instruction (i.e. the ADE), which has been consistently organized into various departments that have evolved with federal and state policies. Under the leadership of the State Superintendent of Public Instruction, ADE administrators have defined their mission as

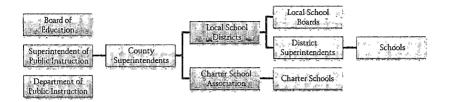

Figure 2.1 Organization of Arizona state education

being 'to serve Arizona's education community, ensuring every child has access to an excellent education' (ADE, 2015b: 1).

These state government and education stakeholders have influenced public instruction across Arizona in a variety of ways, both impacting the financing of Arizona's education system. Despite the stated missions of these three major educational entities, educational spending in Arizona has long been dismal. Fifty years ago, Pickering (1966: 13) studied the landscape of Arizona education and asserted, 'What people say about education and what they do may vastly differ. What they do about education and what they are willing to pay for are the same'. With consistently falling per-pupil funding since the 1960s, Arizona has recently maintained the lowest per-pupil funding in the nation, irrespective of the mechanism used to determine this figure (Hoffman & Rex, 2009). Influenced by the governor's budget, the school funding formula approved by the state legislature and other state-level regulations and guidelines, decades of scant educational funding have resulted in low-paid and inexperienced teachers, larger-than-average classes sizes and fewer administrative staff members in both local school districts and charter schools (Hoffman & Rex, 2009) (Figure 2.1).

Local school districts and charter schools

After the three macro-level entities, the responsibility for public instruction flowed next to the 15 county superintendents, then to the 230 school district boards and superintendents, and finally to the 2000 individual schools in Arizona (ADE, 2015c; Pickering, 1966). Pickering (1966: 16) explained Arizona's delegation of educational responsibilities from the state to the local context: 'From the earliest territorial days to date, the local school district has been the fundamental organizational unit. Each district has always been a separate entity whether it has been within, beyond, or among city limits'. With wide geographic expanses between student populations in the territorial days, paired with organizational provisions for education in the 1912 state constitution, rural and urban districts often formed around extended families and communities. According to Pickering (1966: 16), 'The influences of school districting have been provincial, political, economic and personal. Many of the districts have guarded their rights from state and especially federal encroachment with great care'. This historical and personal development of school districts has led to the 230 school districts currently operating in the state of Arizona (ADE, 2015c), a figure down from 292 from 50 years prior due to some regional efforts to consolidate the numerous independent school boards, districts and schools (Pickering, 1966).

Following the passage of House Bill 2002 in 1994, charter schools entered and became an integral fixture in Arizona's educational system, providing parents with public instructional alternatives to local school districts. *Charter schools* are publicly funded, independent schools that are operated based on terms of charters with local or national authorities. With the first charters issued in 1995, these schools have increased in presence in the state's educational landscape over the past two decades, now representing 30% of Arizona schools and serving 17% of Arizona students across urban, suburban and rural settings (Arizona Charter Schools Association [ACSA], 2015; Cobb & Glass, 1999). Consistently maintained as a platform for the conservative party to provide alternatives within public instruction, school choice and the corresponding charter school movement have continued to grow over the past two decades, making Arizona the state currently with the greatest percentage of charter schools in the US (ACSA, 2015). With 526 charter schools operated independently of public school districts, supporters of charter schools formed the Arizona Charter School Association to support, advocate and lead the large and growing charter school initiative (ACSA, 2014).

Within local communities in Arizona, there exists a demographic divide between school districts and charter schools. Amid the growth of charter schools, Cobb and Glass (1999) discovered ethnic segregation in Arizona charter schools as compared to adjacent public schools, with charter schools maintaining a larger proportion and percentage of White students. Additionally, these scholars found that students attending charter schools with larger populations of students of color were typically on vocational secondary or alternative schooling tracks that did not lead to post-secondary educational opportunities. A recent study funded by charter school supporters (Aportela & Laczko-Kerr, 2013) uncovered similar demographic trends, with Arizona charter schools enrolling significantly lower percentages of Latino and Native American students and greater percentages of White students than public schools. Nonetheless, the charter movement continues to gain momentum in the state, with many local school districts turning to the charter school model to tap into funding sources and maintain school-based autonomy (ACSA, 2015).

Teachers and teacher preparation

More than a century before the debate over charter schools, state legislators recognized the need to prepare teachers for Arizona schools.

Similar to the territorial origins of public instruction in Arizona, higher education in this southwestern state began in 1885 when the Thirteenth Territorial Legislature passed legislation that provided land and fiscal support for universities (Pickering, 1966). Founded in the central region of the state in 1886, Arizona State University was home to the first teacher preparation institution, known as the Territorial Normal School at Tempe. Teacher preparation came to southern and northern Arizona, respectively, with the founding of the University of Arizona in Tucson in 1891 and Northern Arizona University in Flagstaff in 1899. To date, these three public universities produce the majority of teachers in Arizona, as 'in contrast with the eastern and mid-western parts of the United States, private colleges have not flourished in Arizona' (Pickering, 1966: 25).

Following state legislation in 1927, community colleges provided an additional avenue for aspiring teachers with a network of county- and city-level junior colleges. Additionally, for-profit universities have gained momentum in the teacher preparation landscape in the past two decades in Arizona, including the Phoenix-based University of Phoenix and Grand Canyon University, offering primarily online teacher certification programs. Together, community colleges, 4-year public universities and for-profit universities create the pipeline of teachers for Arizona schools (Gau et al., 2003).

Nonetheless, the state's population grew significantly at the turn of the 21st century due to both migration from cooler US climates and immigration from Mexico and other nations. Scholars questioned whether the supply of teachers from Arizona institutions of higher education could meet the demand for teachers in K-12 schools. Gau et al. (2003) investigated the nature and extent of the so-called 'teacher shortage' in Arizona in the early 2000s. The increasing student population foreshadowed a substantial demand for teachers, leading to the assumption of a teacher shortage; however, researchers found that overall, the state had a sufficient number of teachers but that specific regions further removed from urban centers (e.g. rural regions such as western Phoenix suburbs and Yuma) and specialty areas with complex contexts and challenges (e.g. EL, special education) had shortages that were expected to worsen. Gau et al. (2003: 6) found that 'Teachers are not applying in adequate numbers for positions generally perceived to be difficult, either because of their location or because of student characteristics'. Whereas scholars described an integral supply in the small pool of certified teachers who had previously left the classroom, they proposed other solutions from both traditional and alternative teacher certification programs.

In addition to increasing the teacher supply through traditional university programs, Gau et al. (2003: 7) called for state leaders to 'strengthen state-level efforts and out-of-state recruiting' and 'remove and/or streamline certification requirements'. With alternative paths to teaching certification that recruited teachers beyond the state of Arizona, in contrast to the traditional paths to teaching certification situated at Arizona universities with primarily in-state students, stakeholders expected to fill teacher shortages in high-need communities and placements. One such source of alternatively certified teachers came from Teach For America (TFA), a non-profit organization with a large and growing presence in Arizona and broader US education. Founded in 1990, this national movement aimed to close the achievement gap along racial and socioeconomic lines, enlisting elite college graduates for placement as novice teachers in districts and charter schools in low-income urban and rural regions across the US (TFA, 2014a). Starting in Arizona in 1994 with 20 novice teachers, referred to as *corps members*, TFA Phoenix has grown substantially over the past two decades. Now the organization boasts over 300 corps members and 600 alumni working in Arizona education, partnerships with numerous Phoenix-area urban and suburban districts and charter schools and growing alumni involvement in educational decision-making in both state and local contexts.

Despite tapping into both traditionally and alternatively certified teachers to staff Arizona classrooms in the 1990s and 2000s, a scarcity of Latino teachers and teachers qualified to teach ELs persisted. Gau *et al.* (2003) documented a mismatch between teacher and student race, with specific attention to the growing population of Latino students and the marked dearth of Latino teachers and role models for children and adolescents. Further, they predicted the shortfall in EL-qualified teachers, stating, 'It would require nearly six years to meet the current shortfall of LEP [limited English proficient] qualified teachers before even beginning to address new demands expected from attrition and growth of the Hispanic population' (Gau *et al.*, 2003: 17). To meet teacher shortages in predominantly Latino communities, some Phoenix-area districts and charter schools looked to TFA to provide underprepared novice teachers for placement in classrooms with ELs (Heineke & Cameron, 2011, 2013; Hopkins & Heineke, 2013). Within this broader historical context of Arizona education, I now specifically hone in on the history of EL education, starting with the epoch of bilingual education prior to the passage of Proposition 203 in the year 2000.

Pre-Proposition 203: Bilingual Education in Arizona

Previously Mexican territory before 1854, Arizona has long been home to large Latino and Native American populations who speak Spanish and hundreds of indigenous languages (McCarty, 2011; Milem *et al.*, 2013). Despite the rich linguistic diversity of the original residents of Arizona, English became the medium by which both Latino and Native Americans were assimilated upon formal statehood in 1912. In 1919, state legislation mandated English only in Arizona public schools, specifically targeting non-native speakers of English in segregated contexts known as '1C classes' (Rolstad *et al.*, 2005: 48). Sheridan (1986: 224) described these state-mandated beginning-English classes as having a narrow and low-level focus on discrete language skills with the primary goal being to 'incorporate "foreign" students into the mainstream of U.S. society'. Because of the skill-based focus on vocabulary as separate from content learning, this language policy resulted in poor academic achievement for Latino children, as they dropped out of school, never transitioned to age-appropriate content instruction and continued to progress more slowly throughout their subsequent schooling (Rolstad *et al.*, 2005; Sheridan, 1986). These 1C courses remained the primary instructional option for ELs in Arizona public schools until 1965.

Bilingual education for English learners

Bilingual education efforts emerged with the civil rights movement in the 1950s and 1960s, which fought for the equal rights of minority and disenfranchised groups and resulted in the Civil Rights Act of 1964. In 1965, Congress approved the Elementary and Secondary Education Act (ESEA), which aimed to equalize educational opportunities. Title VII of the ESEA, the Bilingual Education Act, was signed into law in 1968 and provided public school districts with funding, training and resources for the teaching of languages other than English. Across the US, linguistically diverse groups pushed back against English-only education to further the agenda for bilingual education and demand adequate support for ELs. In California, the Chinese-American immigrant community called attention to the lack of support provided in English-only instruction. Using educational discrimination by national origin as the basis for a civil rights case in 1974, *Lau v. Nichols* expanded the rights of non-native speakers of English in schools, requiring adequate support for language learning and bilingual education. The subsequent Equal Educational Opportunities Act (EEOA) of 1974 highlighted schools' responsibility to 'take appropriate action to overcome language barriers that impede equal participation by its students in its instructional programs' (§1703). Further judicial action (*Castañenda v. Pickard*, 1981) supported bilingual programming across the nation, requiring schools to (a) develop programs for ELs based on sound theory and research, (b) provide trained teachers and sufficient resources to implement the program and (c) evaluate the efficacy of the program and refine instruction based on evaluation data.

These federal legislative and judicial actions supported the development of bilingual programs in Arizona.[1] In 1969, following the Bilingual Education Act of 1968, the state legislature passed the first bilingual education statute, permitting school districts to voluntarily provide bilingual instruction across the K-3 grades but providing limited financial appropriations (Sacken & Medina, 1990). After an unsuccessful attempt in 1973 to remove the K-3 limitations and increase fiscal appropriations, bilingual advocates from universities and public schools converged with state legislators in 1984 and put forth a bill to extend, strengthen and require bilingual programs (SB 1160, 1984, as cited in Sacken & Medina, 1990). Despite the original intentions of making bilingual education mandatory for ELs extending through 8th grade, creating bilingual teaching certification standards and requiring ADE monitoring for effective program compliance, the bill passed only after significant revisions. In line with the name change of the bill from *Bilingual-Bicultural Education Program* to *Bilingual Programs and English as a Second Language Programs*, the revisions removed requirements for native language instruction and teacher certification standards and stated that 'all districts [would] be permitted to choose freely between bilingual or English-only programs' (Sacken & Medina, 1990: 394). Nevertheless, the state language policy extended opportunities for bilingual education, including bilingual programs in intermediate and middle grades and additive models of dual-language instruction.

The shift to bilingual education extended options for Arizonan ELs beyond the skill-based English-only instruction previously offered through 1C courses. Building on the linguistic assets of the large Latino and Native-American populations across the state, educators designed and implemented bilingual programs in Spanish and indigenous languages, corresponding to the student population in the local school district. Focused on Spanish bilingual programs for Latino ELs in Arizona, results from a meta-analysis to investigate the effectiveness of bilingual education from 1985 to 2000 demonstrated ELs' higher achievement when enrolled in English and Spanish as compared to ELs enrolled in monolingual programming (Rolstad *et al.*, 2005). Using ethnographic research in the Rough Rock reservation, McCarty (2002) documented the community's development of Navajo bilingual/bicultural education; despite the challenges of recruiting bilingual teachers and securing bilingual materials, she found that the program supported cultural reclamation and linguistic maintenance, which in turn served to reinvigorate and reunite the community. Overall, state-level student achievement data collected and analyzed by the ADE demonstrated that 'the students identified by the schools to be learning through bilingual techniques scored higher than those in ESL programs' (Haver, 2013: 27); however, bilingual opponents questioned those data and began a crusade for English-only education in Arizona schools.

The English for the Children movement

Despite the successes of bilingual education, English-only proponents campaigned against native language use in Arizona and across the US

(Crawford, 2000; Lillie & Moore, 2014). The contemporary *English-only movement* formed in the mid-1980s and gained momentum through the 1990s, being simultaneous with the surge in immigration from Latin America to the US (Crawford, 2000). In attempt to abolish public education for ELs in languages other than English, millionaire Ron Unz sponsored state-level legislative initiatives for official policies in schools in what he introduced as the *English for the Children* movement. Claiming that bilingual education resulted in the lack of academic achievement of ELs due to Spanish-medium instruction, they provided voters with the legally mandated alternative of English-dominant instruction. The literature and advertising widely disseminated by English for the Children, which opponents have called unclear and misleading, led to the overwhelming support of propositions in California (1998; Proposition 227), Arizona (2000; Proposition 203) and Massachusetts (2002; Question 2). In addition to an emphasis on English at the state level, the federal No Child Left Behind Act (NCLB, 2001) replaced the Bilingual Education Act of 1968 with the *English Language Acquisition, Language Enhancement, and Academic Achievement Act* (Title III), reinforcing English as the preferred medium of instruction in classrooms. Although the reauthorization did not constitute a federal policy mandating English only, the change reflected the governmental insistence on English monolingualism to demonstrate academic achievement (Wright, 2005b, 2005c, 2014; Wiley & Wright, 2004).

Ron Unz, a software entrepreneur from the Silicon Valley with political aspirations, began the English for the Children campaign in his home state of California (Wright, 2005a). Unlike the voluntary option of bilingual education in Arizona, California had required bilingual education for ELs until the passage of Proposition 227 in 1998. Despite the lack of state-mandated bilingual education in Arizona, English-only proponents wanted to completely eliminate bilingual education as an option for local school districts, claiming the inefficacy of Spanish-medium instruction in promoting English language development and academic achievement (Haver, 2013). In this way, Ron Unz merged paths with a group of predominantly US-born Latino Arizonans to promote their shared English-only priorities; whereas movement members recalled a grassroots effort to improve education (Haver, 2013), outsiders discerned this claim as a façade with Ron Unz spearheading the campaign efforts (Wright, 2005a). Drawing from the successful California movement, the Arizona anti-bilingual group utilized a *citizens' initiative*, collecting the required number of signatures to add Proposition 203 to the ballot with 13 other initiatives in November 2000 (Combs, 2012). Whereas English-only proponents praised the efforts to eliminate ineffective bilingual programs (Haver, 2013), bilingual proponents described the citizens' initiative as a 'means of circumventing state legislative special interest ... [for] wealthy entrepreneurs who exploit their appeal to further person or political agendas' (Combs, 2012: 61).

The English-only movement and Proposition 203 campaign proved successful: Voters passed the measure by 63% to all but eliminate bilingual education for ELs in Arizona. The highly politicized campaign divided educators and residents across the state, using $187,000 from Ron Unz to produce 'misleading and inflammatory sound bites' (Combs, 2012: 62), which both sides recognized as a strategy to tap into anti-immigrant sentiments prevalent at the time (Crawford, 2000; Haver, 2013). Drawing from policy and media documents, Wright (2005a: 672) described the English-only campaign as a 'political spectacle' with Unz engaging in verbal combat via 'vehement media attacks' against bilingual scholars and advocates. Similarly, Johnson (2005) uncovered rhetorical strategies used by English-only proponents in newspapers and voter materials during the campaign, exposing metaphors that denigrated bilingual education and those who supported it. Overall, couched in assimilative and monolingual ideologies, the campaign discourse emphasized the failure of bilingual education and situated minority-language students as victims, while tapping into the news media to enshrine English as the key to the 'American Dream' (Johnson, 2005; Wright, 2005a). Regardless of the tactics, the English for the Children movement won the war over EL education in Arizona, and Proposition 203 brought about a new era of language policy in practice.

The Flores case, 1992–2000

Simultaneous with the ideological, political and pedagogical struggle between bilingual and English-only supporters that typified the Arizona language policy context in the 1990s, a legal battle ensued that continued to affect EL education for the next two decades. Originating in the border town of Nogales and based on educational practices in the Nogales Unified School District, the dispute arose when parents of ELs recognized the meager funding of public instruction for their children enrolled in bilingual and EL program models (Combs, 2012; Sacken & Medina, 1990). In 1992, years before the public controversy began over the medium of instruction in Arizona classrooms, litigators filed a class-action lawsuit brought on behalf of EL students, parents and guardians across the 15 counties of the state (Combs, 2012; Hogan, 2014). Using the federal EEOA as a legal context, the *Flores* case charged the State of Arizona with inappropriate instructional accommodations and methodologies to support students from non-native English backgrounds, thus impeding their equal participation in schools (EEOA, 1974). Particularly, the litigation focused on inadequate funding for EL education in public school districts, with the plaintiffs contending that the additional 6% over the base-level funding for other students (i.e. $150) provided by the state of Arizona failed to sustain effective and research-based programs for ELs (Combs, 2012; Hogan, 2014).

After years of legal rulings and proceedings, in January of 2000, a federal judge found in favor of the plaintiffs, asserting that Arizona had violated the EEOA regarding denying ELs access to appropriate and adequately funded programs and methodologies. Tim Hogan, the primary litigator for the Flores plaintiffs, explained the 2000 federal ruling:

> Defendants were violating the EEOA because the state's funding for EL programs was arbitrary and capricious and bore no relation to the actual funding needed to insure that EL students in the Nogales School District were achieving mastery of required essential skills. (Hogan, 2014: 30)

Based on the federal court's ruling, the state of Arizona entered into a legally binding consent order with the plaintiffs, agreeing to specific measures intended to improve the curriculum and instruction provided to ELs across the state (Combs, 2012; *Flores v. Arizona*, 2000; Hogan, 2014). Just months before the passage of Proposition 203 in Arizona, EL education advocates appeared to have won a significant battle; however, the *Flores* case was far from over and would continue to affect language policy for the next decade.

Proposition 203 and Structured English Immersion

In line with the ideologies and goals of the English for the Children movement, Proposition 203, passed in 2000, narrowed the instructional options for ELs, specifically limiting local educators' options to provide bilingual education. The two-page policy document framed the importance of the legislation by describing English as the language of American and Arizonan public practice, thus 'allowing them [ELs] to fully participate in the American Dream of economic and social advancement' (ADE, 2000: 1). The triumphant citizens' initiative balloted as Proposition 203 formally became part of the Arizona Revised Statutes (Section 3, Title 15, Chapter 7), titled English Language Education for Children in Public Schools. In these revised statutes, policy regulations repeatedly stipulated English as the medium of instruction in Arizona: 'All children in Arizona public school shall be taught *English* by being taught in *English* and all children shall be placed in *English* language classrooms' (emphasis added; ARS 15-752: 1). Despite the profuse monolingual rhetoric, nebulous language within Proposition 203 led to varying interpretations and implementation (Wright, 2005a).

Within the broad insistence on the value and use of English monolingualism, the authors of Proposition 203 utilized specific discourse in the policy document to mandate English-medium instruction in classrooms and schools. Two years after the California campaign, Arizona English-only proponents learned from the perceived issues following Proposition 227 implementation, specifically in California's waiver provisions that allowed parents to sign documentation for their children to participate in bilingual programming. In this way, Arizona English-only advocates deliberately drafted Proposition 203 to tighten these loopholes that allowed bilingual education for ELs toward further promoting monolingualism for immigrant populations (Wright, 2005a). While maintaining certain waiver provisions, including those for children who (a) demonstrated proficiency in English, (b) were 10 years or older or (c) had special needs, Proposition 203 included a provision that allowed for the rejection of parents' waivers: 'Teachers and local school districts may reject waiver requests without explanation or legal consequence' (ARS 15-753: 2). In this way, although the language policy regulations proved successful in greatly reducing bilingual programs across the state, some school districts strategically utilized waivers to their advantage to continue bilingual education for ELs (Combs *et al.*, 2005; Wright, 2005a).

Other provisions in the official language policy document further restricted local school districts in providing instructional options for students, utilizing both subjective language and fear tactics (Wright, 2005a). Authors first broadened the definition of *English proficient*, allowing for subjectivity in applying the EL label in an attempt to reduce options for bilingual education: 'English learner … means a child who does not speak English or whose native language is not English, and who is not currently able to perform ordinary classroom work in English' (ARS 15-751: 1). Additionally, the policy document demanded harsh punitive actions for any educator engaged in bilingual practice, including being removed and 'barred from holding any position of authority anywhere within the Arizona public school system for an additional period of five years' (ARS 15-754: 2). With these policy clauses, Proposition 203 authors attempted to restrict opportunities for local educators to formally or informally engage in bilingual education.

In addition to monolingual ideologies driving instructional restrictions, Proposition 203 put forth SEI as the approach to teaching ELs in schools. To comply with federal law forbidding submersion of ELs in English-only classrooms (*Lau v. Nichols*, 1974), policy regulations designated that ELs would be placed in a one-year SEI program, which used English as the medium of instruction with specific teaching strategies geared to students still learning the language (e.g. pre-teaching vocabulary, manipulatives). Because federal law required EL programs to be soundly theory- and research-based (*Castañeda v. Pickard*, 1981), Arizona looked to SEI, which EL-education experts defined as a model in which teachers maximize instruction in English and use and teach English at a level appropriate to the abilities of the ELs in the class (Ramírez *et al.*, 1991). Proposition 203 officially defined SEI as 'an English language acquisition process for young children in which nearly all classroom instruction is in English but with the curriculum and presentation designed for children who are learning the language' (ADE, 2000: 1). Despite the nebulous description of the instructional model, the ultimate goal of SEI was to quickly transition ELs to English fluency and transfer them to mainstream classes with scant cost to the Arizona taxpayer.

Immersion is an approach to language instruction that is 'a form of bilingual education in which students who speak the language of the majority of the population receive part of their instruction through the medium of a second language and part through their first language' (Genesee, 1987: vii). Immersion approaches have been utilized and researched in thriving educational systems, including Canada, Hungary, Australia, Spain and Finland, with findings demonstrating programmatic efficacy in fostering students' bilingualism (Johnson & Swain, 1997). Proponents of SEI in the US have referred to the widely documented success of Canadian French immersion to justify its use and effectiveness with ELs in American schools (Baker & de Kanter, 1983), despite staunch criticism of inappropriate overextension by both US and Canadian researchers (Hernández-Chávez, 1984; Johnson & Swain, 1997). One of the highest-funded programs in the Canadian school system, French immersion originated from upper-class, language majority (i.e. English-speaking) parents who desired French bilingualism for their children; with the French language valued in the Canadian government, economy and society, immersion enriched students of the English-speaking majority with the French language (Genesee, 1987; Johnson & Swain, 1997; Lapkin, 1998; Schmidt, 1998).

Conversely, mandated by government policy for typically lower-class, language minority children, SEI emphasized English as the hegemonic language that aimed to replace students' native languages at a fraction of the cost of bilingual education (Hernández-Chávez, 1984). Disparities between instructional approaches have cast a shadow on the validity of SEI as an effective approach for language development, with Arizona scholars asserting that state-sponsored monolingual and assimilative ideologies led to SEI as the selected program model, regardless of the lack of conceptual or empirical support for the related instructional practices (Combs *et al.*, 2011). With extreme discord in Arizona's academic community around the ideologies and political origins of the restrictive language policy and the resultant program model for EL instruction, scholars continued to investigate and critique the implementation of SEI in classrooms, schools and districts across the state.

Local school districts looked to the ADE to provide guidance for policy implementation; however, information varied widely depending on the interpretation of the three different State Superintendents of Public Instruction who held the office in the years following the passage of Proposition 203. Lisa Keegan, the ADE leader in 2000, divulged having little interest in the law and issued scant direction beyond the two-page policy document (Wright, 2005a). The ambiguous language within the policy document resulted in widespread confusion, and 'districts scrambled to implement the new law but suffered from a lack of information, time, personnel, and resources to do so' (Rolstad *et al.*, 2005: 44). After Keegan left office in 2001, appointee Jaime Molera issued guidebooks that answered questions while allowing for flexibility in implementation, including sanctioning waivers for bilingual programs (Wright, 2005a). Taking office in 2002 after running on a platform of strict enforcement of Proposition 203, Tom Horne, along with his deputy chief and English-only advocate Margaret Garcia-Dugan, tightened implementation through English-only rhetoric and top-down compliance enforcement (Wright, 2005a). In addition to varying interpretation by state administrators, Wright (2005b, 2014) found that policy regulations contradicted mandates of other federal and state policies, nullifying various facets of Proposition 203 when considering the intersection with legislation such as NCLB. These inconsistent policies, as well as varying interpretations and expectations, led to confusion among educators in local communities.

Overall, studies converged on the misinformation and confusion following Proposition 203, which in turn led to varied implementation and ineffective teacher preparation (Combs, 2012; Rolstad *et al.*, 2005; Wright, 2005a, 2005b, 2014). With lenses on teachers and teacher certification, empirical studies discovered that teachers in designated classrooms were ill-equipped to provide adequate supports for ELs in English-medium classrooms. Combs and colleagues (2005) examined the effects of SEI on teachers, leaders and students in one urban school serving a large population of ELs, finding that SEI teachers remained largely unaware of the model and demonstrated a lack of preparedness to teach effectively. Spanning out to consider SEI teacher preparation across the state, Wright and Choi (2006) surveyed third-grade teachers to ascertain how language policy change influenced their teaching effectiveness with ELs; findings revealed confusion over what was and was not allowed by language policy and what practices constituted quality instruction for ELs. Specifically, teachers reported a lack of guidance regarding SEI, resulting in blurred lines between SEI and mainstream instruction, as well as possible submersion where ELs were left to sink or swim. Researchers attributed the lack of teacher awareness and preparedness to the widely varied and haphazard nature of the SEI endorsement training that hundreds of local educational agencies rushed to create following the language policy change (Combs *et al.*, 2005; Moore, 2012).

Other post-Proposition 203 empirical studies focused on the varied implementation of the SEI program in practice across the state. Comparing districts across the state, Wright (2005b, 2014) discovered that SEI implementation varied drastically based on the professional backgrounds of district-level administration. With EL education dichotomized between complete indifference to strict enforcement of SEI mandates, findings indicated the political nature of policy interpretation in local practice with ELs. Johnson (2012) conducted a 3-year ethnographic study of one district's shift to SEI. He documented educators' struggles with the restrictive policy, which differed from the district's historic emphasis on bilingualism. Whereas monolingual ideology pervaded much of district practice, some teachers negotiated mandates to find space for students' native language. Nevertheless, fear and formal restrictions highly limited bilingual instruction and education across the state. Investigating a bilingual school, Combs and colleagues (2005) found that ADE leaders' policy interpretation seriously reduced the number of students eligible for the school's dual-language program, forcing ELs into SEI settings despite the stress caused to students and parents. Overall, scholars documented efforts to eliminate bilingual programs across the state, including the Navajo immersion programs that were supposedly exempt from the state policy (Combs, 2012; Wright, 2005b, 2014).

The Flores case, 2000–2006

Within this contentious ideological and political context of monolingual education, the legal battle between Arizona EL education advocates and ADE administrators continued. SEI implementation research scholars and EL advocates asserted the inherent civil rights violations for both students and parents, such as the refusal to provide parents with translation services, which resulted in federal civil rights complaints and investigations (Combs et al., 2005; Wright, 2005b, 2014). Additionally, the Flores case continued in the backdrop of post-Proposition 203 Arizona. Following the 2000 federal finding and resulting resolution in favor of the plaintiffs, the defendants failed to meet their required obligations and changes to EL education.

Cost studies emerged throughout this 5-year span between 2000 and 2005 as the plaintiffs and defendants disagreed on adequate funding for EL programs. According to Hogan (2014), one cost study conducted by ADE consultants estimated the cost of providing SEI as required by Proposition 203 at approximately $1200 per EL pupil, juxtaposed with the $150 allocated at the time. With the cost study threatening a needed $50 million increase to the state budget, the legislature passed House Bill 2001, which tentatively raised the per-pupil EL funding to $350 and ordered another cost study. Conducted by the National Conference of State Legislatures (NCSL, 2005), the draft report projected up to $2500 per EL needed for effective programming in high-need districts. After the ADE dismissed these findings as invalid and refused changes, the plaintiffs returned to court, resulting in $20 million in fines on the state for not complying with his original judgment five years prior; the hefty financial sanctions finally prompted the state legislature to take action (Hogan, 2014).

House Bill 2064 and English Language Development

The next major language policy in recent Arizona state history, the state legislature passed House Bill 2064 in 2006, building on extant policy to further constrict EL education. Continuing to emphasize one-year-to-English-proficiency, the legislation called for a 4-hour ELD block as the model for first-year ELs and created an EL Task Force to design cost-effective program models for ELs at all proficiency levels. Whereas Proposition 203 had clear origins in the citizens' initiative supported and funded by the English for the Children campaign, House Bill 2064 maintained nebulous foundations. The timing and discourse of the 2006 legislation indicated a connection to the above-described Flores Consent Order, particularly the discussion on EL student funding and emphasis on cost efficiency for EL program models (Combs, 2012). Additionally, the varied interpretation and implementation of Proposition 203 and SEI reportedly upset the State Superintendent of Public Instruction, Tom Horne, who wanted more prescription as to a set *model* for SEI that schools had to follow, along with added compliance measures to enhance rigidity in implementation (Hogan, 2014). With implications from both the Flores case and the troubled SEI implementation, paired with omnipresent assimilative and monolingual ideologies within the conservative state legislature, House Bill 2064 put the design of EL education in the hands of the nine-member task force.

The English Learner Task Force

The creation of the EL Task Force in 2006 proved an unprecedented move in the history of Arizona state education. Prior to 2006, the central facets and organization of Arizona's education system had remained consistent since the territorial days before statehood: The State Board of Education, the State Superintendent of Public Instruction and the State Department of Public Instruction (i.e. ADE) had utilized state-level policies to guide the education practices of counties, school districts and individual schools (Pickering, 1966). With House Bill 2064, the state legislature created an authoritative entity within the macro level of state education. By affording the task force unilateral control over the design and monitoring of SEI program models, the membership gained executive power over EL education across the state.

The task force consisted of nine members appointed by political leaders, including three members appointed by the Superintendent of Public Instruction and two members appointed by each the governor, president of Senate and speaker of the House of Representatives, respectively (House Bill [HB] 2064, 2006). As described in her book on the English-only movement in Arizona, two-term delegate Johanna Haver explained that task force members included both educators and non-educators: 'Both Superintendent Tom Horne and Governor Janet Napolitano picked people with experience in education. The House and Senate chose education experts and politicians' (Haver, 2013: 116). With these multiple perspectives, the legislation charged the task force to develop and adopt research-based, cost-efficient program models aligned to federal and state laws for implementation in school districts and charter schools, as well as an ongoing review of the models following initial implementation.

In line with the ADE demands for more oversight in language policy, House Bill 2064 also created the Office of English Language Acquisition Services (OELAS) with administrators charged to publish rules, monitor for compliance and train teachers and administrators (HB 2064, 2006: 11–12). In this way, OELAS administrators maintained responsibility for implementing the model designed by the task force through compliance monitoring and training at universities, school districts and charter schools.

In her 2013 book, Haver provided internal details on the task force's process of program design. The appointed members first elected a chairman – a non-educator who 'came across as a good choice because he had experience in leading other government-related committees and knowledge of the policymaking procedures of the Arizona legislature' (Haver, 2013: 117). The group invited various practitioners from urban, rural and border districts who consistently expressed opposition to a 4-hour model with only ELs in a classroom, describing the challenges such a system would create for student learning (e.g. teacher as sole model of English proficiency, lack of curriculum for teaching grammar skills). Nevertheless, Haver (2013: 119) noted how the legislation guided the program design process: 'As Margaret Garcia–Dugan [a task force member] often stated, HB 2064 and Proposition 203 both require separation of the ELLs from the other students, whether anyone agrees with it or not'. In his document analysis of the language policy process following House Bill 2064, Lawton (2012) noted that Garcia-Dugan served as the primary advisor who guided legislators in drafting the bill, which was conveniently used to deflect her own and the broader EL Task Force's responsibility. The wearer of many English-only hats in state-level educational policy, she also served as the co-chair of the English for the Children – Arizona campaign and Tom Horne's Deputy State Superintendent of Public Instruction (Haver, 2013).

In addition to practitioners, education professors representing each of the three state universities came to share their expertise and perspectives to inform the program design process, including Dr Christian Faltis from Arizona State University, Dr Luis Moll from University of Arizona and Dr Norbert Francis from Northern Arizona University. Well versed in theory and research on second language acquisition and bilingual education, the professors emphatically noted the value in and need for native language instruction when teaching ELs. Nevertheless, the appointed members of the task force had invited these university stakeholders as a gesture of inclusivity without being obliged to heed their expert educational perspectives. Haver (2013: 119) reflected, 'This [advocating for bilingual education] was an exercise in futility. Bilingual education was now against the law in Arizona, and the panel they were talking to [task force members] had no power to make the changes they wanted'. Inaccurately referencing the illegality of bilingual education via Proposition 203 in 2000, the authoritative political entity of the EL Task Force claimed a lack of power to incorporate research-based theory and practice into the resultant ELD model.

Despite the fact that Proposition 203 allowed for native language support and that House Bill 2064 only mandated the 4-hour skill-based model for first-year ELs, the task force interpreted the legislation differently to revoke possibilities for the requested flexibility in program models. In other words, Arizona legislation stipulated (a) only one year in the ELD setting (HB 2064, 2006) and (b) options for native language support in classroom instruction (ADE, 2000). Because of what they asserted as legislative limitations, the task force instead prioritized the recommendations of self-proclaimed SEI experts, particularly Kevin Clark; a California-based consultant, Clark emerged following Proposition 227 to support California districts in transitioning from bilingual education to SEI (Clark, 1999). In the broader field of EL education, where most recognized scholars and experts spoke out against SEI as an approach to teaching and learning, Clark maintained a relative monopoly as an educational consultant in California and Arizona, as he embraced restrictive language policy to shape and define classroom practice. Haver (2013: 121) recalled, 'He convinced most members in attendance at the meeting that he could help them reach their goal of developing educationally sound SEI models that corresponded to HB 2064'. In this way, the perspectives of Kevin Clark significantly shaped the program design process and resultant model (Clark, 2009; Haver, 2013).

The resulting model, referred to by most stakeholders as ELD, reflected increased prescription in EL education. Whereas the original SEI approach called for by Proposition 203 was nebulous and resulted in varied implementation across the state, the ELD model aimed to ensure compliance with rigid regulations for four hours of skill-based language instruction (Combs, 2012; Johnson, 2012; Wright, 2005a, 2014). Scholars aimed to contradict the research behind the ELD model, which centered on the *time-on-task principle*; this purported that extensive time using English skills would then transfer to students' increased English proficiency (ADE, 2007). Opponents specifically targeted the EL Task Force, Kevin Clark and their program design process utilizing the first prong of *Castañeda v. Pickard* (1981), which required that programs for ELs be based on educational theory and research deemed sound by qualified experts (Combs, 2012; Faltis & Arias, 2012; Long & Adamson, 2012). Despite the historic tendency of the courts to defer to educational practitioners and scholars, Faltis and Arias (2012) found that the task force instead used anti-bilingual education consultants and school district personnel as expert witnesses, thus limiting the research base of the 4-hour prescriptive model focused on discrete English skills. Interestingly, task force member Haver (2013) confirmed in hindsight the substantial and undue influence of consultant Kevin Clark.

The Flores case, 2006–present

Litigators joined the dispute over the resulting ELD model designed by the task force, using the Flores case to continue to advocate for EL instruction in Arizona, but only after a federal court reversed the 2000 legal decision. Following the passage of House Bill 2064 in 2006, State Superintendent Tom Horne argued that the state should not be forced to comply due to changed circumstances in state language policy, citing the passage of both Proposition 203 and House Bill 2064 since the 2000 Flores consent decree (Hogan, 2014). After arguing unsuccessfully to the judge and the court of appeals, Horne took his case to the US Supreme Court (*Horne v. Flores*, 2009, as cited in Hogan, 2014). After almost a decade of inaction by state leaders following the 2000 legal decision, the original Flores judgment against the state of Arizona was vacated. The justices determined that the inadequate funding of the Nogales Unified School District did not constitute a statewide violation of the EEOA. That is, rather than holding implications for the education of ELs across Arizona, the ruling could only be applied to the local context of Nogales, a border community in southern Arizona. In this remarkable turn of events, the Flores case returned to the district court and maintained focus on the educational practice in Nogales rather than at the state level.

Despite the disappointment of the Supreme Court verdict, Hogan and his colleagues utilized the continuing Flores litigation and the district court proceedings to fight the 4-hour ELD block that resulted from House Bill 2064 and the EL Task Force (Hogan, 2014). Again drawing from the federal EEOA legislation and the *Castañeda v. Pickard* (1981) court case, lawyers contended that the ELD block segregated ELs without research-based pedagogical purpose and denied equal access to the content curriculum, such as mathematics, science and social studies. Two years after the district court trial, the judge issued a ruling in favor of the defendant, thus relieving the state of Arizona from the original judgment and consent order issued in 2000 (*Flores v. Huppenthal*, 2013, as cited in Hogan, 2014). In his ruling, the district court judge asserted that the Flores lawsuit was not the vehicle to leverage all educational issues in the state of Arizona (*Flores v. Huppenthal*, 2013, as cited in Hogan, 2014). Unsatisfied with this outcome and in staunch disagreement with the judge that the 4-hour model did not violate the EEOA, Hogan and colleagues have appealed that ruling (Hogan, 2014).

Over two decades since the original class-action suit in 1992, *Flores* has continued to affect language policy in practice to the present day.

Other related educational policies

Whereas the language policy shift to the more restrictive 4-hour ELD block did not receive national attention, another simultaneous and contentious educational policy issue brought Arizona into the media spotlight. In 2010, Superintendent Tom Horne launched an effort to ban ethnic studies in Arizona K-12 classrooms. The same leader who had pushed for a prescriptive SEI model to ensure local compliance with Proposition 203 (Hogan, 2014), Horne specifically targeted Latino students and teachers participating in the Mexican American studies program in the Tucson Unified School District. Despite the program's positive impact on Latino and EL students' achievement and graduation rates, Horne cited an anti-American curriculum and prompted state legislation to eradicate ethnic studies across the state (Cabrera *et al.*, 2014). After one unsuccessful attempt to ban ethnic studies with Senate Bill 1069, introduced adjacent to Senate Bill 1070, which brought international scrutiny for the so-called 'show-me-your-papers' immigration law, the ban on ethnic studies became official with House Bill 2281 in 2010 (Sandoval & Tambini, 2014). Horne wasted little time in dismantling Tucson's Mexican American Studies program with what scholars critiqued as a targeted move grounded in assimilative ideologies and racist political discourse rather than concern for student learning (Cabrera *et al.*, 2014; Cammarota & Aguilera, 2012; Orozco, 2012).

Although the state's ban on ethnic studies stirred up public scrutiny across the nation, in 2010 many Arizona residents had focused educational policy concerns on the adoption and implementation of the Common Core Standards (CCS). A national movement to raise standards across states to better prepare K-12 students for college and careers in a changing global economy, the 'New Standards' sparked debate and controversy regarding the role of the federal government in education policy, which has historically been reserved for individual states (Bomer & Maloch, 2011; Porter *et al.*, 2011). Arizona's Board of Education adopted the CCS in 2010, and the ADE began work to prepare for full implementation in Arizona classrooms, schools and districts in the 2011–2012 school year (ADE, 2010). Nonetheless, the controversy and debate continued due to disagreement with federal overstep into local control, which districts and communities had previously maintained for educational decision-making throughout Arizona's territorial and state history (Pickering, 1966). In response to criticism in the growing debate across the state and nation, Governor Jan Brewer utilized an Executive Order (2013-08) to rename the standards in 2013, changing the CCS to the *Arizona College and Career Readiness*

Standards. Representing the same policy originally adopted in 2010 by the State Board, these newly named standards continued to guide curriculum and instruction in schools.

Discussion: Past Educational Policies and Practices

The past century of educational policies in the state of Arizona has shaped the contemporary context of EL education. Situated on land that was formerly Mexican territory, Arizona has progressed over the state's history to gain the xenophobic reputation as 'America's racist state' (Cammarota & Aguilera, 2012: 485) with assimilative and monolingual ideologies pervading state educational policies (Combs *et al.*, 2005; Combs, 2012; Lawton, 2012; Lillie & Moore, 2014; Wiley, 2012; Wright, 2005a, 2005b, 2014). With the institutional insistence on English-only education cresting with House Bill 2064 in 2006, language policy in Arizona has become the most restrictive in the US (Gándara & Hopkins, 2010; Mahoney *et al.*, 2010).

Looking back at the past two decades, the shifts within the education of ELs in Arizona have appeared on the surface to be dramatic and contentious. With bilingual programs once offered in urban, suburban and rural school districts across the state, tapping into the students' native languages such as Spanish and Navajo (Combs *et al.*, 2005; McCarty, 2002; Rolstad *et al.*, 2005), Arizona stakeholders appeared to value bilingualism and bilingual education. Nonetheless, behind the scenes, policy players engaged in legislative moves to maintain voluntary use of bilingual education, limit state funding for EL education and reduce requirements for teacher preparation and certification (Lawton, 2012; Sacken & Medina, 1990). The citizens' initiative of Proposition 203, funded by the English for the Children campaign, further institutionalized assimilative and monolingual ideologies by tapping into the anti-immigrant sentiments prevalent among residents in this border state (Crawford, 2000; Haver, 2013). Meanwhile, EL education advocates continued to challenge the state to adequately fund the programs, whether bilingual or monolingual, using federal legal precedents to mitigate state policy and argue their case (Combs, 2012; Hogan, 2014).

In 2008, following the passage of House Bill 2064, the creation of the EL Task Force and the subsequent design and implementation of the ELD model of instruction, students labeled as ELs across the state were separated from their mainstream, English-proficient peers to receive four hours of explicit instruction in the discrete skills of the English language, such as vocabulary and grammar (ADE, 2008). Despite multiple federal and state language policy moves across the three branches of government, including judicial actions via the Flores case, legislative actions such as House Bill 2064 and the executive actions of the EL Task Force, Arizona appeared to have reverted back to the model of EL education from almost 100 years prior. Reminiscent of the '1C classes' mandated for non-native speakers of English in 1919, the ELD approach in 2008 required ELs be placed into separate classrooms for skill-based, content-devoid, English-medium curriculum and instruction (Rolstad *et al.*, 2005; Sheridan, 1986). In the next chapter, I utilize policy documents and recent research to detail this current instructional approach to teaching ELs in Arizona, commonly referred to as ELD.

Note

(1)   For the purposes of this text, unless otherwise noted, bilingual education refers to Spanish–English educational policy and practice, given the large proportion of ELs in Arizona who speak Spanish.

3 Contemporary Context of English Learner Education

One of three educational contexts with restrictive language policies in the US, Arizona followed California and preceded Massachusetts in passing legislation that severely reduced bilingual programming options for students labeled as English learners (ELs). Following the original mandate for English-medium public instruction in 2000, Arizona's language education policy has increased in prescriptions and limitations over the past 15 years, such that Arizona's mandated 4-hour block of skill-based English language instruction for all ELs (i.e. English Language Development [ELD]) is now considered the most restrictive language policy context in the US (Gándara & Hopkins, 2010; Mahoney *et al.*, 2010). Whereas Chapter 2 outlined the historical trajectory of educational and language policies guiding the education of ELs in Arizona, this chapter focuses on current language policy in practice. I have specifically utilized policy guidelines and extant literature to describe the implementation of ELD mandates in schools and classrooms related to language assessment, classroom instruction and teacher preparation.

Test In, Test Out: The Central Role of Language Assessments

Central to the education of ELs in Arizona is the reliance on language assessments. Whereas extant literature and research has focused primarily on the controversial 4-hour block of skill-based language instruction wherein ELs are segregated from their English-proficient peers, instruction is directly related to assessment. Within Arizona language policy regulations, mandated assessments have guided ELD implementation with students, including initial identification of ELs, subsequent placement in ELD classrooms, exit from program participation and reclassification from EL to English proficient (Arizona Department of Education [ADE], 2011). Additionally, state leaders have utilized assessment data to measure school and district performance for accountability purposes, determine supplemental funding for EL services and evaluate ELD program effectiveness (ADE, 2011). The two assessment tools – the Home Language Survey (HLS) and the Arizona English Language Learner Assessment (AZELLA) – are explored here.

Home Language Survey: Assessment as gatekeeper

The EL identification process has consistently started with the HLS. When parents register children in school, school officials provide the HLS as part of the intake forms and initial paperwork for Arizona school enrollment. Utilized by the majority of the US, the HLS began the standardized two-step procedure for EL identification to meet federal requirements (No Child Left Behind [NCLB], 2001). The HLS serves as the initial referral, followed by the administration of an English language proficiency test. Goldenberg and Rutherford-Quach (2012: 22) defined the HLS as 'a brief 3- or 4- question instrument ... that asks parents what language or languages are spoken in the home, the language first spoken by the child, and the language most often spoken by the child'. If parents provided a response other than English to any of the HLS questions, then educators assumed that students might be limited in English proficiency and would require further testing to determine eligibility for EL services. In this way, the HLS served as a gatekeeper to EL services: Parents' reports and students' subsequent proficiency test performance held the key to whether students received appropriate instruction and supports required by federal laws (Goldenberg & Rutherford-Quach, 2012).

Arizona language policy outlined the standardized procedure for the initial referral of students who may be entitled to EL supports. House Bill 2064 called attention to this first step in the identification process yet remained nebulous to allow flexibility for the Superintendent of Public Instruction. The policy stated, 'The primary or home language for all new pupils who enroll in a school district or charter school shall be identified in a manner prescribed by the Superintendent of Public Instruction' (House Bill [HB] 2064, 2006: 4). In the EL Task Force's ELD model, language policy further detailed the procedure: Administer the HLS to determine whether students require the initial label of *PHLOTE* (i.e. students who speak a primary home language other than English). Using the manner prescribed by the Superintendent of Public Instruction, any parental response that signaled a language other than English resulted in PHLOTE ascription (ADE, 2013). School officials then administered the English proficiency test (i.e. AZELLA) to PHLOTE students; students who did not demonstrate English proficiency were ascribed the label of EL (ADE, 2008). See Figure 3.1 for state procedure for identifying EL students (ADE, 2013).

Prior to July 2009, the Arizona HLS asked three questions:

- What is the primary language used in the home regardless of the language spoken by the student?
- What is the language most often spoken by the student?
- What is the language that the student first acquired?

In July 2009, ADE administrators reduced the statewide HLS to one question: '*What is the primary language of the student?*' (Goldenberg &

Procedures for Identifying English Language Learner (ELL) Students

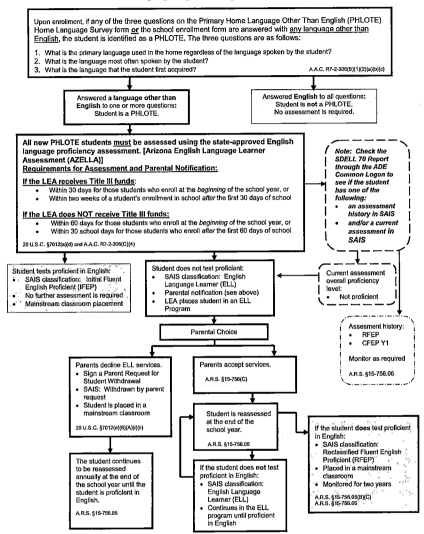

Figure 3.1 Procedures for identifying English language learner students

Rutherford-Quach, 2012). Because policy regulations required initial screening for home language but left the procedure to the state superintendent (HB 2064, 2006), the shift from a three- to a one-question survey required no formal approval prior to implementation. Although ADE administrators argued that primary language was the sole factor indicative of limited English proficiency (Goldenberg & Rutherford-Quach, 2012), the US Office of Civil Rights (OCR) disagreed. Recognizing the potential to under-identify students in need of and entitled to EL services, the OCR filed suit against the state, asserting, 'Students who are English language learners (ELLs) and eligible to receive English language acquisition services are not being served, because they are not being identified' (OCR, 2009: 1). With federal actors successful in the legal action, the resolution required the reinstatement of the three-question HLS by the 2011–2012 school year (OCR, 2009).

Simultaneous to the federal probe of Arizona's one-question HLS, Goldenberg and Rutherford-Quach (2012) conducted two empirical studies to evaluate the validity of the one-question HLS for EL identification. Situated in two urban Arizona districts – one medium and one large in student population – researchers investigated the efficacy of the one-question HLS by surveying parents with additional questions to glean more information on students' primary language. Findings indicated that the one-question HLS significantly under-identified students eligible for EL services, as English-dominant bilingual students could still be developing English language proficiency (ELP). Merging findings from the studies, they purported that 11%–18% of students eligible for EL services might remain unidentified due to the single-question screener. Additionally, they discounted the state's *fail-safe mechanism* that was utilized to justify the one-question screener. Despite the state's assertion that teachers could refer students for testing in addition to EL classification using the HLS, authors found that teacher referral would not capture most unidentified students. Overall, Goldenberg and Rutherford-Quach (2012: 29) came to the poignant conclusion that '[many] students likely to need English learner support services will not receive them'.

Arizona English Language Learner Assessment: Assessment as sole measure of proficiency

If parents' reports of students' language on the HLS indicated potential limited English proficiency, students then took the AZELLA, Arizona's standardized assessment of ELP. Grounded in federal requirements for standardized language proficiency testing (NCLB, 2001), AZELLA represented a series of criterion-referenced tests written for five grade bands (i.e. Kindergarten; Grades 1–2; Grades 3–5; Grades 6–8; Grades 9–12) measuring listening, speaking, reading and writing (ADE, 2011). The ADE outlined four purposes of the AZELLA in Structured English Immersion (SEI) programming:

a) To determine student placement for EL services
b) To measure student progress in ELD
c) To establish exit criteria for students from the EL label
d) To monitor the English proficiency of re-classified students (ADE, 2011)

Following PHLOTE determination from the HLS, Arizona House Bill 2064, enacted in 2006, defined the mandated second step in the EL identification process. The policy stated:

> The English language proficiency of all pupils with a primary or home language other than English shall be accessed through the administration of English language proficiency assessments in a manner prescribed by the Superintendent of Public Instruction. The test scores adopted by the superintendent as indicating English language proficiency shall be based on the test publisher's designated scores. (HB 2064, 2006: 4)

Similar to the nebulous nature of the statement regarding primary language screening, the ambiguous wording of the state legislation allowed the state superintendent to guide the selection of an ELP assessment tool as well as to set the cut scores to determine eligibility for services.

The AZELLA, the state-selected assessment provided by Pearson Education, comprised sub-tests divided by language domain: listening, speaking, reading and writing. The composite of the subtest scores resulted in the numeric ascription of one of five ELP levels: (a) *pre-emergent*, (b) *emergent*, (c) *basic*, (d) *intermediate* and (e) *proficient* (ADE, 2008). Any student who scored in a category other than proficient (i.e. pre-emergent, emergent, basic and intermediate) was 'classified as an English language learner and shall be enrolled in an English language education program' (HB 2064, 2006: 5), pending parental acceptance or refusal of services (see Figure 3.1; ADE, 2013). School personnel reassessed ELs at the end of each school year (HB 2064, 2006), with an optional assessment mid-year for formative purposes (ADE, 2008). The AZELLA composite score, which combined students' scores on the various subtests, held great weight in the education of ELs as 'SEI classroom entry and exit is determined solely by AZELLA score' (ADE, 2008: 1). Just as students' AZELLA scores determine placement in the ELD program, their numeric classifications of ELP determined program exit.

After a composite score of *proficient* on the AZELLA, which could take multiple years to achieve, a student was reclassified from EL to fluent English proficient and transferred to English-medium mainstream classrooms (HB 2064, 2006). Arizona educators utilized AZELLA scores to monitor reclassified students for two years (HB 2064, 2006; NCLB, 2001). During the two years of federal- and state-mandated monitoring, student's AZELLA scores maintained the high-stakes nature that served as the sole predictor for program and classroom placement. If students continued to demonstrate proficiency by testing above the designated cut scores, then they maintained placement in mainstream classrooms; however, if students scored below the designated test score for proficiency, then they were removed from mainstream classrooms and returned to ELD classrooms.

As described in House Bill 2064 (2006: 11), 'Pupils who fail to demonstrate English proficiency on the reassessment test in the two years following their exit from Structured English Immersion, subject to parental consent, shall be reenrolled in Structured English Immersion'.

The assumption behind the language policy regulations was that students scoring proficient on the AZELLA were capable of actively participating and achieving academically in mainstream classrooms. Researchers have challenged this assumption, specifically examining the validity of the AZELLA in determining ELP and testing the predictive ability of the AZELLA for students' achievement. Florez (2010, 2012) investigated the validity of AZELLA cut scores, finding questionable validity in accurately identifying ELs' language proficiency. Florez first considered issues with cut scores, including (a) test developers' procedures utilized to determine cut scores through a procedure no longer used by national assessment organizations, (b) test developers' failure to establish qualifications of judges who set cut scores using conceptual judgments and (c) state administrators' choice to modify cut scores from test recommendations.

Empirical evidence also demonstrated that cut scores over-identified kindergarten students and under-identified older children. García et al. (2010) examined the validity of the AZELLA in predicting students' academic achievement as measured by standardized tests. In the first year of the ELD mandate, researchers found that the AZELLA was not predictive of academic achievement at higher grade levels. Calling into question the reliance on one test for EL education, they concluded, 'The use of the AZELLA over-predicts the transitioned student's capacity to succeed academically in the regular classroom and places a critical barrier to obtaining an equal education in Arizona' (García et al., 2010: 13).

Simultaneous to the studies conducted by Florez (2010, 2012) and García et al. (2010), the OCR investigated whether AZELLA cut scores were indicative or predictive of academic achievement, with a specific focus on ELs who exited ELD programs prepared for mainstream classrooms. Using data from a sample of students who took the first two iterations of the AZELLA (i.e. AZ-1 used 2007–2009, AZ-2 used 2009–2012), the OCR determined that Arizona administrators removed ELs prematurely from ELD classrooms and federally mandated EL services (OCR, 2012). Following the successful OCR suit in 2010, the resolution agreement of 2012 required Arizona educators meeting with parents of prematurely reclassified students to determine appropriate placement for EL services. In the meantime, state administrators revised the assessment to increase rigor and provide valid cut scores that were more indicative of language proficiency and academic achievement. The resulting revisions represented the third iteration of the AZELLA (i.e. AZ-3), the state's sole assessment of ELP in 2013.

High-stakes language assessments: Assessment for accountability

In addition to using AZELLA scores to determine ELs' classification and educational programming, administrators utilized the language assessment for purposes of accountability with federal policy and compliance with state policy. Administrators at the ADE, specifically in the Office of English Language Acquisition Services (OELAS), outlined the use of AZELLA with implications for language policy and practice: (a) district and school performance measures for federal accountability purposes, (b) district and school performance measures for state compliance purposes, (c) supplemental funding for EL services and (d) indications of ELD program effectiveness (ADE, 2011).

With federal-level guidelines (NCLB, 2001) and state-level mandates (HB 2064, 2006) for EL assessment and instruction, AZELLA scores provided data to measure performance at the school and district levels. At the federal level, AZELLA scores served accountability purposes to (a) provide longitudinal data analysis of EL performance (ADE, 2011), (b) demonstrate progress on Annual Measurable Achievement Objectives (AMAOs) and (c) assign school labels based on EL student achievement (ADE, 2011). At the state level, language assessments combined to outline compliance requirements for districts and schools, including required forms (e.g. HLS, 2-year monitoring form) and mandated procedures (e.g. EL identification, EL reassessment). Whereas ADE administrators emphasized assessment documents and procedures, instructional implementation of the 4-hour ELD model also took center stage for schools and districts to demonstrate compliance with language policy. Instructional mandates are discussed in the next section.

Isolate and Instruct: The English Language Development Model

After providing a system for labeling and placing in EL education by Arizona's two-pronged assessment procedure, language policy then provided guidelines for teaching and learning in ELD classrooms. State leaders described the ELD setting as 'a classroom in which all of the students are limited English proficiency as determined by composite AZELLA scores of Pre-emergent, Emergent, Basic or Intermediate. The purpose of the classroom is to provide four hours of daily ELD instruction' (ADE, 2014: 1). As described in Chapter 2, the ELD approach to instruction resulted from the language policy shift outlined in House Bill 2064 (2006), which formed the EL Task Force of appointed participants charged to design a research-based program and prescriptions for SEI (ADE, 2008). This section utilizes language policy and extant literature to outline details on the ELD approach, including the self-contained classroom setting, four hours of skill-based language instruction and changes to the models that have comprised EL education across the state of Arizona in the past five years.

Self-contained settings: English learners separated from mainstream peers

Because ELs' placement in ELD classrooms is contingent on their English proficiency as determined by AZELLA composite scores, educators must isolate ELs in language-focused instruction with other students still in the process of acquiring English. Prior to the design of the ELD model by the task force, state legislation mandated the separation of ELs from English-proficient students in House Bill 2064 (2006: 7): 'The models shall be limited to programs for English language learners to participate in a Structured English Immersion program not normally intended to exceed one year'. By limiting participation to labeled ELs, rather than incorporating inclusion with English-proficient students, the language policy designed an inherent mandate to segregate students into instructional settings based on English proficiency. Further, only when a student demonstrated English proficiency on the AZELLA could they be 'transferred to English language mainstream classrooms' (HB 2064, 2006: 11). Building on these guidelines provided by lawmakers, the EL Task Force members detailed mandates to dictate how school administrators organized students into classrooms.

In addition to the separation of ELs from English-proficient peers, the new ELD models required the separation of ELs based on ELP levels as measured by AZELLA composite scores. The SEI Models document (ADE, 2008: 4) outlined, 'The primary determinant of the appropriate student grouping for SEI Classrooms is the English proficiency level of the students. The proficiency levels and grade levels of the ELLs must be used in order to determine appropriate student placement'. In elementary schools, prioritization guidelines centered on overall proficiency and grade level, organizing students by proficiency levels within grade and possibly across grade. In this way, at schools with large numbers of ELs, all students with overall proficiency levels of pre-emergent and emergent might be in one classroom, separate from students who scored basic or intermediate. At schools with fewer ELs, one ELD classroom might house all proficiency levels either within one grade level (e.g. third grade) or across grades (e.g. Grades 3, 4 and 5). Secondary settings differed in the prioritization of students' proficiency sub-levels using the specific AZELLA subtests. Assuming that the skill-based language blocks were separated into periods (e.g. reading, writing, conversation), guidelines required student grouping by that specific language domain score within and across grades. See Table 3.1 for ELD student grouping guidelines (ADE, 2008).

Scholars and critics have described many issues related to this particular facet of Arizona language policy that places ELs into ELD classrooms apart

Table 3.1 Student grouping guidelines

Setting	Grouping prioritization	Grouping example
Elementary	Overall proficiency level within grade	Grade 1 ELD, basic composites
	Overall proficiency level band with grade	Grade 1 ELD, all composites
	Overall proficiency level band within grade band	Grades 1 and 2 ELD, all composites
Secondary	Proficiency sub-level within grade	Grade 6 reading, basic sub-score
	Proficiency sub-level within grade band	Grades 6–8 reading, basic sub-score
	Overall proficiency level within grade	Grade 6 ELD, basic composites
	Overall proficiency level within grade band	Grades 6–8 ELD, basic composites
	Overall proficiency level band within grade band	Grades 6–8 ELD, all composites

from their mainstream peers. Gándara and Orfield (2012) considered the segregation by multiple dimensions, including how the policy organized students into categorical classrooms based on ethnicity, language and poverty across both schools and classrooms. Authors conceptualized restrictive language policy as further exacerbating school-level segregation with classroom-level segregation. Arizona as a state and within major metropolitan areas has historically been culturally, linguistically and socioeconomically segregated by region. This socio-historical segregation has resulted in schools with predominant population compositions, such as how the Cartwright district in western Phoenix – composed of predominantly low-income Latinos – compares to the Chandler district in suburban Phoenix – with predominantly middle-class Whites (Gándara & Orfield, 2012). In addition to this three-dimension scheme of segregation by culture, language and socioeconomic status, critics argue and pose conceptual issues with social, emotional, linguistic and academic facets of EL student development and achievement.

Detrimental social and emotional implications of separating ELs from their peers have emerged as key critiques of the restrictive language policy. Scholars have merged around student segregation as isolating, stigmatizing and marginalizing ELs (Faltis & Arias, 2012; Gándara & Orfield, 2012; García, 2011). An original member of the EL Task Force, Eugene García (2011: 50) has since described that the segregation required in the language policy and resulting ELD model 'reduces their [ELs'] social and cultural well-being, silencing and marginalizing them in the greater school context and diminishing their sense of belonging'. Using a review of research on segregation and linguistic isolation, Gándara and Orfield (2012: 2) found that 'excessive segregation of Arizona's Latino and EL students is most probably harmful to their achievement and social and emotional development'; such inhibitions to positive academic and social-emotional functioning has contributed to increases in school failure and dropout rates in secondary settings. In elementary settings, students have been placed in ELD classrooms to receive only the mandated language instruction, but scheduling challenges result in continued separation from mainstream peers for lunch, recess, special areas and extracurricular activities – leading to social separation, and social marginalization, for the entire school day (Faltis & Arias, 2012).

Linguistic issues have also been central in critiques of the ELD model, considering the direct correlation with separating children and adolescents based on language proficiency. With ELs separated from their English-proficient peers, often for the extent of the full school day (Faltis & Arias, 2012; Lillie et al., 2012; Lillie & Markos, 2014), students receive limited or no opportunities to integrate and interact with native English speakers as fluent models (García, 2011; Iddings et al., 2012). In this way, the classroom teacher has remained the only fluent model of English proficiency for students (Faltis & Arias, 2012). Drawing on prior research on second language learning (Faltis, 2006), Faltis and Arias (2012) described the conditions that best support ELs' learning and language development:

> Through interaction with English speakers, English learners are obliged to produce language that increasingly approximates English, because English speakers often ask for clarification, check for understanding and rephrase language to confirm understanding. This kind of negotiated interaction pushed English learners to test hypotheses about language and to pay attention to language structure and language meanings. When English learners are provided these rich opportunities for negotiating meaning and using language for communication with others about school topics and academic content, oral and written English proficiency increase, along with academic learning. (Faltis & Arias, 2012: 33)

Instead, classrooms composed of all ELs, often at the same level of ELP as determined by AZELLA composite scores, fail to provide language acquisition environments conducive to multiple scaffolds for students' immersion in authentic language use.

Because of the lack of access to content curricula in ELD classrooms, academic issues outlined by scholars have particularly centered on the statement that ELD classroom placement was 'not normally intended to exceed one year' (HB 2064, 2006: 7). Prioritizing the instruction of discrete language skills determined as prerequisite foundations for academic learning (ADE, 2008), ELD classrooms focused on language rather than content, resulting in equity issues as ELs fell behind peers in core academics (Faltis & Arias, 2012). The on-the-ground reality is that the ELD setting is not moving the majority of ELs toward English proficiency in one year (Combs, 2012; Faltis & Arias, 2012; Gándara & Orfield, 2012). Combs (2012: 80) described the conundrum: 'If students do not achieve proficiency in one year, however, they could remain segregated in remedial classrooms a second, third, even fourth year'. By denying ELs access to academic curriculum and instruction in literacy, mathematics, science and social studies, the academic achievement gap between ELs and mainstream peers will continue to grow (Gándara & Orfield, 2012; García, 2011). Based on the *time-on-task* principle, according to which more time spent on English language skills is assumed to speedily lead to ELP, the ELD model separates ELs from English-proficient peers, basically situating ELs in a distinct school within a school (ADE, 2007; Lillie & Markos, 2014).

Time on task: Four hours of English language development instruction

Language policy regulations

The primary characteristic of the ELD model, the 4-hour block of skill-based language instruction, emerged from House Bill 2064 and the resulting development of prescriptive models of SEI designed by the EL Task Force. Whereas the formal legislation only required a minimum of four hours of ELD for 'the first year in which a pupil is classified as an English language learner' (HB 2064, 2006: 7), the task force extended the 4-hour ELD structure to be 'uniform for all SEI models' (ADE, 2008: 3). In this way, all labeled ELs regardless of proficiency level received four hours of ELD instruction per day, organized into five 'English language skills categories' (ADE, 2008: 5) including grammar, vocabulary, conversation, reading and writing. Task force members described the slight differences in *models* as the specific time allocations for language-based content areas, which varied depending on the composite AZELLA score of the student. See Table 3.2 for the organization of language skills in ELD models of instruction.

The five language-based content areas (e.g. grammar, vocabulary) stemmed from the *language star* framework introduced to the task force

Table 3.2 Time increments in 4-hour instructional block

Composite AZELLA Level	Conversation	Grammar	Vocabulary	Reading	Writing
Pre-emergent and emergent	45 min	60 min	60 min	60 min	15 min
Basic	30 min	60 min	60 min	60 min	30 min
Intermediate	15 min	60 min	60 min	60 min	45 min

by consultant Kevin Clark during the development of the SEI models. In addition to the time-on-task principle that led to the decision to require the extended four hours for all students (ADE, 2007), task force members utilized the language star to design and explain the specific adoption of the ELD model.

> 'ELD' means English language development, the teaching of English language skills to students who are in the process of learning English. It is distinguished from other types of instruction, e.g., math, science, or social science, in that the content of ELD emphasizes the English language itself. ELD instruction focuses on phonology (pronunciation – the sound system of a language), morphology (the internal structure and forms of words), syntax (English word order rules), lexicon (vocabulary), and semantics (how to use English in different situations and contexts). (ADE, 2008: 1)

Distinct from SEI models used in California and Massachusetts, which focus on teaching content (e.g. science) to ELs while simultaneously scaffolding for language development (Echevarría *et al.*, 2013), the ELD model dichotomized content and language learning – mandating skill-based language instruction as prerequisites and apart from the learning of academic content. See Figure 3.2 for the Language Star framework utilized to guide the design of the ELD model.

State administrators provided additional mandates for ELD classrooms teachers to guide instructional planning, implementation and materials within this 4-hour block with the five language-based content areas. Within a given mandated content area in the 4-hour block (e.g. a 1-hour class on grammar), administrators mandated the use of ELP standards and the Discrete Skills

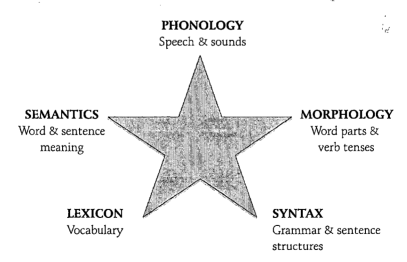

PHONOLOGY
Speech & sounds

SEMANTICS
Word & sentence
meaning

MORPHOLOGY
Word parts &
verb tenses

LEXICON
Vocabulary

SYNTAX
Grammar & sentence
structures

Figure 3.2 Language Star framework

Inventory (DSI; ADE, 2008) for instructional planning. Paired with the extant ELP standards, organized into language domains by listening and speaking, reading and writing, state leaders developed the DSI to guide the explicit teaching of grammar, which the task force and administrators prioritized as 'essential in the language acquisition process for ELLs' (ADE, n.d.: 1). With defined language standards in the state-mandated ELD classroom lesson plans, teachers then had to select textbooks and materials that (a) included only the English language, (b) supported students at their specific ELP levels, (c) aligned to the ELP standards and DSI, (d) facilitated and promoted defined language objectives and (e) predominantly featured the specific language skill targeted in the language-specific content areas (ADE, 2008: 7–8). Without standard curricula provided to teachers in ELD classrooms, teachers must find these leveled, targeted and English-medium resources on their own.

Conceptual critiques

To meet federal standards for EL instruction (*Castañeda v. Pickard*, 1981), state administrators had to demonstrate educational theory and research supporting the ELD model (Faltis & Arias, 2012). Consultant Kevin Clark, who emerged on the scene after his SEI implementation work in California, assisted the EL Task Force in the development of the ELD model; drafted a 13-page document with supporting research on time-on-task, discrete English language skills in a particular order; and allocating fixed periods of time to certain elements of language (ADE, 2007). Despite the fact that scholars described it as having multiple flaws and missing important areas of educational research, this document became the primary underlying research base of the ELD model (Martínez-Wenzl *et al.*, 2012). In response to Clark's literature review, Krashen and other leading scholars in the field of second language acquisition responded point by point to debunk the ADE research document (Krashen *et al.*, 2007, 2012). Since that initial response, other scholars have critiqued the research base, calling into question whether education policy and practice in Arizona had met the legal requirements of *Castañeda* (Faltis & Arias, 2012).

With the research base for the ELD model centered on the time-on-task principle, scholars framed conceptual critiques by discrediting the maximum exposure principle through second language acquisition theory (August *et al.*, 2010; Combs, 2012; Faltis & Arias, 2012; Long & Adamson, 2012). Long and Adamson (2012: 51) described the ELD model as 'inconsistent with what SLA [second language acquisition] research has shown about how children learn new languages and about how best to teach them'. First, the model did not incorporate native language, which contrasted with second language acquisition theory supporting the role of students' first language for learning a second (Combs, 2012; Faltis & Arias, 2012) as well as the benefits of bilingualism and bilingual education (August *et al.*, 2010; Martínez-Wenzl *et al.*, 2012). Second, the 4-hour block of skill-based language instruction did not factor in the development of academic language and competence, which has been deemed central to second language acquisition (August *et al.*, 2010; Combs, 2012; Long & Adamson, 2012). Finally, the state's projected one year to achieve ELP contradicted widely accepted understandings that students need 4–10 years to learn a second language (August *et al.*, 2010; Collier, 1989; Faltis & Arias, 2012; Hakuta *et al.*, 2000).

In addition to using theory, critics of the ELD model have considered conflicting research on effective instruction for ELs. Unlike the oft-cited successes of French immersion programs in Canadian classrooms used as a research-based justification for SEI in the US, the ELD approach yields a one-size-fits-all model with specific instructional prescriptions to overtly teach discrete language skills (Combs, 2012). García (2011: 49) asserted, 'In Arizona law, ELD consists of improving phonology, morphology, syntax, lexicon, and semantics. Nobody learns a living language this way'. ELD policy mandated teachers to adhere to principles to accelerate English learning in practice, such as correcting students' linguistic errors, using only English in the classroom and requiring students to use complete sentences (Combs, 2012). Nevertheless, extant research on effective EL instruction has supported a contradictory set of principles, such as using first language to build instruction, tapping into families' funds of knowledge, merging language with academic content and providing ample opportunities for authentic and meaningful language use (Iddings *et al.*, 2012).

Empirical research

In addition to the copious conceptual critiques of the ELD approach to EL teaching and learning, a handful of empirical studies have probed the implementation and efficacy of the restrictive SEI models since their inception in 2008. One qualitative study engaged a team of researchers in seven weeks of ethnographic data collection in five Arizona school districts in the second year of ELD implementation in 2009–2010, aiming to document characteristics of the 4-hour ELD model in practice (Lillie *et al.*, 2012; Lillie & Markos, 2014). Findings from two elementary school districts indicated that the 4-hour policy resulted in (a) full-day segregation from mainstream peers, including lunch where students sat by classroom; and (b) scant time for content area instruction, with 40 minutes on average for mathematics (compared to 240 minutes on prescribed language instruction) and no science or social studies. Findings from three secondary districts demonstrated similar separation and stigmatization; although older ELs received non-ELD instruction in other class periods, they were typically with the same classmates, physically isolated from mainstream peers in separate class sections and often in different buildings. Additionally, due to mandated ELD classes, high school ELs 'are faced with the real possibility that they will not graduate as a result of their placement in the SEI model' (Lillie &

Markos, 2014: 227). Across both elementary and secondary settings, teachers and leaders (a) enforced English-only policies and procedures, (b) lacked appropriate resources and materials, (c) adversely corrected students' errors and (d) conceptualized ELs as fundamentally different than non-ELs.

Among quantitative studies, Rumberger and Tran (2010) analyzed achievement gaps between EL and mainstream students in reading and math in Grades 4 and 8. In addition to finding sizeable achievement gaps, they found that states with more restrictive language policies, specifically Arizona, had larger gaps, particularly in Grade 4. García et al. (2012) also found Arizona ELs' test scores lag behind those of students in states with less restrictive language policies. Additionally, when comparing Arizona EL achievement data before and after the ELD model, they found 'little to no progress in closing the achievement gap between ELL and non-ELL students' (García et al., 2012: 2).

Rios-Aguilar et al. (2012a) analyzed the longitudinal academic achievement of ELs in one urban Arizona school before and after ELD, as well as comparing EL data between ELD and mainstream settings; they found that 'ELLs who participated in mainstream classrooms and in other instructional arrangements have higher academic achievement compared to ELLs who participated in the 4-hour ELD block' (Rios-Aguilar et al., 2012a: 47). García (2011: 49) pointedly described the consequences of this empirical evidence: 'This puts Arizona in violation of the U.S. Supreme Court decisions that require states to give proof of the success of their ELL programs'. In other words, data demonstrating the ineffectiveness of the ELD model contradicts the requirement for program revision based on evaluation data (*Castañeda v. Pickard*, 1981).

Policy shifts

Despite conceptual critiques and empirical studies demonstrating the challenges and inefficacy of ELD implementation, state leaders have made few alterations to the 4-hour model since its original implementation in 2008–2009. Although state legislation opened the door for program changes, calling for annual review of information and data to 'delete, add, or modify the existing models' (HB 2064, 2006: 8), EL Task Force members opted not to make changes to the mandated 4-hour structure despite practitioner and scholar requests due to implementation-related challenges like those described above (Leckie et al., 2013). Instead, the task force maintained the overall design of the ELD model, inciting OELAS administrators to increase the rigidity of implementation. With the original ELD model outlined in an eight-page document (ADE, 2008), additional instructional mandates and compliance guidelines emerged to further restrict and monitor local educators' practice.

During this time of increasing oversight and top-down monitoring from the state, scholars and advocates continued to push back against policy regulations, heightening scrutiny in the academic and political sectors through journal publications (Language Policy, 2012; Teachers College

Record, 2012), edited texts (Faltis & Arias, 2012; Moore, 2014) and federal legal actions (OCR, 2009, 2011). Although scholars have continuously critiqued the instruction mandated by ELD, their research and lawsuits have occasionally placed more students in ELD classrooms. For example, the federal legal actions focused on the HLS and AZELLA lawsuits resulted in federal judicial resolutions on the side of OCR and EL education scholars and advocates; however, the resulting resolutions significantly increased the number of labeled ELs and therefore returned tens of thousands more children to ELD classrooms, those same educational settings that scholars have argued so vehemently against. Often housed at the three Arizona universities, many of these ELD critics have found themselves negotiating restrictive policy roles as instructors for the state-mandated teacher preparation courses. How language policy has an impact on teacher education is described in the next section.

Structuring English Immersion: Teachers and Teacher Preparation

Without access to native language support and bilingual materials typically utilized to support students' language development in other states, the onus of providing appropriate and effective instruction for ELs has fallen on one set of shoulders – the classroom teacher's (Gándara & Maxwell-Jolly, 2006). With federal law prohibiting the use of submersion, or sink-or-swim language instruction (*Lau v. Nichols*, 1974), the well-prepared teacher became the primary lever that differentiates the English-medium immersion versus English-only submersion. Recognizing the centrality of the teacher to avoid submerging children, policy regulations included explicit attention to teachers and teacher preparation (Arias, 2012). To be considered *highly qualified* to teach in the 4-hour block in ELD classrooms, a public school teacher need a bachelor's degree and valid Arizona teaching certificate (i.e. intern, provisional, reciprocal, standard), as well as a bilingual, ESL or SEI provisional or full endorsement (ADE, 2008, 2014). In this section, I outline policy and extant literature on teacher preparation in state-mandated coursework and teachers' practice in classrooms and schools.

Teacher preparation: The Structured English Immersion endorsement

When Arizona lawmakers passed House Bill 2064 in 2006, the resulting language policy did not only attempt to restrict and script practice with ELs in K-12 schools but also extended mandates influencing the preparation of teachers at communities colleges, universities and other local educational agencies (Arias, 2012). Policymakers ascribed responsibility for teacher training to the State Board of Education, formally relegating the determination of qualifications for the provisional and full SEI endorsements and the approval of university coursework and other training agencies (House Bill 2064, 2006: 13–14). In this way, appointed members of the State Board of Education had control over the prescription of required content and allotted time for the state-mandated endorsements, as well as the oversight to monitor the programs and bodies that facilitated the content with educators across the state.

Using the power granted by the official language policy document, the State Board of Education approved provisional and full SEI endorsements to be phased in with in-service and pre-service teachers between 2006 and 2009 (Arias, 2012). Originally, an SEI endorsement required 60 total clock hours for all in-service Arizona teachers, including 15 hours for the provisional and 45 additional hours for the full endorsement (ADE, 2005). With House Bill 2064, the SEI endorsement extended to 90 clock hours for new teachers, with 45 hours for the provisional and 45 for the full endorsement (ADE, 2011). In addition to assigning mandated clock hours and outlining procedures to roll out the language policy for teacher preparation, the State Board of Education designed curricular framework with learning objectives, sub-objectives and specific time allotments (ADE, 2005, 2011). The curricular frameworks then served as blueprints for board members to approve the teacher preparation provided by colleges, universities and other training agencies.

For board approval, courses and workshops had to follow the curricular frameworks for provisional and full endorsements, each with specific content and objectives organized across 45 clock hours. Within both frameworks, state administrators designated only a handful of hours for teachers to learn about the foundations of second language acquisition, ELP standards and facets of language assessment. For example, following the curricular frameworks, teacher educators should only allot approximately 30 minutes for teachers to 'list language acquisition theoretical principles' (ADE, 2005: 1). Lacking in theoretical foundations, the curricular frameworks instead focused primarily on strategies, reserving at least 50 hours for SEI strategies, such as 'preview/review, content areas reading and writing strategies' and 'vocabulary developmental approaches in the content areas' (ADE, 2005: 1). With the curricular frameworks largely unchanged since pre-ELD, the emphasis has remained primarily on sheltered strategies for scaffolding language in content instruction (Echevarría et al., 2013). See Table 3.3 for a content overview of curricular frameworks for provisional and full SEI endorsements.

Teacher educators have struggled with the restrictive language policy regulations regarding SEI coursework. In 2006, after the initial implementation of the newly mandated endorsement coursework, Moore (2014) found that school districts, universities and other educational agencies rushed to put together curricula to gain approval from the State Board of Education and meet the high demand of training all Arizona

Table 3.3 Curricular frameworks for SEI endorsements

Endorsement	Objectives and hours	Sample sub-objectives
Provisional endorsement (45 hours)	Language standards (3 hours)	Examine format of ELP standards
	Assessment (3 hours)	Analyze and use AZELLA data
	Foundations of SEI (3 hours)	Know basic SEI terminology
	SEI strategies (24 hours)	Identify and use multiple strategies
	Flex time (12 hours)	Use at instructor's discretion
Full endorsement (45 hours)	Language standards (1 hour)	Use standards to plan instruction
	Data analysis and application (3 hours)	Track students' language progress
	Formal and informal assessment (3 hours)	Create multiple assessments
	SEI foundations (1 hour)	Outline role of culture in learning
	SEI strategies (25 hours)	Plan lessons using prior knowledge
	Home/school scaffolding (3 hours)	Identify sociocultural influences
	Flex time (9 hours)	Use at instructor's discretion

teachers. Despite the curricular frameworks with specific objectives and time allotments, the wide array of providers led to inconsistent training for teachers. Juxtaposed with these findings, Arizona teacher educators have recently found the difficulty in designing effective EL teacher education coursework in line with the scripted curricular framework mandated by the state (Arias, 2012; Markos & Arias, 2014). With over eight years since the initial implementation, the board had increased the detail and scrutiny of SEI courses, specifically focused on pre-service teacher education. Arias (2012: 13) attested that the 'scripted curriculum left little room for instructors to include components that the research reports to be high-quality education for teachers of ELLs'. Without alignment to EL teacher education research, the *one-size-fits-all* approach to preparing teachers appeared ill-suited to adequately equipping EL teacher candidates for the ELD classroom (Arias, 2012; Markos & Arias, 2014).

In addition to scholarly criticisms of the SEI endorsement for teachers, particularly from Arizona teacher educators forced to prepare teachers within the rigid framework (Arias, 2012), investigators have compared the efficacy of teacher preparation across bilingual, English as a Second Language (ESL) and SEI endorsements. Previously, some teachers opted for university programs of study in ESL or bilingual education; now, the ADE required all teachers to receive the SEI endorsement at a minimum. Equivalent to two university courses of state-prescribed teacher training (ADE, 2008). In contrast to the two courses required for the SEI endorsement, bilingual and ESL endorsements entailed seven and six courses, respectively (Combs, 2012). As a result, more teachers opted for the minimum requirement of the SEI endorsement, rather than the more extensive and time-consuming bilingual and ESL endorsements, which were often perceived and even presented as unnecessary (Hopkins, 2012). In fact, Arias (2012) found that since the board rule change in 2006, teachers have opted for the SEI endorsement at double the rate of bilingual and ESL endorsements.

The extensive bilingual and ESL endorsements provided ample and thorough preparation for Arizona teachers of ELs, with expert faculty designing and facilitating learning experiences to build in-depth knowledge and skills for bilingual or ESL settings (Arias, 2012; Hopkins, 2012). Nevertheless, the minimal time frame for the SEI endorsement, paired with the mandate that all teachers receive SEI endorsements regardless of teaching assignment, has resulted in teachers lacking sound preparation. Evidence indicates that SEI-endorsed teachers are less prepared and equipped for work with ELs than those certified in ESL or bilingual education (de Jong et al., 2010; Hopkins, 2012; Lillie et al., 2012; Murri et al., 2012; Rios-Aguilar et al., 2012a). In contrast, Arizona teachers with ESL and bilingual certification (a) utilized more effective instructional strategies, (b) held more positive perceptions of ELs' abilities (de Jong et al., 2010; Rios-Aguilar et al., 2012a), (c) promoted students' funds of knowledge (Murri et al., 2012) and (d) negotiated policy in practice (Lillie et al., 2012) significantly more than teachers with the minimal SEI endorsement. In sum, despite being considered *highly qualified* to teach in the unique and demanding ELD classroom context, teachers with SEI endorsements tend to bring incomplete research-based knowledge and skills to support ELs' learning and development.

Teachers and teaching: Policy implementation in classrooms and schools

With SEI endorsements required for all Arizona teachers and not specific to ELD classroom settings, policy regulations also influence in-service teacher preparation. State administrators housed in the OELAS monitor for compliance with Arizona's restrictive language policy (HB 2064, 2006). Administrators determine compliance through on-site monitoring visits, selecting approximately 25 school districts and charters schools for auditing each year (out of the 230 school districts and 526 charter schools in Arizona; Arizona Charter Schools Association [ACSA], 2015; ADE, 2015c). School districts with the 50 highest EL populations in the state require compliance monitoring every four years, whereas smaller population districts and charter schools are audited less frequently. On-site monitoring includes 'classroom observations, curriculum reviews, faculty interviews, student records, a review of English language learner programs and an analysis of programmatic effectiveness' (HB 2064, 2006: 12). Following each on-site audit, OELAS administrators report compliance within 45 days and possibly draft a corrective action plan within 60 days. State funding is contingent on compliance with official language policies and corrective action plans.

Central to compliance monitoring were regular and coordinated ELD classroom observations. OELAS administrators visited classrooms to observe ELD instruction and ensure adherence to mandates described in the previous section, including (a) separation of ELs from mainstream peers; (b) four hours of skill-based language instruction; (c) language-based content areas of grammar, vocabulary, conversation, reading and writing; (d) use of ELP standards and DSI to plan instruction; and (e) English-only classroom materials and environment (ADE, 2013). A more controversial facet of classroom-based compliance monitoring, OELAS administrators also evaluated teachers' English fluency by documenting teachers' errors in grammar and pronunciation (Leeman, 2012). Despite that monitoring of teachers' ELP was not an official policy requirement, Arizona administrators maintained that informal measures of teachers' proficiency yielded teachers' speaking of flawless English in front of ELs (Hanna & Allen, 2013). If state administrators determined that teachers lacked fluency in English, those teachers were required to attend Saturday language classes or were removed from classrooms (Jordan, 2010; Zehr, 2010).

Compliance mandates have guided teachers' classroom practice since the inception of the restrictive language policy known as ELD in the 2008–2009 school year; however, teachers' practice has not been rigidly dictated by language policy mandates. Teachers' perspectives, experiences and preparation merged to influence how they perceived and negotiated language policy in practice. In a large-scale study surveying 880 ELD teachers across 33 Arizona schools, Rios-Aguilar et al. (2012a) found that educators questioned the efficacy of the ELD approach to EL education. Teachers reported the 4-hour block as somewhat effective, with most indicating scant acceleration of ELP and lack of access to academic content. Comparative analyses demonstrated that elementary ELD teachers were more critical about both student segregation and the 4-hour model than secondary ELD teachers.

Smaller qualitative studies of bounded cases of teachers have expanded beyond perceptions to investigate teachers' appropriation of language policy based on prior experiences and preparation. Mackinney and Rios-Aguilar (2012) studied the case of one urban middle school, using interview data to consider the implementation of language policy in practice. Findings indicated the variance in implementation within one school, as teachers' policy appropriation varied based on their backgrounds and experiences with language and education. Within a rural elementary school on the Arizona–Mexico border, Brat and Cain (2013) probed how bilingual teachers implemented language policy in practice in a unique bilingual community. Findings demonstrated teachers' appropriation inside of ELD classrooms, utilizing native language and strategies learned through professional preparation in bilingual education. Both studies confirmed that Arizona teachers actively make decisions about how to implement language policy in classrooms, including non-compliance and actively utilizing bilingual education strategies and second language acquisition knowledge – despite the strict compliance mandates and enforcement efforts by state and district administrators. Additionally, bilingual teachers with thorough preparation in bilingual education demonstrated more willingness than SEI-endorsed teachers to advocate for ELs and native language instruction within the privacy of their classrooms (Brat & Cain, 2013; Mackinney & Rios-Aguilar, 2012).

Whereas prior preparation and experiences with bilingual education affected veteran teachers' appropriation, research has also explored how novice teachers with minimal preparation or experience implemented policy in practice. Teachers are considered *highly qualified* to teach in ELD classrooms with intern teacher certificates and provisional SEI endorsements (ADE, 2014); thus, schools and districts have recruited and placed novice teachers in ELD classrooms with little to no preparation to teach ELs. Heineke and Cameron (2011, 2013) specifically probed the perspectives of Teach for America (TFA) teachers placed in ELD classrooms with (a) intern teaching certificates after earning undergraduate degrees and completing a 5-week teacher training and (b) provisional SEI endorsements through an online course provided by the ADE. Whereas TFA alumni with multiple years of experience demonstrated knowledge and commitment to teaching ELs (Heineke & Cameron, 2011), novice TFA corps members in their first years of teaching entered the ELD classroom without understanding ELD or ELs (Heineke & Cameron, 2013). Without prior knowledge or experiences from their brief teacher preparation, they relied on the state's language policy mandates to guide practice.

In addition to investigations of teachers' policy perspectives and appropriation through surveys (Rios-Aguilar *et al.*, 2012b) and interviews (Brat & Cain, 2013; Heineke & Cameron, 2011, 2013; Mackinney & Rios-Aguilar, 2012), scholars have probed the perspectives and experiences of school leaders. Grijalva and Jiménez-Silva (2014) sought the perspectives of eight principals to explore issues and impacts of language policy on and in schools. Principals followed the majority of the ELD mandates but skirted the specific minute requirements and allowed for integration across language content areas. In addition to concerns related to segregation, funding and lack of content teaching shared by Arizona scholars, principals described fear of the ramifications for non-compliance with language policy. Merging research on teachers and leaders at one urban elementary school, Heineke (2009, 2015) investigated teachers' appropriation of language policy during the first semester of ELD practice in the 2008–2009 school year. School actors, including classroom teachers and instructional support staff, expressed that they struggled simultaneously with the limited guidelines for the new ELD model and ample compliance mandates and fears. The collaborative teacher study group allowed educators to consider policy demands in practice, although the state's compliance visit shaped the small-group discourse.

Teachers' experiences with language policy (Brat & Cain, 2013; Heineke & Cameron, 2011, 2013; Mackinney & Rios-Aguilar, 2012; Rios-Aguilar *et al.*, 2012a, 2012b), as well as the perspectives of other school leaders (Grijalva & Jiménez-Silva, 2014; Heineke, 2009, 2015), have provided windows into the local implementation of Arizona's restrictive language policy in practice. Nevertheless, prior research has not considered and merged local and state layers and players of language policy in practice, spanning out to consider ELD classroom teachers, school leaders, district administrators, state officials, EL Task Force members, state legislators, teacher educators and community leaders. In the next section, I describe the methodology of the current study to yield a holistic understanding of language policy in practice in the southwestern state of Arizona.

The Current Study: Methods and Contributions

Restrictive language policy necessitates research that captures the complexities of language use across educational layers, where various players co-construct policy in practice through dynamic interpretation, negotiation and appropriation (Levinson & Sutton, 2001; Menken & García, 2010; Ricento & Hornberger, 1996). To conceptualize the various layers, which span micro- (e.g. classroom, school) to macro-level contexts (e.g. state government), Ricento and Hornberger (1996) described the language policy *onion*: Classroom practitioners make up the center layers and intermediary players comprise the layers out and around, including school leaders, district administrators, state administrators and community leaders (Hornberger & Johnson, 2007). In this way, comprehensive policy investigations must begin with micro-level practice in local classrooms and build out to schools, districts, state entities and communities to understand how individuals co-construct policy through active decisions and negotiations of macro-level structures (Ricento & Hornberger, 1996). Accordingly, whereas past research in Arizona has honed in on one particular policy layer, my study provides a cross-sectional approach to multiple layers and players.

Research design

I designed this qualitative study of multi-layered language policy in practice utilizing facets of the *vertical case study* approach (Bartlett & Vavrus, 2014). Although originally conceptualized for comparative educational research, the vertical component of this methodological approach to studying policy allowed for 'simultaneous attention to and across micro-, meso-, and macro-levels' (Bartlett & Vavrus, 2014: 131). In this way,

I designed a qualitative case study concurrently situated at multiple sites to investigate the dynamic complexities across local and non-local contexts of language policy in practice (Bartlett & Vavrus, 2014; Erickson, 1986; McCarty, 2011; Menken & García, 2010).

In line with the language policy onion framework, the vertical case study began with micro-level *classroom teacher* practice in the local context of Greenwood, Arizona (Hornberger & Johnson, 2007; Ricento & Hornberger, 1996). (All location and participant names are pseudonyms.) A large and diversely populated suburb in the Phoenix metropolitan area, downtown Greenwood has remained a central hub for Latino families across the past century, recently diversifying to welcome a large number of refugee populations from around the world. Situated in this central region of the suburban community, the Jackson Elementary School District (JESD) provides educational services to the large, growing and diversifying population of ELs. Toward capturing the micro-level layers of language policy in practice, this study included the perspectives and experiences of three ELD classroom teachers, three school leaders and four district administrators.

Still focused on the Greenwood community but spanning outside of the JESD, the meso-level of educational policy in practice included stakeholders in institutions of higher education and charter schools. Desert Community College (DCC) welcomed and trained aspiring teachers, offering the first course of the two-course SEI endorsement. Partnering on-site with the community college, an Arizona 4-year university offered the second SEI course. Situated five miles from the JESD central office, National School provided parents in the community with school choice apart from JESD and other nearby public school districts. To attend to these meso-level layers of language policy in practice, this study included the perspectives and experiences of one charter-school leader, one community-college instructor and one 4-year-university professor.

Integral to the vertical case study design, I then spanned out from the local context of Greenwood to consider the macro-level layers and players influencing Arizona language policy in practice (Bartlett & Vavrus, 2014). These included structures and stakeholders who regularly engaged in policy work related to EL education with reach across the state: two EL Task Force members, two ADE administrators, four state legislators and five community advocates. See Table 3.4 for an overview of participants in the study, purposively selected to provide a sample across language policy layers in Arizona.

Data collection

The crux of the data collection focused on the daily work of various policy players, as described through first-person accounts via in-depth digitally recorded and transcribed interviews. Conducted primarily on-site where the players engaged in their daily practice, the interviews provided

Table 3.4 Study participants and contexts

Layer	Player	Context
Classroom	3 ELD classroom teachers	Greenwood, Arizona
School	3 public school principals	Greenwood, Arizona
District	1 ELL department director; 3 ELL department staff	Greenwood, Arizona
State education	2 Department of Education administrators	State of Arizona
	2 task force members	State of Arizona
	2 teacher educators	Greenwood, Arizona
	1 charter school leader	Greenwood, Arizona
State government	2 state senators (education committee)	State of Arizona
	2 state representatives (education committee)	State of Arizona
	5 community organizers and lobbyists	State of Arizona

real-world, contextualized opportunities for participants to describe their backgrounds, perceptions and practice – situated in their classrooms, schools, district offices, community college settings, university settings, community organizations or government buildings (Erickson, 1986).

Despite the multiple sites of data collection within this vertical case study, including conversations with varied stakeholders ranging from teachers to legislators, the interview protocol centered and aligned the data collection across layers (Bartlett & Vavrus, 2014; Seidman, 2006). In this way, I used the interview protocol to provide the basic structure for all interviews but varied the questions slightly and allowed participants to take control of the direction of the dialogue (Mishler, 1986; Seidman, 2006). First, participants shared their personal stories and professional trajectories to build rapport and background in response to open-ended questions. Then, the questions shifted to collect players' unique perspectives and experiences on Arizona language policy and practice in the past, present and future. I utilized follow-up prompts and questions to inquire and explore perspectives and experiences related to language policy in practice.

Whereas interview data provided the core of the data corpus, additional evidence supported interpretations of the complex and dynamic nature of the multilayered language policy in practice (Erickson, 1986; Levinson & Sutton, 2001). Because the micro level of language policy takes center stage in both the conceptual and methodological frameworks of this study, additional purposefully recorded *contextual* data provided thick descriptions with which to situate findings and understandings related to policy in practice (Bartlett & Vavrus, 2014; Erickson, 1986; Hornberger & Johnson, 2007; Levinson & Sutton, 2001; McCarty, 2011; Menken & García, 2010; Ricento & Hornberger, 1996; Rogoff, 2003; Tharp, 1997). By conducting the in-depth interviews at the sites where players engaged in regular practice with language policy, I was able to collect additional contextual data on the classroom, school, district and beyond (Bartlett & Vavrus, 2014; Erickson, 1986) in the form of photographs, both audio-recorded and written observational field notes and reflective memos following all field-based interviews.

Additional evidence in the form of documentation data supported investigation of the multiple layers of language policy (Erickson, 1986; Menken & García, 2010). I utilized various forms of documentation, such as policies, templates, agendas and reports, as a means of examining the policies that directly affected policy players. I cataloged numerous documents from the JESD, ADE and State of Arizona websites that clarified the mandates, guidelines, curricula and other pertinent resources related to ELD policy and practice. I also read local newspapers and archived articles pertinent to the study topic, typically in the realm of education or immigration. Finally, policy reports from state and national actors also contributed to the documentation database.

Data analysis

Conducted across multiple sites, this vertical case study yielded a large corpus of qualitative data for interpretive analysis (Erickson, 1986). I organized the iterative analytic process into three phases: (a) immerse myself in the holistic data corpus, (b) hone in on specific layers and players and (c) return to the data via multiple iterations to merge findings across layers and players. I began by reading the interview transcripts, documentation data and observational field notes across the 26 participants in the local and non-local settings, from which I drafted and continuously revised the coding scheme of emergent themes from the data, reflecting on both the interpretive and iterative nature of the data analysis (Erickson, 1986). The final thematic coding scheme included five overarching categories with 15 codes and 55 sub-codes, organized using the NVivo 10 qualitative research software.

I then returned to the data for a second iteration to deeply explore layers of language policy in practice, organized into chunks by local layers (i.e. classroom, school, district), state-education layers and state-government layers (Bartlett & Vavrus, 2014; Menken & García, 2010). Starting with the local layer and expanding outward, I engaged in three analytic steps within this phase: (a) analyzing data using coding scheme, (b) drafting player profiles and (c) writing assertions (Erickson, 1986; Seidman, 2006). Using the final coding scheme developed from the first iteration of the data corpus, I thematically analyzed data related to various facets of people, places, policies, issues and influences on Arizona language policy in practice. Then, using individual participants' perspectives and experiences described in interviews, I crafted narrative profiles 'to present the participant in the context, to clarify his or her intentions, and to convey a sense of process and time' (Seidman, 2006: 119). After coding all data sources and drafting all player profiles within the layer, I analyzed each of the 55 sub-codes to write and test assertions for the 15 codes.

After completing interpretive analyses *within* layers, the final phase zoomed out to consider the data *across* layers, to capture trends across multiple policy players using the holistic lens of Arizona language policy in practice (Bartlett & Vavrus, 2014; Erickson, 1986; Menken & García, 2010). Drawing from the codes, profiles and assertions across layers and players, I drafted, tested and revised assertions inclusive of all data to connect and consider the interplay of language policy in practice. I also utilized various reports and queries on the NVivo software to aid in the analyses and triangulation of this larger corpus of data. The resulting findings, presented in the upcoming chapters using individual, within-layer and across-layer analyses, were sent to participants to member check for validity.

Discussion: The Present State of Arizona Education

With the passage of Proposition 203 in 2000, Arizona became the second state to implement restrictive language policy in EL education after California just three years earlier. To skirt submersion, the monolingual policy called for SEI, which initially provided little to no direction to guide classroom instruction. The passing of House Bill 2064 led to a state-level EL Task Force to design more explicit models and·guidelines for SEI. The resulting model, referred to as ELD, centered on the maximum exposure to language skills. Originally implemented in the 2008–2009 school year, the ELD approach utilized standardized language assessment scores to label and place ELs in classrooms separate from their mainstream peers for 4-hour daily blocks of skill-based English language instruction. Considered highly qualified upon receipt of state-mandated SEI endorsements, ELD teachers provided conversation, vocabulary, grammar, reading and writing instruction in ELD classrooms.

Despite the predominance of conceptual literature in the past years on the ELD approach to the teaching and learning of ELs in recent years in Arizona, a handful of empirical studies have investigated issues related to assessment, instruction and teacher education. Among those empirical studies, researchers have considered the perspectives and experiences of particular groups of policy players, such as teachers (Heineke, 2015; Heineke & Cameron, 2011, 2013), principals (Grijalva & Jiménez-Silva, 2014) and EL task force members (Leckie *et al.*, 2013). To date, no single study has presented comprehensive findings across layers for those affected by and effecting Arizona language policy. To address this gap, in this qualitative study I included the perspectives and experiences of multiple players engaged in the education of ELs in Arizona, using data collected from teachers, leaders, administrators, teacher educators, legislators and community organizers (Erickson, 1986). By presenting the holistic and detailed findings in a manner that captures the complexities of EL education in Arizona, this monograph joins other comprehensive contributions to the field of language education policy in the US (e.g. Freeman, 2004; McCarty, 2002; Menken, 2008) and around the world (e.g. Chimbutane, 2011; Davis, 1994; Hornberger, 1988).

Conducted five years after significant restrictions to Arizona language policy and grounded in sociocultural theory (Rogoff, 2003; Vygotsky, 1978), the vertical case study probes the multiple layers and players of language policy in practice with the classroom teacher at the center (Bartlett & Vavlrus, 2014; Hornberger & Johnson, 2007; Ricento & Hornberger, 1996). Using the analogy of the multilayered policy onion, I present the study findings in the next part of the text, organized into four chapters by policy layers and players: (a) ELD classroom teachers, (b) school and district leaders, (c) state-education administrators and leaders and (d) state legislators and community leaders. Situated within the complex and interconnected layers and players of this restrictive language policy context, each chapter foregrounds one layer of policy to deeply explore and probe players' perspectives and experiences that merge to influence the education of ELs (Rogoff, 2003; Tharp, 1997).

Part 2

Findings

4 Starting at the Center: English Language Development in Classrooms

This introductory findings chapter explores one local context of Arizona language policy in practice. The sociocultural paradigm conceptualizes educational policy as a complex and dynamic process that is co-constructed by multiple layers and players (Hornberger & Johnson, 2007; Levinson & Sutton, 2001; Menken & García, 2010; Ricento & Hornberger, 1996). Teachers are at the center of language policy as they interpret, implement and appropriate policy in everyday practice to mediate the teaching and learning of English learners (ELs) (Hornberger & Johnson, 2007; Menken & García, 2010; Ricento & Hornberger, 1996). Based on my study in the community of downtown Greenwood[1] in the Phoenix metropolitan area, I begin sharing the findings from EL classroom teachers (Ricento & Hornberger, 1996). To ground the policy investigation in the sociocultural context, I first utilize descriptive narrative of the local setting, including the history of this Phoenix suburb and the demographics and details of the Jackson Elementary School District (JESD). I then present qualitative narrative cases to introduce three English Language Development (ELD) teachers and their experiences in and perspectives on classroom practice with ELs. After using thick description to provide windows into the daily policy work of teachers (Hornberger & Johnson, 2007; McCarty, 2011; Menken & García, 2010), I close with discussion that foregrounds classroom-level policy work while simultaneously drawing attention to the various layers in the background (Rogoff, 2003; Tharp, 1997), which will be explored in depth in the following findings chapters.

Community and Schools of Greenwood, Arizona

As in much of the southwestern region of the nation, once part of Mexico prior to the cession of land to the US in the Treaty of Guadalupe Hidalgo in 1848, Latino settlers were the first residents of the Greenwood region. Situated in the then US territory of Arizona, Greenwood began as a rural desert settlement of farmers and ranchers, the area initially serving as a place for farmers to come together to give and get products and services in the late 1800s. As Arizona settlers developed ways to sustain life and industry in the desert, such as the canals and railroads that brought water, goods and people beyond the primary settlement of Phoenix, Greenwood continued to grow in size with ranchers raising livestock and farmers tending multiple products from sugar beets to cotton (Greenwood Bureau, 2014). With relatively fertile land due to the location near an Arizona river valley, agriculture thrived in Greenwood more so than in other southwestern communities. Officially founded in 1892, Greenwood was described as a 'quiet, religious community based on strong family values' (Greenwood Bureau, 2014: 1).

Incorporated as a town in 1910 when the population hit the 1000 mark, Greenwood was then miles away from the established city of Phoenix, leading residents to develop their own downtown community with banks, churches, factories and restaurants. Residential neighborhoods popped up around the downtown community, with farms and ranches still finding a home in this desert city. Greenwood continued to grow as a city throughout the 20th century, including various waves of population growth. After a slight increase in the 1940s due to increased industrial jobs for World War II, the population nearly doubled in the 1950s, primarily with Midwesterners and others from across the US coming to enjoy the warm weather and low-cost lifestyle. A steady increase in this suburban population continued throughout the latter half of the 20th century. The late 1990s and early 2000s brought an immense increase in business and tourism to the city limits of Greenwood with concert venues, hotels, shopping malls, bars and restaurants erected in the expansive open tracts of land in the desert (Greenwood Bureau, 2014).

The growth in business and tourism on the outskirts of Greenwood also translated into a boom in the overall population of the city, doubling the number of residents in the last 20 years with the peak in the late 1990s. Today, Greenwood is home to over 200,000 people and continues to grow steadily – up approximately 4% from 2012 to 2013 (City of Greenwood, 2014). Of the Greenwood population, the main demographic groups are residents who classify themselves as Caucasian or Latino, making up approximately 52% and 36% of the population, respectively; the remaining 12% of the population comes from African American, Native American, Asian and multiracial backgrounds. Additionally, 30% of residents speak a language other than English at home (US Census Bureau, 2010). See Figure 4.1 for demographics of the city of Greenwood. Greenwood is considered to be a middle-class suburb; the median household income averages around 50,000 dollars with the average home price at approximately 160,000 dollars (US Census Bureau, 2010) (Figure 4.1).

Positioned between historic railroad tracks and ranches and contemporary freeways and sports venues within the larger city of Greenwood, downtown Greenwood displays relics of the past century

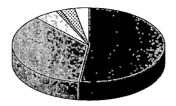

White Non-Latino   Latino   Black   American Indian   Asian Pacific   Multiracial

Figure 4.1 Demographics of the city of Greenwood, Arizona

of growth and change in the region. Walking down the brick, tree-lined streets, historic and contemporary buildings and lifestyles merge to define the changing suburban city. Within the 10 square blocks of the historic region, one can find bungalows-turned-businesses from the early 1900s, main-street-style shops from the mid 1900s, and expansive edifices from the late 1900s and early 2000s. The southern side of Main Street houses main-street-style buildings complete with striped awnings and vintage signs welcoming visitors and residents to eat and shop for antiques, western wear and other specialties. The northern side of Main Street demonstrates the growing urbanity of the region with a large civic center, banks, government offices, luxury lofts and parking structures. Nestled behind the modern constructions, the Crosby Court Corridor consists of four parallel tree-lined roads featuring early-1900s bungalows converted into coffee shops, antique stores, clothing boutiques and specialty stores.

Across the boulevard from the bungalow-style businesses on the northern edge of downtown Greenwood, the JESD offices are situated on a large campus in the Crosby Court Corridor. Surrounded by early 20th-century residential bungalows with declining historic curb appeal, the district offices rise from behind a large metal fence with gates that close and lock by chain and padlock during non-business hours. The former campus of an elementary school, the JESD compound houses educational edifices dating back to 1920. The main building, a 21st-century structure, features a polished desert brick façade that houses the leading administrators for the district, including the superintendent of schools. Offices in the satellite buildings house mid-level administrators and assistants, situated in former classrooms of the open-air elementary school campus originating from the mid-1900s. Additionally, originally welcoming downtown Greenwood children in the early days of incorporation, the 1920s schoolhouse remains a relic on the JESD campus.

From this, the center of operations for the district, administrators oversee the educational, business and human resource practices of schools in and around the downtown Greenwood region. One of multiple school districts within the city of Greenwood, this elementary district provides education to over 13,000 students ranging from pre-K-8 (JESD, 2014a). Schools vary in grade range and services, including pre-K–3, grades 4–8, and pre-K–8 buildings. Typical in the state of Arizona, high schools in Greenwood are organized and led by a separate district. At the JESD offices, the office of the superintendent manages three divisions responsible for human resources, business and education; the latter includes the English Language Learner (ELL) Department consisting of 12 employees organized into three teams focused on students, teachers and parents and families.

JESD is situated in the historic district of the large and growing urban-like suburb, and a greater percentage of Latinos attend JESD schools than other districts in the city; approximately three-quarters of students in the district are Latinos. A historically Latino school district, changing residency patterns have increased the cultural and linguistic diversity in area schools with 36 home languages represented (JESD, 2014b); this includes a growing number of refugee students housed in religious organizations in particular neighborhoods in downtown Greenwood. With over half of students speaking English at home, 35% of JESD students speak Spanish at home, whereas 4% speak one of 34 languages, including Arabic, Vietnamese, Filipino and Kirundi (JESD, 2014b). See Figure 4.2 for native language breakdown in the JESD. Within this cultural and linguistic diversity, approximately 15% of students in the district are labeled as ELs (JESD, 2014a). Almost 90% of JESD students are considered to be living in poverty, based on the federal qualification rates for free and reduced lunch (JESD, 2014a) (Figure 4.2).

Making up approximately half of the employees in JESD, approximately 800 teachers and other school-based educators support the learning of this diverse student population (JESD, 2014a). At each school site, a principal and assistant principal manage teachers, instructional coaches, librarians and other educators. Recognizing the limited number of options for teachers to obtain certification in Arizona, with only three public universities in the state and many for-profit and online institutions, the district prioritizes

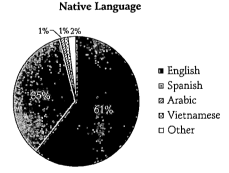

Figure 4.2 Native languages in the Jackson Elementary School District

and engages in out-of-state recruitment and hiring to attract educators from across the country to teach in downtown Greenwood. Additionally, JESD is a long-standing partner of Teach for America (TFA) Phoenix, an alternative path to a certification program that places top college graduates in high-need schools across the region (TFA, 2014a). These teachers, many of whom are placed in ELD classrooms, commit to two years of teaching in Greenwood classrooms while pursuing teaching certification (Heineke & Cameron, 2011, 2013).

English Language Development Teachers in Greenwood Classrooms

Within the community of Greenwood, Arizona and the JESD, ELD classroom teachers engage in language policy work in their everyday practice with the diverse ELs in this Phoenix suburb. Ranging in grade-level placement and years of teaching expertise, the cases of Paula, Tammie and Annie provide windows into the experiences and perspectives of the policy players at the center of Arizona language policy in practice. In this section, I use thick narrative description to explore novice policy players in JESD classrooms: (a) Paula, a first-year teacher; (b) Tammie, a second-year teacher; and (c) Annie, a third-year teacher. See Table 4.1 for details on the classroom-level participants.

Table 4.1 Classroom-level participants

Pseudonym	Grades	Gender	Ethnicity	Language abilities
Paula Street	6, 7, 8	Female	Black	English, Spanish, Asanti
Tammie Johnson	3	Female	White	English
Annie Nethercutt	1	Female	White	English, Spanish

Paula, first-year teacher: A perspective on English language development in the middle-school classroom

Situated in downtown Greenwood, approximately a two-mile drive west on Main Street from the historic corridor, Mountainside School is home to over 900 students ranging from grades pre-K–8. Families walk or drive to Mountainside from a range of homes immediately surrounding the school, including early 1900s bungalows to the south of campus, nestled among stretches of strip malls and convenience stores; mid-1900s ranch-style homes to the north of campus, complete with horses and other livestock; and late 1900s territorial-style homes in subdivisions to the south and west of campus.

The large outdoor campus at Mountainside School features a brown brick façade and turquoise trim, with breezeways leading students, faculty, parents and visitors between various buildings for primary, intermediate and middle-school grade levels. Among the larger school population, approximately 16% of students are labeled as ELs; these 141 students receive four hours of skill-based language instruction in one of nine ELD classrooms. To begin the 2013–2014 school year, the JESD experienced a 40% increase in ELs district-wide, primarily due to the reclassification of ELs who had exited ELD based on Arizona English Language Learner Assessment (AZELLA) scores deemed unacceptable by the Office of Civil Rights.

At Mountainside, the increase in ELs resulted in the addition of a middle-school ELD classroom for the 2013–2014 school year. The sixth-, seventh- and eighth-grade classroom provided a homeroom for a wide array of early adolescents, who varied by grade and developmental level, native language, language proficiency level, immigration status and more. With the total class number fluctuating between 22 and 28 students throughout the school year, the 24 students at mid-year consisted of nine sixth-graders, nine seventh-graders and six eighth-graders. Native languages represented included Spanish, Vietnamese, French and Arabic, including two English-dominant students mislabeled due to the HLS. Because state and district policy required ELD classroom placement for all students who score 'anything other than proficient' on the AZELLA (JESD, 2014c), ELs varied in English proficiency, including pre-emergent, emergent, beginning and intermediate. Students also contrasted by immigration status, ranging from two newcomer students from Vietnam and Mexico to US-born students who had been at Mountainside since kindergarten.

Paula Street moved to Arizona in May of 2013 from Ohio, where she had received her bachelor's and master's degrees in social work, specifically focused on policy and research in community social justice. An African American female and native English speaker with conversational abilities in Spanish and Asanti, Paula finished graduate school and decided to join TFA. Through her 2-year commitment to the organization, she aimed to attain teaching experience before embarking on a long-term career in social work, specifically targeted toward researching and advocating for education. Paula was placed in the Phoenix region and hired by Mountainside School, originally slated to be a primary teacher during her first year as a corps member in the 2013–2014 school year. Shortly before the commencement of the school year, the principal reassigned her to the newly formed ELD classroom in the middle school. Paula described her lack of awareness of ELD policy and practice prior to teaching: 'At the time, I actually wanted to do it. I didn't know what it was. I just thought it was the English class, so I said yes. So to my surprise, it's something totally different.... I had no idea'.

Because of her lack of EL- and ELD-related knowledge at the beginning of the school year, she explained her initial reliance on the explicit instructional time blocks for reading, writing, grammar, conversation and vocabulary (JESD, 2014d).

> At the very beginning, I didn't know hardly anything about the ELD classroom. I knew the basics of the SEI model. I didn't know anything about application. It [instruction] was very much so choppy. We focus on one thing in vocabulary, one thing in reading, one thing in grammar. I was like, 'These kids are hating this'.

Paula recognized her use of the district training to guide her implementation of ELD policy in practice, using rote and scripted approaches for teaching language skills. In the conversation and vocabulary blocks, she described audio-lingual methods for language drills with students but found students did not receive these well or engage in them, as 'they were not robots'. In addition to English-medium drills, Ms Street recalled punishing students for using their native languages, based on the suggestion of her district-level EL instructional coach. She elucidated, 'When you hear them [speaking another language], my coach told me, "Talk to them right away, and let them know that they can get negatives or you need to have a consequence"'. Using her behavior management system, she distributed positive cards as reward for speaking English and negative cards as a deterrent from speaking other languages.

Reflecting on ongoing practice with students in her self-contained middle-school classroom, paired with her evolving understanding of her role in language policy in practice, she explicated her shift in approach to teaching and learning as the school year progressed. Paula realized that she was reinforcing the social and linguistic subjugation inherent in ELD policy, specifically mandates that separated ELs from peers based on linguistic background. She recollected, 'Just the way my kids responded to it [negative cards for native language use], I saw them start to act differently toward me. I stopped doing that'. Instead, she described her shift in practice to allow students to use native language in the classroom to demonstrate the value of bilingualism, paired with honest and straightforward dialogue with students about Proposition 203 and the purpose of the ELD classroom. Through these conversations, students despondently shared the social stigmas within the school and expressed desire to move into a 'normal' or 'regular' classroom.

> There's a serious social impact for them [students] and for adults who may look at them and say they can get over it [being in an ELD classroom] because they need to learn English. When you're outcast, when you feel like you're outcast that does something to confidence.

Connecting students' self-confidence to current and future academic achievement and resilience, Paula recognized her role in fostering social, linguistic and academic development to improve students' high-school performance, reduce drop-out rates and increase the likelihood of college.

Paula described implementing ELD requirements through 4-hour-long 'subject areas of ELD' (JESD, 2014c: 1): (a) oral conversation and vocabulary, (b) reading, (c) grammar and (d) writing. After entering the classroom in the morning, students began with oral language and conversation for the first hour of the day; attempting to build vocabulary through authentic dialogue, Paula provided prompts for students to engage in discussions, typically grounded in current events in Arizona, the US and the world. In the second hour-long block designated for reading instruction, Ms Street explicated her regular use of the gradual release of responsibility to engage students in vocabulary development and reading strategies in whole group, small group and individually; small-group and individual work time included differentiation by language proficiency level. After an early lunch, students returned to the classroom for the grammar block, which included the integration of science. Paula expounded on a grammar lesson focused on chemical bonds:

> They have to read about chemical bonds. During the grammar [block], we are going to do an experiment, or we'll watch an experiment. The way I integrate a grammar part, usually we do that on a day we have to do the interrogative sentences. They're asking a question, you have to place a question by making a hypothesis. We're going to do all that and I'll teach the grammar lesson, and then we'll do the experiment.

Following grammar, writing concluded the 4-hour ELD block, where Paula attempted to merge language-specific subject areas 'to bring in everything together for the whole day' as well as integrate social-studies content; for example, she described having students write about US intervention in other nations.

As a first-year teacher, Paula recognized her struggle to meet the needs of the diverse students in her middle-school classroom, working within the prescriptive structure of the state-mandated, 4-hour blocks for ELD classroom instruction.

> It is a monster to differentiate between proficiency, grade level, interests, and just their [students'] needs too. It's very difficult. They [administrators] tell you all the time, differentiate. Now, the district is pushing to include content like science and such. Just think about all those variables going on, and you [the teacher] got to figure out: How do you do this?

Despite observing the inequity in denying content area instruction to ELs, Paula reflected on the difficulties related to the district's new push to integrate science and social studies. Although state and district-level players defined the ELD program model as one 'designed to accomplish its goal in a period of one school year' (JESD, 2014c), her middle-school classroom included long-term ELs who had been 'lacking in content for years' as well as recent immigrants with interrupted educational experiences.

> When I was being told to give content, it was more just so, 'Okay, I have a reading about science.' Anyone knows if you don't have prior knowledge in this [topic], if you haven't learned about it, I might as well give you a paper full of German writing. You don't know. You don't have any connections with it. That's when I determined that I have to teach science, like exclusively teach, 'This is an atom. This is a molecule. This is a periodic table.' Because if I just give you a paper and say, 'Okay, let's circle the nouns. Let's look for the adjectives.' They're like, 'What? We don't know what this is. This is gibberish for me'.

In addition to the challenges of teaching science and social studies without prior exposure to academic content and language, Ms Street recognized her lack of professional preparation as a science or social studies teacher. With her eighth-graders mandated to take a state standardized test for science, she lamented the negative impact due to lack of preparation for grade-level science content – on the part of both teacher and students.

Contemplating her lack of professional knowledge around middle-school content, Paula considered her teacher preparation prior to entering the ELD classroom at Mountainside, which included an online Structured English Immersion (SEI) course and the 5-week TFA summer institute. By completing the 5-week teacher training as well as the 15 hours of online coursework to receive a provisional SEI endorsement, state policy regulations considered Paula to be 'highly qualified' to teach in an ELD classroom, with the stipulation that she complete the remaining 75 hours of SEI coursework. Despite her 'highly qualified' label, she felt unequipped for her placement:

> Before this, I was [prepared for] social work, period. I just came in [to teaching] thinking like, [teaching] English, anybody can do it… I was overwhelmed because I didn't have that training. Once I really understood what I was supposed to do and the implications and the policies behind it [ELD], I was, even now, I'm overwhelmed because it's so much that you're required to do by yourself. It's frustrating because I like to be prepared, and I wasn't.

Paula earned the additional hours for the full SEI endorsement as embedded in two courses in her master's degree program at a nearby 4-year university. Craving specific guidance on ELD classroom practice from her university instructors in the College of Education, Paula described learning about the history of the restrictive language policy as well as generic sheltered strategies geared toward mainstream teachers: 'The majority of the students in my class, my colleagues, they don't teach the entire ELD class. They only have ELs inside their classrooms. It's just more so, "Remember use some pictures because you may have ELs"'.

As a first-year teacher, Paula identified ample classroom-based support from mentors at TFA, Mountainside and JESD. Due to the unique context of middle-school ELD, TFA struggled to match her with the appropriate coach and instead gave her multiple, including those with backgrounds in special education, English language arts and social studies. She described TFA support as 'more of a burden than a help' in that they asked time, data and artifacts without providing EL-specific support in return. School-level structures provided her with a new teacher mentor as well as supports from the middle-school team of teachers. As the only ELD teacher in middle school, Paula felt disconnected and disconcerted, because team meetings centered on data analysis using the same measures to compare and contrast students without attention to the different instructional context of ELD. Paula described other teachers looking at her like she did something wrong in her classroom instruction: 'Sometimes that makes me feel, pushes me almost to the point of depression, because I feel like we're putting all this work and sometimes you don't see the direct result of what you are trying to teach'. ELD-specific supports came from her district EL coach, Peter, who focused primarily on compliance with state policy. In addition to one classroom observation, they had met on two occasions to talk through frustrations and challenges in the classroom. Paula explained the support of district-level EL players: 'I feel like they're just coming in to see if I'm complying, which is what they're supposed to do. It's not really a teaching situation'. With various mentors inside and outside of the school and district, all with different areas of foci and expertise, Paula felt that their perceived support only contributed to her stress.

The vast array of student diversity, lack of preparation for the language-specific context, multiple policy and practice demands and various mentors provided a sampling of the challenges faced by this first-year teacher in the self-contained middle-school ELD classroom at Mountainside. Paula confided, 'Emotionally, it's hard for me... Sometimes you feel like you're going to have an anxiety attack... It's so much. It's so much. I just can't relieve the stress, all the difficulties'. Pondering her second year of teaching, she considered following the guidance of colleagues, those who expected her to quit early in the 2013–2014 school year and continued to counsel her to request a non-ELD placement for the 2014–2015 school year. Despite her school principal providing her with an out of the ELD classroom, Ms Street planned to continue in her placement, recognizing the disservice of another unprepared first-year teacher for her students, many of whom would continue in the middle-school ELD classroom.

Tammie, second-year teacher: A perspective on English language development in the elementary classroom

Nestled in the northern portion of the Greenwood historic district, directly around the corner from the JESD offices, Longview School is home to approximately 900 students, ranging from pre-school through middle school. It is situated within the Crosby Court Corridor neighborhood of downtown Greenwood, and most surrounding homes are historic bungalows built as early as 1915. With decorative signs calling attention to the historic bungalows of Crosby Court, aging homes feature chain-link fences, added carports and overgrown yards. In contrast to the higher prices of homes in newer Greenwood subdivisions nearby, Longview family homes range in price from 50,000 to 90,000 dollars.

Originally constructed as Jackson Grammar School in this historic community in 1912, the campus has expanded to include additional buildings and complexes, reflecting both the historic and contemporary priorities of Greenwood (Greenwood Bureau, 2014). The large brown brick buildings have been connected by a series of covered sidewalks, protecting students and faculty from the harsh Arizona sun during the year-round school year. Students labeled as ELs make up 17% of the school's students with a total of 129 children enrolled in ELD classrooms across the school. The school has a faculty of approximately 50 educators, the majority White women, and Tammie Johnson described a positive school culture fueled by passionate teachers and leaders whose commitment and dedication to education 'becomes infectious'.

Originally from Boston, Tammie held non-education-related undergraduate and master's degrees from northeastern US universities. After completing her master's degree in writing, she joined TFA to commit two years to teaching in a low-income region of the US. As a part of the organization's placement process, she ranked the 50 regions in order of her preference (TFA, 2014b). Tammie preferred to stay in Boston or another region near her home and family in New England, but the organization placed her across the country in the southwestern region of Phoenix. Recognizing the short-term commitment to the cross-country living situation, she moved to Arizona, committing to TFA, accepting a job with JESD and enrolling in a master's and teaching certification program at TFA's university partner. Due to the high need for ELD teachers in Phoenix-area schools, the regional TFA staff required all corps members to take an online SEI course before moving to Arizona: 'Everyone who is in TFA [Phoenix] is required to get a [provisional] SEI endorsement just to ensure if there is a need for an ELD teacher that they also are considered highly qualified'. Originally slated to be a special education teacher, Tammie accepted placement as an ELD teacher after being hired by JESD administrators in the summer of 2012.

Despite taking online coursework for the provisional endorsement on the Arizona Department of Education (ADE) online portal, Tammie had no knowledge of ELD prior to starting her first year of teaching in the JESD during the 2012–2013 school year. She recounted a conversation with the school-level leader who hired her for the ELD classroom teaching position:

> I had to just flat out ask my principal, because they put me in ELD 3/4, and I honestly didn't know what that meant. I didn't realize that was something that happened in schools. I don't have an education background... I thought it was three-quarters of my class was ELL. I was really confused. I really had no idea... I had to ask my principal what is ELD, and then finding out that it was English Language Development, then I realized that it was going to be all ELLs.

After being placed as an ELD teacher at Longview School, Tammie commenced the required district-level training for new ELD teachers, facilitated by district administrators and coaches in the ELL Department at the JESD, where she found herself in the company of primarily novice teachers: 'Not just first-year ELD teachers, they were first-years and they were placed as ELD [teachers], which I thought was just insane'. Tammie remembered being surrounded by primarily out-of-state teachers, many of whom were also hired by the JESD human resources department as a part of the district's partnership with the TFA organization and commitment to hiring a set number of novice teachers each school year.

The district-level ELD training focused on compliance with state-level language policy, outlining the rigid time allotments within the 4-hour block for reading, grammar, writing, vocabulary and conversation and stipulating requirements for lesson plans using English language proficiency (ELP) standards, language objectives and learner evidence (JESD, 2014e). According to Tammie, JESD administrators, both inside and outside the ELL Department, prided themselves on being the only district in the state in 100% compliance, which they aimed to maintain as they moved into future years of monitoring by ADE administrators. In addition to training in the state-mandated model of ELD instruction, Tammie recounted the district EL administrators' compliance expectations as monitored by EL instructional coaches:

> If they [district-level EL coaches] came in, they would expect that if your schedule said that you were in reading, that you would be doing reading... I kind of got a little bit scared, but I guess in a good way, because I'm kind of like, 'Okay, I know what I have to do'.

As a new teacher without the specific knowledge and skills around second language acquisition and EL teaching and learning, Tammie welcomed the structure to guide her daily practice in the 3/4 split ELD classroom in her first year of teaching at Longview: 'I was trying to make the best for my kids, and I think I maybe got the hang of it by the end of the year'.

The compliance mandates from the district helped Ms. Johnson to make meaning of the complexity of her 3/4 split classroom. With students in two grade levels, from various language backgrounds and with multiple English proficiency levels, she struggled to implement the prescriptive ELD approach. As the only ELD teacher in third or fourth grade, she recalled her first year of teaching as characterized by a lack of school-site support without a grade-level team with which to connect, plan and collaborate. In addition to Tammie's struggles with instruction and isolation, she recognized the social stigma experienced by her students in the split-grade classroom focused on language: 'Girls would come crying from recess because people would say, "Oh, you're stupid, you're in Ms Johnson's class"'. The taunts from other students transferred into classroom practice, where Tammie met discouraged children when teaching discrete language skills, recounting students' insistence that 'we're doing something stupid because we're the stupid class'. Her on-the-job learning, paired with the support of TFA mentors who challenged her to push expectations beyond skill-based language instruction, led Tammie to question the language policy structures around why her students did not receive rich explorations of content learning like other third- and fourth-grade classrooms.

These realizations transferred over to her second year of teaching at Longview School in the 2013–2014 school year. With an increase in the number of ELs across the school and district due to a change in AZELLA cutoff scores, Tammie became Longview's third-grade ELD teacher, situated in a self-contained classroom setting rather than the 3/4 split from the previous year. She described her 18 students as being similar only in terms of the common EL label as they represented four language backgrounds (i.e. Farsi, Somali, Karen, Spanish), ranged from pre-emergent to intermediate in English proficiency as measured by AZELLA, varied from monolingual in their native languages to on-grade-level in English-medium reading and included 'special ed, dual-qualified ELL and special ed kids'. Despite the complexities, Tammie exuded excitement in the shift to third grade due to the increased role and support from her grade-level team: 'It's just been really amazing because we're able to really plan [instruction] together and make sure that all of our kids are getting what they need to be successful'. In addition to having regular collaborators in her colleagues, she felt that the targeted grade-level support from both her team and TFA mentors led to consistent and high expectations for content learning in line with mainstream third-grade classrooms.

Unlike the rigid hour blocks implemented in her first year of teaching, Ms Johnson portrayed a third-grade classroom with four hours of integrated language and literacy learning. Merging oral language, reading and writing,

Tammie described her differentiated support for diverse students' language development using the gradual release of responsibility through whole-group, small-group and independent work. By integrating the blocks of time within the larger 4-hour structure rather than strictly maintaining the 1 hour per language-based content area as written in her district-mandated lesson plans, she aimed to appropriate additional time for guided reading, which she perceived as central to literacy development:

> The most growth I've seen is in my guided reading groups, and the [ELD] blocks don't allow for that. It's almost like I have to cheat and make sure that I'm technically hitting a writing standard while I'm doing reading groups because it's writing time. There's ways around it [time mandates], and I would say that I'm way better at finding those ways around it than I was in the first year [of teaching ELD].

In the weekly lesson plans that she submitted to district administrators (JESD, 2014e), Tammie maintained the separate blocks, specifying ELP standards in listening and speaking, reading and writing (ADE, 2012); however, based on the collaborative work with her third-grade team, she professed to teaching from grade-level standards and holding corresponding expectations for student learning and achievement. Tammie described her strategic use of both Common Core Standards (CCS) and the ELP Standards required for ELD classroom teachers: 'I have to keep my eye on the ELD standards because that's what they're going to be tested on, but if their reading [ability] is at grade level, then they should be passing the AZELLA. Period. End of story'.

In addition to appropriating language policy in her classroom by integrating blocks and using grade-level content standards, Tammie critically considered decisions by district and state policy players, including district-level grading policies and the state-level ELD mandates. Within the JESD, district officials declared that ELD teachers were not allowed to assign report card scores corresponding with mastery of learning standards:

> They [district administrators] said we're not allowed to give a three [demonstrating mastery] because ELP standards are not at grade level. If you're telling me that that's fair, it's certainly not. I think that it's up to the teacher, really, to make sure that these kids are being exposed and held to that standard of higher expectations.

Recognizing the unjust nature of the policy that divided opportunities for children based on their native language, Tammie questioned JESD and Arizona policy players' expectations for ELs, specifically considering the mandated hour of grammar instruction focused on prescriptive and discrete language skills.

They're [district administrators] super excited for our ELD kids because they have that whole hour of grammar kind of thing. They think that it'll be beneficial for them, and I'm not arguing one way or the other, I just would be interested to see down the road how much this grammar actually does improve their [students'] skills as a real person. Not as a test taker, as a learner... I don't think that our expectations are high enough for our kids to be successful outside of the ELD classroom. They know a noun, verb, and adjective and can put together a sentence, but is that setting them up for success as a student without the ELD support or without the program itself?

Building on her probe of direct grammar instruction, Tammie also critically assessed the notion of her diverse ELs held to a 1-year timeline to demonstrate English proficiency on a highly standardized assessment of the English language (i.e. AZELLA).

Using her own experiences across two years as an ELD teacher in Greenwood, Tammie shared her equal hesitation around policies related to teacher preparation and placement. Critically considering her original placement in an ELD classroom, a collaborative effort by policy players working at TFA Phoenix, the JESD and Longview School, she pondered,

That's where it really starts – is getting those highly qualified teachers [into ELD classrooms], and this would be putting me out of a job, but last year I shouldn't have been placed as a 3/4 ELD teacher. I really shouldn't have been. I was doing my kids a disservice, seriously. I was a first-year teacher. I was in way over my head. I did the best job I could.

Ruminating about her experiences in teacher education for ELs, specifically her SEI endorsement coursework as a part of her master's and certification program, Tammie shared that ELD teachers needed specific preparation: 'Not just an asterisk that's like [a strategy] for ELLs, like I'll use pictures for vocabulary, but seriously knowing how to teach ELL'. Supplementing the broad EL knowledge and skills gleaned from instructors in the mandated SEI coursework, district-level ELD training, facilitated by district administrators and coaches in the ELL Department, focused solely on compliance to state-level mandates: '[The JESD] did a good job of setting me up to be, as Arizona would see it, a great ELD teacher in terms of they do A, B, and C requirements'. Pulling together her perspectives on policies related to teacher placement, preparation and training, Ms Johnson held a contrasting perspective from state and district players: 'Our best teachers should be in ELD classrooms, they should be, and I don't think that's what Arizona's practicing right now'.

Despite her qualms related to policies for ELD teachers and teaching, Tammie credited her two years of ELD classroom teaching as effectively preparing her for any educational context. She planned to stay in education beyond her 2-year commitment to the TFA organization, specifically working with ELs regardless of her next destination as a classroom teacher. Wanting to move closer to home and family in the northeastern US, Ms Johnson toyed with the idea of staying an additional year in Greenwood or taking an ESL teaching position in Massachusetts.

Annie, third-year teacher: A perspective on English language development in the primary classroom

Annie Nethercutt supported six- and seven-year-old children in one of the two first-grade ELD classrooms, situated in the primary grades building of Longview School, accessible by indoor corridor to kindergarten, grade-one and grade-two classrooms. Per state and district policy, schools grouped ELs 'by their English proficiency level for a minimum of four classroom periods' (JESD, 2014c). Unlike upper grades that utilized one ELD classroom for all levels of ELP, Annie taught the first-grade class with predominantly pre-emergent and emergent ELs as measured by AZELLA. With numbers fluctuating throughout the school year, Ms Nethercutt's first-grade classroom welcomed approximately 24 students around mid-year – 22 Latino students from Spanish-speaking backgrounds and two students from the Middle East who arrived speaking their native languages of Farsi and Arabic. All students came from immigrant backgrounds, either immigrants themselves or children of immigrants, with five families recently arriving in the US. Annie explained that many parents left high-status careers in their countries of origin to take low-paying jobs in Greenwood, primarily to afford their children a good education, which resulted in respect and desire for and dedication to learning and behaving well in school.

Ms Nethercutt came to Longview School at the beginning of the 2013–2014 school year after two years of teaching at nearby Advance School, also in the JESD. A third-year teacher, she moved from the Pacific Northwest following a 4-year undergraduate degree in psychology and sociology as a part of the TFA organization. Originally from a high-poverty neighborhood of Portland, Oregon, Annie grew up in a White, working-class family, joining TFA as a way to give back to an educational system that had opened doors for her as a student. Desiring to leave the northwestern US for somewhere new, she put Phoenix as her highly preferred placement, which was at the time considered a 'high-need' region for TFA organizational priorities (Heineke & Cameron, 2013). Originally slated by TFA to teach elementary special education, Annie was hired as an ELD teacher by the principal at Advance School, the only opening at the school and primary area of need in the district. Annie reported having no knowledge of ELD upon being hired, despite being considered highly qualified to teach in that context. Starting her novice teaching career with 35 pre-emergent kindergartners and scant applicable knowledge and skills for the ELD classroom, she described herself as a 'rule follower' to the compliance mandates pushed by JESD administrators. After looping with her students into first grade in her second year of teaching, Ms Nethercutt moved to Longview for her third year of teaching, seeking to work with her original principal from her first year of teaching.

In the first-grade ELD classroom at Longview Elementary, the beginning of the school year began quietly. With 20 of her 24 students labeled as pre-emergent from their performance on the AZELLA, corresponding to the initial stage of second language acquisition characterized by the silent period, Annie found that many of her students preferred listening over speaking. Although she expected this from her newcomers, the majority of students had attended kindergarten at Longview. After talking with the kindergarten teacher who had the pre-emergent ELs in the prior school year, Annie surmised: 'There weren't a lot of supports and scaffolding through their silent periods.... There also wasn't as much pushing as needed to be done to get them to really converse and have those conversations'. She aimed to provide instructional scaffolds to push children to use language, such as using writing and drawing to support oral language production, as well as building trust for students to feel safe and comfortable to take risks with language. Despite the challenges posed by the large number of pre-emergent ELs, Annie reflected on the progress since starting the school year: 'The growth that you see in an ELD classroom is phenomenal'. She aspired to continue that growth to move all students into mainstream classrooms for second grade.

Seeking to reach the goals she set for her students, Annie divulged planning instruction in collaboration with her team using grade-level standards to guide teaching and learning. The Longview first-grade team, which included both ELD and mainstream classroom teachers, collaboratively planned 'grade-level, very integrated units... with curriculum that is Common Core aligned'. In addition to providing ELs with grade-level content in both literacy and mathematics, mainstream classroom teachers also explicitly focused on vocabulary and language development. Annie and her team particularly embraced the math time that fell outside of the 4-hour structure and therefore allowed for more flexibility to 'do what's best for kids'. Utilizing the unmonitored hour of time in the late afternoon of the school day, teachers organized leveled math groups across the first grade, which mixed native English speakers from mainstream classrooms with students labeled as ELs in ELD classrooms. In this way, Longview teachers pushed back against the segregation inherent in language policy to allow students to learn with peers, with ELs able to interact with English-proficient students. Recognizing the importance of the encouragement and support provided by her school principal, Annie expounded on the value for her students socially, linguistically and academically.

Within the 4-hour ELD block in the morning and early afternoon of each school day, Annie communicated how she individually maneuvered mandates to match her conception of teaching and learning with young ELs. She explained, 'What I do, and what they [district administrators] expect of us, it's a little bit different. I really am of the belief we should be doing everything [considering] what's best for kids. That's not necessarily what's easier for adults'. Rather than separate learning into four separate hour-long blocks, Annie described integrating language and literacy into content-based units, where students utilized vocabulary and grammar in meaningful ways as attached to content concepts and ideas. Additionally, she dedicated ample time to guided reading groups, which targeted students' reading fluency and comprehension and included attention to developmental writing supports. Annie's integrated approach to ELD teaching required ample time to document, as she wrote one set of lesson plans to guide her classroom practice and another set to submit to the district to demonstrate compliance with language policy. She explained, 'It [extensive planning time] is one of the challenges, but at this point, it's very easy for me. Everything that I do is in compliance because I know how to work the system'. To demonstrate her compliance to district players, she documented vocabulary and grammar instruction in 15-minute increments throughout the 4-hour integrated block; she also cited both the Discrete Skills Inventory (DSI) and ELP standards (ADE, 2013), despite using the CCS as the primary source to guide instructional planning for first-grade content.

In addition to the state-mandated blocks of ELD instruction, Ms Nethercutt challenged district-level interpretation of language policy, such as teaching methodologies and Spanish-language guidelines. First, district administrators required teachers to use particular methodologies 'that they say are empirically-based and really support language development'. After unsuccessfully requesting the research to back up the methodologies, such as the drilling of discrete grammar skills, Annie chose not to reproduce these approaches in her classroom. Second, Annie described threats of teachers being fired for using Spanish in the classroom:

> If I'm getting observed or someone [from the district] is coming in here [to my classroom] and they saw that [me using Spanish], they literally tell people, 'You could be fired for that'. Technically, I know I couldn't be. I read the law. It's like, 'You can do it [use native language] for support'.

Knowing that Arizona language policy allowed for targeted native language use (ADE, 2000), Annie described how she utilized her Spanish proficiency to support newcomers, point out cognates and verb tenses and build students' identities; however, she only did this when by herself with students in the classroom. Annie recognized the importance of the knowing the law rather than implementing the language policy as dictated by the district.

> Many of our ELD teachers have not even read the law to understand what the law truly says. I'm fairly knowledgeable in that because I've done some [policy] case studies within that... It's just not fair as our district to be able to say, 'These are these mandates, and this is how we're interpreting this law. That's the end of the story'... Is this what they [state administrators] are really telling us to do? Because that's not part of the law.

Despite her negotiation of the policy demands in the local context, Ms Nethercutt noticed the double-edged sword of appropriating policy, as state and district administrators could construe her students' growth and test scores to demonstrate the efficacy of the ELD model.

Annie appropriated ELD policy in practice within the classroom layer, but she also pushed back against compliance demands through her interaction with district players. Reflecting on her initial training as a first-year ELD teacher, she described, 'What I received here in our district was mostly surrounding compliance'. The training remained stagnant across Annie's three years in the district; rather than evolving to bolster the professional growth of ELD teachers, district administrators and coaches repeated the compliance-focused content each year for the large number of new teachers. In addition to training, the classroom-based support provided by the district-level EL instructional coaches fixated on compliance; Annie explained, 'Everything that they [district coaches] are pushing down to us [ELD teachers] and assessing teaching within has to do with compliance'. Seeking to share her concerns with district players, Annie recounted arranging a meeting with Cynthia, the ELL department director, who blamed the stagnancy in training and support on school leaders' placement of primarily first-year teachers in ELD classrooms. Not accepting the displacement of responsibility, Annie appraised the JESD administrators:

> They [district players] are not being vision-driven, which is something that I have a very huge issue with our [ELL] Department currently in our district. What is our vision? Is it compliance? If it's compliance, [rather] than instruction, you can't expect them to have quality instruction. You're not giving them [teachers] the support that they need.

Using the TFA discourse around the need for a clear vision to drive educational practice (Heineke & Cameron, 2013), Annie critiqued the singular focus on compliance that she perceived to drive the district layer of EL education in the JESD.

The state-mandated SEI teacher preparation accompanied the district-level training for ELD teachers. Prior to and during her first year of teaching, Annie took three SEI courses – one online through the ADE and two hybrid (i.e. in person and online) at a nearby university in her master's degree and certification cohort with other first-year TFA corps members. She described her graduate coursework: 'The preparation I received from my master's program I felt was very lacking considering we have such a high number of English language learners in this area'. The SEI course curriculum focused on the Sheltered Instruction Observation Protocol (SIOP), which centered on teaching content to ELs in mainstream classroom settings (Echevarría et al., 2013). As Annie explained, 'They [SEI courses] were not really rooted in my experience here in my [ELD] classroom'. She described learning about generic strategies related to ELs, as well as the history of language education in Arizona shortly before and shortly after Proposition 203 (ADE, 2000). Multiple years after the shift in language policy (ADE, 2008), the professor did not have knowledge of the ELD policy or context; therefore, he not only did not utilize the state policy to guide teacher learning, but he also looked to Annie as the expert to share her experiences and inform her peers about ELD. In this way, she felt out of her wheelhouse being positioned as the ELD expert when she was a novice struggling to support the learning and development of 35 pre-emergent and emergent kindergartners with little knowledge or skills to teach them effectively.

In addition to analyzing teacher preparation for ELD classrooms, Annie critiqued Arizona language policy by highlighting the inequities resulting from ELD mandates. Starting with current inequities, such as ELs not receiving content instruction, she went on to consider the long-term impacts on preparing the state's workforce, stating, 'The educational system that we have in Arizona right now is not preparing our students for the jobs that they should be taking'. Annie proposed her solution for her first graders:

> I want them to be able to be out of this [ELD] program. I want this [ELD] program to be eliminated from the state. I fundamentally believe that English language learners need a ton of direct instruction and a ton of support; however, everything that I've ever read has said that the most successful English language learners are the ones that are in programs that are surrounded by students that are proficient, native [English] speakers, and are being supported, and in places where their culture is valued, and their [native] language is valued.

Despite her desire to abolish the policy that segregated students in the spirit of monolingual assimilation, she critically probed how her students' assessment data may have supported state administrators in purporting the success of ELD, although she appropriated policy in a manner distinct from the approach designated by the EL Task Force.

Now perceived by peers and administrators as a 'veteran' ELD teacher in the JESD, Ms Nethercutt decided to persist in the classroom, planning to stay in the Greenwood community for the long term as an elementary ELD teacher. Although many TFA corps members left the Phoenix metropolitan area after their 2-year commitment to the organization (Heineke *et al.*, 2014), and many ELD teachers opted for general education settings with less policy demands and instructional challenges, Annie chose to make EL education her chosen profession. She highlighted the primary reason for her retention in the classroom: 'The kids and the families. I love the growth that we have here. I love that the families are such wonderful people. They truly, like I said, believe in the education'. She felt the need to improve her professional practice in service of immigrant families who had sacrificed to provide their children the promise of a well-rounded education. In addition to the commitment to students and families in Greenwood, Annie attributed her retention to the strong support and mentorship from her school administrator, as well as her learned ability to maneuver the policy demands in the ELD classroom.

Discussion: Language Policy (P)layers in English Language Development Classrooms

This chapter has introduced the JESD and Greenwood as the local context to investigate Arizona language policy in practice, specifically foregrounding the experiences and perspectives of the classroom-level ELD teachers (García & Menken, 2010; Hornberger & Johnson, 2007; McCarty, 2011; Menken & García, 2010; Ricento & Hornberger, 1996; Tharp, 1997). Through 'thick descriptions of policy interpretation and implementation at the local level' (Hornberger & Johnson, 2007: 511), the narrative cases provide snapshots of everyday classroom practice as ELD teachers negotiate policy to support the teaching and learning of ELs in Greenwood, Arizona. In foregrounding the classroom with qualitative narratives of three ELD teachers, various policy layers and players emerge in the background as influencing teachers' daily practice with ELs (Tharp, 1997). By using the sociocultural framework and qualitative methods to investigate policy in practice, the complexity and dynamism of the Arizona language policy context becomes apparent (Hornberger & Johnson, 2007; Levinson & Sutton, 2001; McCarty, 2011; Menken & García, 2010; Rogoff, 2003; Tharp, 1997).

Looking across the cases of ELD teachers, themes emerge in the consideration of how broader policy layers and players influence daily practice in Greenwood classrooms. All coming from out of state with non-education backgrounds as a part of the TFA program, teachers entered classrooms with no knowledge of the ELD policy context, despite having completed a

15-hour SEI online course offered by the ADE and TFA summer training in Phoenix. Prior research has investigated the implications of novice TFA corps members teaching in ELD classrooms, who have consistently been found to be underprepared for the complex teaching context (Heineke & Cameron, 2011, 2013; Hopkins & Heineke, 2013). Hopkins and Heineke (2013) described the problematic training provided to TFA corps members through the 5-week summer institute, which included one 90-minute session on ELs and literature that stigmatized ELs as having special needs. With a total of 16.5 hours of EL-specific training via the online course and summer institute, Heineke and Cameron (2011, 2013) discovered first-year corps members in ELD classrooms with little to no knowledge or skills for teaching ELs, thus defaulting to frustration and the rigid implementation of policy mandates. Using the perspectives and experiences of the three teachers in this study, findings confirmed similar repercussions of the troubling trend of placing novice TFA teachers in ELD classrooms.

Taking advantage of the state-level policy that allowed teachers to be considered highly qualified after taking the online course, school and district administrators hired and placed Annie, Tammie and Paula in ELD classrooms as novice teachers with a complex set of variables for teaching and learning: a kindergarten classroom with 35 pre-emergent and emergent ELs; a third- and fourth-grade split classroom with no clear set of standards, curriculum or grade-level team; and a middle-school classroom with sixth, seventh and eighth graders spanning language backgrounds and proficiency levels. Simultaneously maneuvering the complexities of ELD classroom teaching as novice teachers from non-education backgrounds, teachers struggled to find sources of support with district coaches focused solely on compliance with state-level policies, university instructors utilizing syllabi designed broadly for all Arizona teachers, and TFA mentors without EL-related knowledge, skills or lenses. Overall, classroom-level policy players' common perspectives on teacher placement, preparation, training and support from both internal (e.g. school leaders, district administrators) and external actors (e.g. TFA mentors, teacher educators) signaled the lack of infrastructure to support EL teaching and learning at the local and state contexts, even after five years of implementation.

Despite the complexities of the ELD classroom context, teachers maintained their focus on students to interpret, negotiate and appropriate language policy in practice (Hornberger & Johnson, 2007; Levinson & Sutton, 2001). Within the culture of compliance of the JESD, teachers used evolving understandings of EL teaching and learning to make decisions about how to carry out the ELD block. Progressing and developing as novices in the educational profession, teachers differed in their approaches to language policy appropriation as they chose to maintain, recognize or negotiate various policy mandates in the classroom (Heineke & Cameron, 2013). In her first year of teaching, Paula maintained the hourly ELD blocks, finding ways to infuse science and social studies into blocks designated for vocabulary and grammar. In her second year of teaching, Tammie recognized her agency to integrate hourly blocks to make additional time for guided reading. In her third year of teaching, Annie actively negotiated policy mandates to integrate language and literacy learning, utilize native language supports, and combine ELs with English-proficient students to support grade-level teaching and learning using CCS. With consent from school administrators to work with non-ELD teachers at their grade level and make the policy work for the students in their classrooms, teachers found ways around state and district compliance mandates, such as writing separate sets of lesson plans to submit to district coaches with ELP standards cited and hourly blocks maintained.

This chapter foregrounded the ELD classroom, shaped and framed by other layers of language policy (Hornberger & Johnson, 2007; Ricento & Hornberger, 1996). In the upcoming chapters, I foreground other layers to investigate the actions and interactions between players in the school, district, state and community contexts (Tharp, 1997). Drawing from the experiences and perspectives of ELD classroom teachers, Chapter 5 spans out to the local context of language policy in practice to investigate school and district layers and players, including school and district leaders. Chapter 6 explores state-level education layers, foregrounding EL Task Force members, ADE administrators, teacher educators and leadership from Arizona's growing system of charter schools. Finally, Chapter 7 brings in the lens of state-level government, considering state senators and representatives engaged in ongoing legislation guiding Arizona education, as well as community leaders in education, law and business. By foregrounding each layer while simultaneously backgrounding the many interconnected layers and players, the findings as a whole present the complex and dynamic interpretation, negotiation and reconstruction of language policy in practice (García & Menken, 2010; McCarty, 2011; Ricento & Hornberger, 1996).

Note

(1)   All location and participant names are pseudonyms.

5 Local Policy (P)layers: Classroom, School and District Educators

Teachers engage in language policy work not only in their own classrooms but also within the local context of school and district layers through interaction with school and district players (Levinson & Sutton, 2001). In this way, local policy players in classrooms, schools and districts act and interact to interpret and implement language policy in practice to mediate the education of English learners (ELs; Hornberger & Johnson, 2007; Johnson & Freeman, 2010). Building out from the focus on the English Language Development (ELD) classroom teachers, this chapter delves further into language policy in practice in Greenwood, Arizona. Seeking to understand the complex actions and interactions in local communities, I explore the themes emergent from my investigation of micro-level layers and players using the metaphorical onion of language policy in practice. I first 'peel the onion' to individually describe the language policy players on school and district layers. I then 'slice the onion' to investigate the interpretation and implementation of one cross-cutting issue within the local policy context – teacher placement, support and retention. Finally, I 'stir the onion' to consider the negotiation and appropriation across layers and players (García & Menken, 2010; Hornberger & Johnson, 2007). I close with a discussion of the findings within and across the local context of the Jackson Elementary School District (JESD).

Language Policy in the Jackson Elementary School District

Situated in leadership positions and charged with authority over and guidance of classroom teachers, school and district leaders influenced the practice of ELD teachers and therefore the education of ELs in Greenwood. Three school-level leaders participated in this study, representing a sample from the district: (a) Heather, principal at Jones School; (b) James, principal at Advance School; and (c) Rick, principal at Mountainside School. Leaders worked at three PK-8 schools, strategically selected within the community of downtown Greenwood, rather than at schools situated in more recently developed areas of the city further from the Phoenix metropolitan area and

Table 5.1 School and district-level participants

Pseudonym	Position	Gender	Ethnicity	Language abilities
Heather	School principal	Female	White	English
James	School principal	Male	White	English
Rick	School principal	Male	White	English, Russian
Peter	Instructional coach	Male	White	English, Spanish
Cynthia	Department director	Female	Latino	Spanish, English
Graciela	Data coordinator	Female	Latino	Spanish, English
Delia	Parent coordinator	Female	Latino	Spanish, English

with less linguistic diversity within the student and general population. Four district-level personnel participated in this study with a sample from each of the three teams in the English Language Learners (ELL) department: (a) Cynthia, who directs the department; (b) Graciela, who oversees EL student services; (c) Peter, who coaches ELD teachers; and (d) Delia, who supports ELs' parents. See Table 5.1 for details on school and district-level participants.

In this first findings section, I explore the roles and responsibilities of individual language policy players in the community of Greenwood, Arizona (Ricento & Hornberger, 1996). I describe each school- and district-level participant to introduce their role in language policy in practice, background in education and perspectives on EL teaching and learning. In this way, I provide the context in which to build out the subsequent sections in this chapter so that the reader may understand 'how people make, interpret, and otherwise engage with the policy process' (Levinson & Sutton, 2001: 4). I organize this section based on the study participants' 'connections in the policy chain' (Datnow, 2006: 105). Through the analysis of interview and documentation data, connections emerged between players within the local context of the JESD – both formal associations outlined in district documentation of roles and responsibilities (JESD, 2014f) and informal links co-constructed among participants.

English Language Development teachers

At the center of language policy in practice, teachers engaged in daily policy work via EL classroom teaching and within-school and cross-district interaction with other policy players in Greenwood, Arizona (García & Menken, 2010; Hornberger & Johnson, 2007; Ricento & Hornberger, 1996). To support compliance with state policy, district administrators enforced procedures to ensure that everything related to ELs, including ELD teacher support and supervision, came from the ELL department at the JESD central office. In this way, the EL instructional coach served as the ELD teachers' direct mentor, which participants found helpful but heavily focused on compliance. Employed at particular schools in downtown Greenwood, teachers also sought support, guidance and direction from school leaders, their direct authority within the building. I begin with introductions to school leaders as the more consistent mentor and support system highlighted by teachers in this study.

School leaders

Heather, school leader

With 31 years of experience in education in Greenwood as an elementary teacher and reading coach, Heather was placed as principal of Jones School by the district office in the 2013–2014 school year to turnaround low standardized test scores. She empathized with her faculty, with one-third of Jones teachers being hired by the district's human resources office as novice educators from out of state, then immediately asked to implement new reform efforts at a turnaround school. With a specific lens on EL teaching and learning, Heather recognized the ample challenges, diminished support and limited agency that she had to assist teachers, as the ELL department required ELD teachers to attend separate training in the spirit of compliance with state policies. Explicitly defining her advocacy efforts against Proposition 203 and House Bill 2064, which brought the 4-hour ELD block to Greenwood schools, she disagreed with district administrators' rigid interpretation and implementation policy. She appropriated language policy when possible, such as telling parents to sign their kids out of ELD services or sitting down with teachers to support their integration of language instruction in the 4-hour block.

James, school leader

In his second year as principal at Advance School, along with years of experience in teaching and leading across the Phoenix area, James found more challenges than benefits in the state-level ELD policy. Within the multiple roles of a school leader, Arizona language policy negatively impacted his ability to staff and run his PK-8 school in downtown Greenwood. With the varying numbers of ELs due to changing Arizona English Language Learner Assessment (AZELLA) cut scores, he struggled to organize classrooms, leading to events such as a third/fourth/fifth-grade split ELD teacher walking out mid school year due to the difficult circumstances of the multi-age classroom. Working to maneuver policy demands from the district both inside and outside the ELL department, James supported teachers in the implementation of initiatives such as Common Core Standards (CCS) and Response to Intervention while working within the strict 4-hour ELD structures. Nevertheless, he perceived his impact on language policy as minimal given district administrators had direct oversight of ELD teacher hiring, training and support; however, he visualized district administrators demanding his 'head on a platter' if language policy was not carried out correctly.

Rick, school leader

In his second year as principal at Mountainside, Rick acknowledged that the efficacy of ELD policy in practice depended on the quality of the teacher; however, staffing remained his primary challenge as a school leader due to high turnover in ELD classrooms. He drew from district's ELL department 'minions' for teacher support and other resources for his school to remain in compliance, but he recognized his agency in policy implementation within his school. Rick utilized his role to be 'as creative as possible in his interpretation' and support teachers in recognizing how to mediate policy and practice, such as writing two sets of lesson plans for policy compliance and classroom practice. Despite his support of teachers in maneuvering the policy demands to meet students' needs, he discerned an issue around ELD teacher evaluation. By using content-based standardized test data to compare his teachers across grade levels and drive overall school practice, Rick's method of teacher evaluation, soon to be embraced via value-added measures across the state, situated ELD teachers at a disadvantage. As a bilingual school leader with an academic background in linguistics, Rick described his desire to 'blow it all up' and eliminate ELD from Arizona classrooms.

District administrators

Peter, district instructional coach

ELD teachers and school leaders recognized the direct support of the ELL department, with the EL instructional coach serving as the link in the policy chain between classroom, school and district. After three years of teaching in an ELD classroom in the JESD, two of those years as a Teach for America (TFA) corps member, Peter accepted a position as district-level coach in the summer of 2013, embracing the opportunity to have a broader impact on EL students and teachers. Under the supervision of Cynthia in the ELL department, three instructional coaches collaborated to support 145 ELD teachers across the district, with Peter having specific schools to coach 45 teachers ranging from kindergarten to middle school. With the primary role being to prepare ELD teachers through both district-level training and classroom-based support, he lamented the district's emphasis on compliance with state language policy. With the large number of ELD teachers, 54 of them new to the teaching profession, Peter found it difficult to engage in teacher training and coaching focused on effective teaching and learning of ELs, which he recognized as a detriment that directly impacted EL achievement. As a bilingual individual, with English as his first language and Spanish as his second, he maintained a value of bilingualism but found it difficult to bring into his position as EL instructional coach in a culture of compliance.

Cynthia, district administrator

Peter worked under the supervision of Cynthia, the director of the ELL department, who maintained responsibility for the staff of 12 employees, who included instructional coaches, data analysts and parent/family liaisons. Working under the authority of the district superintendent and division director of curriculum and instruction within the JESD, Cynthia maintained her primary connection to state-level administrators at the Arizona Department of Education (ADE) due to her responsibilities for compliance with language policies and the ELD model. Charged with monitoring and maintaining practice within state mandates, she worked with (a) EL instructional coaches for classroom-level compliance in ELD teaching practices, (b) school leaders for school-level compliance in EL student and teacher placement and (c) data analysts for district-level compliance for AZELLA data collection and analysis. Although she oversaw all three branches of the ELL Department, Cynthia spent much of the 2013–2014 school year supporting the coaches because of the high numbers of novice teachers in ELD placements. As a native Spanish speaker with years of experience as a dual-language teacher, Cynthia's passion continued in dual-language education despite the shift to monolingual policy, and she considered a move to another district with additive program models for ELs.

Graciela, district data coordinator

Under the supervision of Cynthia, Graciela, the EL data coordinator, began as a parent volunteer at Jones School when her children enrolled in the dual-language program prior to the passing of Proposition 203. After the passing of Proposition 203 and the centralizing of EL services to the district office for state compliance purposes, Cynthia hired Graciela to take the responsibility for EL data in the JESD. Due to the emphasis on language assessment within the ELD model, the coordinator oversaw three data specialists who managed all data related to ELs across the JESD. In her district-level role, Graciela interacted regularly with (a) Cynthia, the district-level EL director, to provide data to guide district-level decisions; (b) state-level administrators, to ensure alignment of data procedures with changing state mandates; (c) Pearson, the for-profit company that maintained and scored language assessments; (d) school leaders, to pass along AZELLA data to guide school-level program decisions; and (e) parents, to explain students' placement in ELD classrooms. Citing the direct tie between language policy and assessment, such as student identification, program placement and school budgets, Graciela was cognizant of her role's impact on policy in practice.

Delia, district parent liaison

After teaching for 32 years in JESD, Delia chose to tentatively forgo retirement to work part-time as the parent liaison in the ELL department.

Recruited by Cynthia with external grant funding, she worked with parents across the district to foster strong home-school connections, advise parents about the American school system and build literacy skills through reading and writing practices at home. With the majority of parents being from Latino backgrounds, she utilized her own Spanish bilingualism and passion as a former dual-language teacher to empower parents to foster bilingualism and biliteracy. Using her personal and familial experiences as part of a Mexican immigrant family, as well as her strong anti-Proposition 203 mindset, she recognized the importance of her role in maintaining students' native language, even though the education system attempted to take it away. As a non-classroom-teacher not forced to comply with state language policy mandates, Delia sought out ways to use parents' native language both as a medium of instruction and to demonstrate native language use in the home with children to foster first and second language learning. In addition to Spanish-speaking Latino parents, the changing population in the district brought ample linguistic diversity, as well as cultural backgrounds and social-emotional challenges and issues, which Delia embraced in her mission to help families within the restrictive language policy environment of Arizona.

Language Policy Implementation Affecting Teachers

In this second findings section, I investigate the multilayered interpretation, implementation, and engagement with language policy in practice (Hornberger & Johnson, 2007). Emergent from thematic data analyses of classroom, school and district layers within the local context, I explored policy players' positions and perceptions on teachers and teaching, including teacher preparation, placement, training, support and retention. Across the JESD, teacher-related directives surfaced frequently in dialogue with classroom teachers, school leaders and district personnel. As reflected in the narrative cases in Chapter 4, teachers felt that they (a) entered classrooms without the necessary knowledge and skills to effectively teach ELs, (b) received ongoing training and support solely related to compliance with state language policy and (c) attended teacher education courses that did not connect to the ELD teaching context. Building on classroom-level findings, this findings section probes local policy players' positions and perspectives as they engaged with the cross-cutting issues related to teachers, specifically (a) initial teacher preparation and placement, (b) ongoing teacher training and support and (c) existing teacher retention and attrition.

Initial teacher preparation and placement

Situated within various restrictive language policy regulations, local policy players agreed that staffing ELD classrooms provided significant challenges to practice. In addition to the three classroom teachers who recognized their lack of knowledge and preparation prior to placement in ELD settings, school leaders and district administrators highlighted the difficulty of finding teachers willing to teach in ELD classrooms due to the challenging context, high turnover rate and growing demand for ELD teachers. Whereas Heather utilized her 30 years in the community to frame the historical trend and broad need for all teachers, James explained the specific challenge in ELD classrooms.

> The issue that becomes is that they're [ELD classrooms] the least attractive classes to teach because they're the most complex, and a lot of times we get the least qualified people that want to teach them because other teachers will actually resign before they will teach them [ELs]. So the way our Human Resource Department has worked is that, if certain positions aren't occupied by a certain time, they will take letters of intent, candidates which are first-year teachers and drop them in positions that are not filled, so that's what positions they get stuck in. So you get three grade-level bands for an ELD position for our first-year teacher.

At Advance and other schools in the JESD, existing teachers refused to teach in ELD settings after seeing the challenging context within which ELD teachers had to work. Rick described having to use his 'gold-bladed tongue' to 'con' teachers into staying in ELD classrooms after struggling the first year, as he saw the inherent challenges of the revolving door of novice teachers who never developed professionally in the new and complex classroom context.

In the 2013–2014 school year, the challenges related to ELD teacher placement evolved into a widespread problem across the district after a federal resolution resulted in the reclassification of thousands of ELs in the JESD. As described in Chapter 2, with assistance from the Arizona legal advocates involved with the Flores case, the US Department of Justice and Office of Civil Rights found the ADE to be out of compliance for reclassifying and exiting ELs prematurely. The corresponding resolution agreement (ADE, 2012) resulted in a new version of the AZELLA assessment (i.e. AZELLA 3). From his perspective of working with ELD teachers, Peter explained the impact in the JESD.

> Last year we had 90 teachers in ELD and now we have, I think, 143 [teachers]. We've had an additional 50 teachers join ELD [classrooms]. That's due to a new test they came out with in Arizona, the 'AZELLA 3' they're calling it. They [state administrators] changed the scoring. They made a few [test] items more rigorous, which really put a lot of students who were more on the end to expected to pass it [AZELLA], didn't pass it, and then also some students who were still in that

monitoring phase tested back in [to ELD]. There were just a lot more [new] teachers to ELD [this school year].

Whereas district players recognized the good intentions of the federal-level investigation and state-level resolution, they had to negotiate the on-the-ground consequences of the policy change. Exacerbating the long-standing challenge of staffing, they now looked to fill an additional 54 ELD classrooms with novice teachers, primarily from out of state and without specific preparation for ELs.

As reflected by the three teacher cases in Chapter 4, JESD administrators looked to its partnership with TFA to fill classroom vacancies, specifically the hard-to-staff ELD classrooms. Despite coming to Greenwood predominantly from out of- state with non-education-related undergraduate degrees, TFA corps members were considered by the state of Arizona as 'highly qualified' to teach in ELD classrooms, requiring the minimum of a bachelor's degree, intern teaching certificate and provisional Structured English Immersion (SEI) endorsement (ADE, 2014). Originally founded to fill teacher shortages and recognizing the ELD teacher shortage in their partner districts, TFA required all Phoenix-area recruits to take the online course and receive the provisional SEI endorsement prior to starting the 5-week summer institute (Hopkins & Heineke, 2013). Tammie explained how TFA provided her with the guidance to set her up for the ELD position.

> TFA does a really good job of making sure that their candidates are highly qualified in the school districts that they're being sent out to... Everyone who is in TFA is required to get an SEI endorsement just to ensure that if there is a need for an ELD teacher that they also are considered highly qualified.

In this way, with an undergraduate degree, five weeks of training at the TFA summer institute and a 15-hour online course, the placement of Paula, Tammie, Annie, and other corps members in ELD classrooms helped to resolve the ELD teacher shortage across the district. Without thorough initial preparation in general teaching or specific to ELs, as reflected by teachers' revelations of having no prior knowledge of ELs or ELD upon being hired and placed in ELD classrooms, district and school players now faced negotiating how to train and support the many novice teachers who were new to the restrictive language policy context of Arizona.

Ongoing teacher training and support

Because of the centrality of ELD teachers' practice to maintain compliance with state language policy, the district's ELL department controlled all training and support, directed by Cynthia and provided by three EL instructional coaches. With support organized into cycles with teacher trainings and corresponding classroom coaching, coaches shared the responsibility for training the almost 150 ELD teachers and coaching approximately 50 teachers each. Cynthia disclosed that this teacher–coach ratio was not preferred, but EL enrollment for the 2012–2013 school year dictated the funding for ELL department personnel. With two of the three coaches new to the role in the 2013–2014 school year, as well as at least 54 teachers new to the profession and ELD context, players struggled to find balance within policy confines. Peter described his experiences as a first-year EL instructional coach.

> We have to deal with teachers who might be a little short with us while we're trying to train them, making sure that they are in compliance. Then just going in and in and training and training on the same process – just compliance, compliance, lesson plan, lesson plan, instead of here are strategies to make sure that your pre-emergent students can speak by the end of this year.

Over halfway through the 2013–2014 school year, coaches had not yet completed the first training and coaching cycle, which focused solely on compliance with the ELD model rather than supporting teachers with quality teaching and learning of ELs. With the training and coaching cycles remaining fixated on compliance, Peter recognized the cycle as distressful for coaches, teachers and ultimately students.

Nevertheless, due to ongoing monitoring and supervision by state administrators, compliance remained at the forefront of the work of the district players in the ELL department. Cynthia revealed that although she did not agree with all facets of the ELD model, her role was to ensure compliance as facilitated through the department's philosophy: 'We train you. We coach you. We help you'. Peter expressed the importance of compliance:

> Our district was one of two districts who was audited out of 22 and we were one of the two that were in compliance. The other 20 were out of compliance. Our department is very proud of that fact, and we want to maintain that just because we don't want OCR [Office of Civil Rights] breathing down our neck and all that. That's where we start with the teachers, training them on compliance.

To remain in compliance, district players planned trainings with content directly from the ADE, including materials developed by Office of English Language Acquisition Services (OELAS) administrators and external consultants, including lesson planning with ELP standards, using SEI methodologies and teaching grammar with the Discrete Skills Inventory

(DSI) (JESD, 2014g). Aiming toward the ultimate goal of the compliance-focused support cycle, Cynthia expected conformity in ELD classrooms; she and her staff looked for evidence of compliance in teachers' lesson plans and classrooms. She explained, 'When you enter an ELD class, you know that you are in an ELD classroom – what's on the walls, how we're speaking to the children, group configurations... the methodologies are very scripted in their steps'.

To accomplish this goal, EL instructional coaches provided training to all teachers, followed by coaching with their assigned sub-set of teachers. Using the support of Kevin Clark, the primary consultant for the EL Task Force when designing the ELD model (Clark, 2009; Haver, 2013), district players designed trainings focused on 12 SEI methodologies to teach discrete language skills (JESD, 2014g), specifically focused on the mandated hour-long block of grammar in the ELD model. Acknowledging that many teachers did not receive explicit grammar instruction as students, district coaches first provided a full day of grammar training, followed by sessions focused on SEI methodologies to teach grammar to students, such as language warm-ups and verb tense studies (JESD, 2014g). Compliance coaching followed trainings to ensure transfer to classroom practice. Cynthia elucidated the 'whisper coaching' component in classrooms: 'They [coaches] stand there and as the teacher is teaching they are whispering to the teacher, or go to the teacher and say, "Change this, say this, don't forget about that, you forgot this step"'. With the combined efforts of training and coaching, as well as regular monitoring of lesson plans and other documentation, district players utilized state-level tools and directives to implement ongoing teacher training and support in the JESD.

Existing teacher retention and attrition

Whereas district players in the ELL department maintained control of the EL-related training and support of ELD classroom teachers, school leaders held the ultimate responsibility for retaining teachers in the challenging context of ELD within schools. In this way, school players negotiated policy mandates to provide teachers with on-site support and ameliorate challenges at the classroom and school levels. To support teaching and learning, leaders described serving as a sounding board for teachers, supporting teachers' lesson planning and providing on-site mentoring. Nevertheless, they recognized that they could not negotiate some of the strict structures set up by state and district policies, including the professional isolation at the school and additional requirements in the district. Considering her eight ELD teachers at Jones, Heather explained,

They [ELD teachers] have to go to all kinds of verb-tense grammar training, just continuously... Generally they're pulled from our general training, so they don't get to go a lot of my [school-level] stuff... All the other teachers are getting choices when they go to district PDs [professional developments] and my ELD teachers [get told], 'You're going here and you're going here'.

In addition to being absent from school professional development due to required district ELD trainings, Heather described ELD teachers' isolation from other Jones colleagues, 'My 6-7-8 [grade ELD teacher], she kind of sits off by herself and does her own thing because she can't [collaborate] ... it [ELD] has really put a really big crimp in the PLCs [professional learning communities] working together'. Heather expected to lose all six novice ELD teachers after the 2013–2014 school year, particularly the self-contained middle-school teacher who faced numerous student behavior challenges in addition to the professional isolation.

Along with the inherent challenges of ELD teaching, school leaders identified specific teachers who struggled more than others. Based on their observations from previous years as both principals and assistant-principals in the district, all three school leaders agreed that teachers, both novice and veteran, typically lasted one year in ELD before asking to be moved to a mainstream setting. Rick specifically described his second-grade ELD teacher:

> She's just an absolute hard charger, and she's one [teacher] who is going to do an amazing job in ELD and leave after the first year. She's one of those absolutely high-strung people that will suffer no foolishness and put up with nothing less than [the best]. If she's putting in her all and her best, she expects to see every kid at the high-marks [performance] level, and she's not taking into account that she's got to transcend a language barrier first.

Rick, a principal dedicated to data-driven instruction and evaluation, regularly engaged his teachers in collaborative data analyses using students' content-area assessment scores, even in ELD classrooms where content was not the focus. As reflected in Chapter 4 through the case of Paula, a teacher at Rick's school, the data comparison with grade-level colleagues left teachers with feelings of professional inadequacy and considering leaving the ELD classroom. On the other hand, Rick deliberated how the practice might support ELD teacher retention, rather than attrition.

> I wouldn't want... our expectation [for ELs] to be any different from any other kid. That being said, there needs to be some understanding when [test] results come in... If Arizona's going to start paying teachers for growth, and you have a teacher whose very data minded, and you say, 'You can show the most growth of the students coming from

this background'. You can walk them into it [ELD teaching] and it's their choice.

Rick negotiated the efficacy of the teacher evaluation policy for ELD, recognizing its challenges in retaining teachers like his second-grade ELD teacher and the possibilities for attracting teachers to ELD due to the immense growth that ELs make in one school year.

Among the many factors that local policy players attributed to the challenges around teachers and teaching in ELD classrooms across the JESD, they all agreed that teacher retention and attrition was a major concern in the district. To provide a specific example, James described a difficult conundrum during the middle of the 2013–2014 school year.

> I just had to hire a new 3-5 [third, fourth and fifth grade] ELD teacher who just started last week. So, my last one [teacher], after a semester, resigned. So now I've got, I have to recruit, hire, train, and coach a brand new teacher after doing a lot of coaching and training and recruitment for the other ones [teachers].

In this situation at Advance School, the difficult teaching context of having a mixed-grade classroom with multiple standards, levels and demands and without a specific grade-level team for support led the teacher to walk out mid-year, requiring another novice teacher to fill the vacancy. In this way, teacher attrition perpetuated the cycle of challenges related to teachers and teaching across the local policy context of Greenwood, as the departure of ELD teachers required new teachers to take their positions.

Policy Negotiation and Appropriation in Local Practice

In this third findings section, I consider how different players make language policy through actions and interactions within the local context (García & Menken, 2010). Recognizing the agency of policy players, including classroom teachers, school leaders and district administrators, I investigated various ways of negotiating and appropriating language policy mandates, considering the personal, interpersonal and institutional planes of sociocultural practice (Levinson & Sutton, 2001; Ricento & Hornberger, 1996; Rogoff, 2003). Emergent from data analyses of local players' discourse and documentation, I utilized the construct of *compliance* to investigate how educators interpreted and negotiated mandates within the confines of compliance, as well as utilized the comforts of compliance to maintain implementational space to engage in individual, intra-layer and inter-layer policy appropriation in practice (Hornberger & Johnson, 2007; Johnson & Freeman, 2010).

Individual policy appropriation

Sociocultural theory (Rogoff, 2003; Vygostky, 1978) has recognized that individuals at all layers of policy have agency to independently interpret, implement and therefore make policy through enactment in practice (Hornberger & Johnson, 2007; Levinson & Sutton, 2001; Menken & García, 2010; Ricento & Hornberger, 1996). In this study, individual policy players engaged as 'human agents who act as interpretive conduits' (Hornberger & Johnson, 2007: 528), utilizing their agency to interpret and maneuver language policies to implement in practice in meaningful ways in line with their beliefs, values and contexts (Datnow *et al.*, 2002; Menken & García, 2010). In Chapter 4, the case of Annie demonstrated this individual policy appropriation in her description of closing the classroom door and using Spanish to support individual students. Despite district players' interpretation of language policy, which manifested in a strict English-only policy (JESD, 2014c), Ms Nethercutt knew that state-level policy allowed for native language support and recognized her individual agency to utilize Spanish in her classroom. Her knowledge of language policy (i.e. Proposition 203), paired with her recognition of native language as an effective instructional tool, led Annie to individually appropriate policy in practice through Spanish-medium classroom supports for students.

Zooming out to the broader context of JESD, school-level players also engaged in individual policy appropriation to implement language policy in schools. Although the ELL department claimed control of all ELD programming across the district, school leaders exercised their agency in various ways within policies and procedures at state and district levels, such as the situation James encountered when organizing middle-school ELs into classrooms at Advance School. James explained the policy for placement of labeled ELs into classrooms: 'There's the policy, if there's more than 20 [ELs] in the band, grade-level band, K-2, 3–5, 6–8, that we have to have a separate class for them [ELs] and teach the 4-hour block using the 4-hour model'. At Advance School, AZELLA data from the 2012–2013 school year necessitated that James implement one sixth, seventh and eighth mixed-grade classroom for all labeled middle-school students to start the 2013–2014 school year. He did this begrudgingly, reflecting on his prior experiences as a seventh- and eighth-grade teacher and recognizing the challenges and inequities posed to both teachers and students.

In the middle of the 2013–2014 school year, James received new AZELLA data from Graciela, the EL data coordinator, and recognized the implementational space to negotiate the typically static procedure for ELD class placement (Hornberger & Johnson, 2007; Johnson & Freeman, 2010). After the mid-year AZELLA testing, some of the middle-school students met the needed scoring criteria to be reclassified. During our interview in

January 2014, he explained ELD at Advance School and the use of Individual Language Learner Plans (ILLPs):

> We have a Kindergarten ELD classroom. We have a first-grade ELD classroom. We have a second [grade] ELD classroom. We have a 3–5 [mixed-grade] ELD classroom. And six through eight [grades], we go ILLPs. We had an ELD [mixed-grade classroom for] six through eight [grades], but our numbers dropped below 20, and we immediately redistributed those kids across the three grade levels and did ILLPs.

By using ILLPs, James remained in compliance with district (JESD, 2014h) and state policy (ADE, 2011) while exercising his agency to make mid-year changes to school structures and EL placements. In addition to integrating ELs into mainstream classrooms to provide access to both content instruction and English-proficient peers, James strategically restaffed the teacher formerly occupying the middle-school ELD classroom, making her the school-level instructional coach specifically tasked to support the ELD teachers in their unique teaching contexts.

Intra-layer policy appropriation

In addition to acting alone, which prompts the visualization of closing one's classroom or school door to engage in covert policy work (Datnow et al., 2002; Heineke & Cameron, 2011), local policy players interacted with one another within layers to collaboratively interpret and negotiate mandates (Rogoff, 2003). Seeking out peer support, educators looked to their colleagues to actively engage in the consideration of language policy, the negotiation of various mandates and implementation in practice in line with shared beliefs, values and contexts (Datnow et al., 2002). In Chapter 4, the case of Annie demonstrated this intra-layer policy appropriation when she collaborated with her grade-level team to integrate first graders from across ELD and non-ELD settings in guided math groups. At odds with the mandate to separate students into classrooms by ELP levels and recognizing the value of ELs interacting with native English speakers to support students' social, emotional and linguistic development, Annie and her first-grade colleagues negotiated the rigid ELD structures that segregated primary students for the entire school day and implemented heterogeneous small groups across the grade level for at least one hour of daily practice.

Spanning out to the broader context of JESD, intra-layer policy appropriation also occurred within the district layer. Despite classroom and school players' perceptions that district players based all practice on compliance, ELL department staff engaged in similar interaction to collaboratively interpret, negotiate and implement policy in practice, such as Cynthia and Delia's joint district-level work with EL parents and families. Working within the confines of the ELD approach that Cynthia defined as 'not a flexible model', these two district players toiled to find ways to build what they both valued as central to EL teaching and learning – bilingualism. As bilingual individuals themselves, as well as long-time dual-language educators in the JESD prior to the passage of Proposition 203, their passions continuously remained in bilingual and biliterate education for young Latinos. Recognizing the diminished flexibility of the language policy within classrooms and schools, Cynthia looked outside the schools and corresponding policy confines to work with parents and families, seeking out external funding to allow the hiring of Delia as the EL parent liaison who coordinated family literacy workshops aimed at building PK-3 students' bilingualism.

As an educator opposed to the English-only approach, Delia embraced the implementational space within the district layer of language policy appropriation (Hornberger & Johnson, 2007; Johnson & Freeman, 2010). She explained, 'It's very difficult for me right now with the [restrictive policy] conditions that we have here in Arizona. But that's the hand we're dealt with, and this is why my job is so wonderful'. In her role, Delia provided workshops for parents focused on building children's literacy skills. Although she utilized English-medium texts, due to what she described as the need to align workshops with ELD classroom materials and practices, she brought in the lens of native language support and bridging language to build bilingualism, specifically emphasizing parents' roles and responsibilities in accomplishing children's bilingualism and biliteracy. She recounted her regular narrative with parents:

> Bilingual does not mean just speaking it [native language]. You've got to be able to read it and write it, and unfortunately your child is not going to learn to read and write it until he's in high school, if he chooses okay [to take a foreign language]. So who's going to teach him to read it and write it? You need to be involved with that.

Through her literacy workshops with the parents of ELs, which merged both reading and bilingual strategies, Delia hoped that families from all cultural and linguistic backgrounds across the community would espouse active policy roles to support students' native language development at home despite the monolingual environment at school.

Inter-layer policy appropriation

Just as local players collaborated within layers, they also engaged in collaborative policy work across layers of educational practice, including classroom, school and district-level players (Hornberger & Johnson, 2007;

Johnson & Freeman, 2010). Through inter-layer policy appropriation, educators recognized the need to seek out colleagues for shared negotiation and aligned implementation of language policy in practice. The cases of Tammie and Annie, both ELD teachers at Longview School, demonstrated inter-layer policy appropriation, as their school leader encouraged collaboration across grade-level teams with non-ELD teachers and supported instructional planning to integrate language and literacy instruction across the rigid hourly blocks. With ongoing collaborative efforts across the classroom and school layers, Tammie and Annie described maneuvering additional time for guided reading, integrating grammar mandates to be more developmentally appropriate for children and incorporating grade-level content standards to hold ELs to high expectations.

Extending the collaborative endeavors beyond the school campus, inter-layer policy appropriation also transpired across classroom, school, and district layers, such as the shared initiative to infuse social studies and science content into the 4-hour block in classrooms across the JESD. As described in Chapter 2, the passing of House Bill 2064 led to the creation of the EL Task Force and the design of the ELD model, which declared English proficiency as a prerequisite to academic content learning and insisted on four hours of ELD instruction emphasizing only the English language itself as distinct from other content areas (ADE, 2008). District policy documents also reflected the state-level mandates against the merging of content and language, as JESD administrators defined the ELD program model as a classroom in which 'students will be provided with a total of 4 periods of ELD, 1 period of Math and 1 period of a Special Area. Students will not participate in Science or Social Studies instruction' (JESD, 2014c). Nevertheless, all educators across the local policy context expressed the inequity of ELs not having access to content area learning. With the unrealistic expectation that students would test out of the EL label after one year (ADE, 2008), local policy players recognized that ELs remained in skill-based language settings for multiple years, falling behind their mainstream peers in science and social studies.

Although teachers in and across Greenwood may have independently been teaching content within the ELD block prior to the 2013–2014 school year, the inter-layer policy appropriation focused on content instruction now had the support of and alignment with the district-level players in the ELL department. As described by educators across policy layers, the JESD prided itself in being '100% in compliance' with state language policy. With compliance monitoring as a regular component of district-level practice, where ADE administrators came to classrooms, schools and the district office to review practice in line with state mandates, full compliance led to reduced state-level monitoring and supervision. In this way, the ELL department recognized the implementational space to negotiate policy mandates (Hornberger & Johnson, 2007; Johnson & Freeman, 2010) and infused science and social studies content into the ELD blocks that remained formally labeled as oral language and vocabulary, reading, writing and grammar (JESD, 2014h). Cynthia recounted her explanation to ELD teachers on finding implementational space within language policy:

> I don't agree with the entire philosophy in the [ELD] model, but guys, this is the law and we have to comply. We're going to do the best we can, so we're going to enrich this little piece here, and we're going to put some things here, and we're going to help you.

After the ELL department director utilized the cushion from the state administrators to negotiate demands, EL coaches supported teachers' implementation in practice.

Despite the district administrators finding space to allow for the integration of academic content into the 4-hour block, ELD classroom teachers and school leaders continued to negotiate policy to implement effectively in practice. As demonstrated in the narrative case of Paula in Chapter 4, she recounted attempts to integrate science and social studies into her ELD blocks only to find additional challenges to teaching and learning; for example, the long-term ELs in her middle-school classroom, many of whom had been in ELD classrooms since the primary grades at Mountainside, had little background knowledge on content topics and vocabulary due to exposure to only skill-based language settings in previous school years. Though they were on board with the inter-layer policy appropriation focused on content instruction, school leaders also expressed complexities, such as James' concern for his multi-grade teachers at Advance who needed to utilize multiple sets of content standards to plan instruction for three grade levels of students. In this way, though engaging in the district-level initiative for content instruction, local policy players had to negotiate the complexities and repercussions of changing paths after five years of district insistence on compliance to ELD instruction devoid of academic content.

Discussion: Language Policy (P)layers in the Local Context

This chapter has explored Arizona language policy in practice within the JESD, including the local players working within classroom, school and district layers. Findings demonstrated the complexity of policy work in the local context, as dynamic human agency engaged with static mandates and structures to inform the implementation of EL education (García & Menken, 2010; Hornberger & Johnson, 2007; Ricento & Hornberger,

1996). Within the confines of compliance, which emerged frequently in participants' discourse as they interpreted and negotiated policy, local players both accepted and resisted various mandates. When accepting state policies and engaging in practices to enforce compliance, district and school players positioned ELD teachers as passive policy targets, such as placing novice teachers in ELD classrooms and requiring strict compliance-based training to guide EL teaching and learning (Honig, 2006). When resisting state policies and engaging in practice to negotiate compliance, district and school players positioned ELD teachers as active policy agents, such as enlisting classroom-level support to provide content instruction (Datnow, 2006). When considering the complex and dynamic context of the multiple layers and players within the JESD, classroom teachers, school leaders and district administrators developed ways to appropriate policy in practice in the most restrictive language policy in the US (Gándara & Hopkins, 2010).

By foregrounding the local context of the JESD, findings demonstrated that federal, community and state layers and players influenced and backgrounded local practice (Rogoff, 2003; Tharp, 1997). At the federal layer, the investigation by the US Department of Justice and Office of Civil Rights and the resulting resolution greatly increased the number of ELs needing placement in ELD classrooms in the JESD and across the state; this federal investigation began within the community layer of language policy due to the ongoing work of legal advocates connected to the *Flores* case litigation. Tasked to enforce the ELD model designed by the EL Task Force in line with state legislation, the state layer provided the construct of compliance that local players maneuvered to provide on-the-ground teaching and learning to ELs in Greenwood. These backgrounded layers and players, including ADE administrators, teacher educators, EL Task Force members, state legislators and community leaders, are foregrounded in the upcoming findings chapters to continue to explore the complexity and dynamism of language policy in practice.

6 Administrators and Educators: State Educational Policy in Practice

Simultaneous to local players engaging in language policy work in practice across classrooms, schools and districts, other educators and educational administrators influence the education of English learners (ELs) at the state level. Whether designing the English Language Development (ELD) model, monitoring districts for policy compliance or preparing the state's teaching force, state policy players have broad impact on the language educational practices around the state of Arizona. In this chapter, I foreground the layers and players involved in EL education at the state level, as connected to and contextualized by local practice in Greenwood and other Arizona communities (Rogoff, 1995; Tharp, 1997). Building on the historical and contemporary information presented in Part 1, I begin by introducing the layers and profiling the players who participated in the current study (Hornberger & Johnson, 2007; Ricento & Hornberger, 1996). See Table 6.1 for details on state education participants. I then utilize themes emergent at the state education level to chronicle players' developing perspectives and ongoing experiences first historically throughout two decades of Arizona education and then recently across five years of implementation of the 4-hour ELD approach. I close with a discussion exploring the complexities within Arizona state education, including the alignment, misalignment and dependency across state and local contexts of language policy in practice.

Policy Layers and Players in Arizona State Education

English Learner Task Force

As described in Chapter 2, House Bill 2064 established the EL Task Force, composed of nine members appointed by political leaders (HB 2064, 2006). Language policy charged the task force to develop and adopt research-based, cost-efficient program models aligned to federal and state laws for implementation in school districts and charter schools. The resulting 4-hour ELD block became the state-mandated model for EL

Table 6.1 State education participants

Pseudonym	Position	Gender	Ethnicity	Language abilities
Alex	Task force chair	Male	White	English, German, Latin
Pat	Task force member	Female	White	English, German, Latin
Gayle	ADE administrator	Female	White	English
Gabby	OELAS administrator	Female	White	English, Spanish
Wendy	Community college instructor	Female	White	English, Spanish
Frank	University professor	Male	White	English, Spanish
Wayne	Charter school leader	Male	White	English

instruction, situating the task force as a unique policy layer with executive, legislative and educational roles and responsibilities. After the initial design of the ELD model, task force members held monthly public meetings with presentations from state (e.g. deputy superintendents) and local policy actors (e.g. district administrators) with the goal being to review and discuss needed changes to ELD program models. The task force maintained responsibility for ongoing review until state legislation transferred power to the Board of Education in 2013 (HB 2425, 2013). Two task force members participated in this study: Alex, the task force leader and a non-educator; and Pat, a task force member and former educator. Both participants served on the task force for two 4-year terms, from its inception in 2006 to its termination in 2013.

Alex, task force leader

An economist by trade with 35 years in Arizona public policy, Alex led the EL Task Force for two terms after his appointment by the president of the senate, a long-time friend and colleague. Conceptualizing himself as the only member without an agenda, he utilized his role as chairman to be a 'fair broker to all sides'. During the first 4-year term, he described the intensive workload of monthly meetings and public hearings to glean input and feedback from hundreds of stakeholders across the state, including teachers, school and district leaders, community members and university researchers. Despite being bound by stipulations required by House Bill 2064, Alex described what he viewed as a bottom-up policy movement wherein teachers' experiences and perspectives guided decision-making around the 4-hour ELD block. In his role as chairman, he aimed to guide the task force in using stakeholder feedback to define a clear model of 'what it looked like' so that EL instruction could be replicated in a straightforward manner. After the initial design of the ELD model, he described the shift of the task force to a monitoring body, where regular meetings welcomed comments and concerns from practitioners in the field. Following the first term, the second task force included a new group of appointees outside of Alex, Pat and another member. Recognizing the political nature of the nominations and appointments, Alex recalled the 'mess' of the second term, during which very little got done and which culminated in the shift of responsibility to the board.

Pat, task force member

A two-term member of the EL Task Force, Pat brought her secondary foreign and second language teaching experience in Arizona as well as her experience in international language teaching and learning in Germany and Japan. A German major who became a foreign language teacher through national initiatives in the 1970s during the time of grammar translation and audiolingual methodologies, she lived in Germany for a year, where she taught English and saw the value of language immersion through her daughter's schooling. Upon returning to Arizona and finding no German teaching jobs, Pat shifted to reading and teaching English as a second language (ESL) at a Phoenix-area junior high school, followed by ESL and foreign language teaching at three Phoenix high schools, where she found explicit teaching of English grammar to be helpful for ELs as well as teaching language through the content areas. Pat retired from teaching and shifted focus to her education-focused newspaper column and the English for the Children movement, which aimed to eliminate bilingual education. Her newspaper column, as well as her support of the English-only movement and Tom Horne's election to the office of state superintendent, earned her appointment to the task force. In the first term, she utilized her experiences and observations at schools to guide her decision-making around the ELD block; however, her decisions had consequences that she later regretted. Reflecting on her second term, she described turmoil within the task force, as school and district practitioners' pleas for flexibility and change fell on the deaf ears of powerful and politically connected task force members.

Arizona Department of Education

Since the territorial days before statehood, the Department of Public Instruction (i.e. the Arizona Department of Education [ADE]) has overseen educational policy and practice across the state. Administered by the State Superintendent of Public Instruction, an elected official, the ADE has utilized various offices with deputy, associate and deputy associate superintendents appointed to leadership roles. One of these state-level offices, the Office of English Language Acquisition Services (OELAS), has employed individuals focused on EL education, including an associate superintendent; a deputy associate superintendent; three directors of compliance monitoring, professional development, and accountability;

12 education program specialists; and one administrative assistant (ADE, 2015c). OLEAS was established in 2006 as a part of House Bill 2064, and lawmakers outlined its primary tasks as the publication of program rules, compliance monitoring, technical assistance and teacher training (HB 2064, 2006). Within the broader state level, ADE and OELAS administrators maintained responsibility for implementing the ELD model designed by the task force through compliance monitoring and professional development at universities, school districts and charter schools. Two state administrators participated in this study: Gayle and Gabby, the associate superintendent and deputy associate superintendent who led OELAS policy work.

Gayle, Associate Superintendent

Appointed by the Superintendent of Public Instruction, Gayle's role as Associate Superintendent of Academic Standards situated her in a leadership role charged with overseeing various offices, including OELAS. She began her career in Arizona PK-8 education, with two decades of experience as a primary teacher, school literacy coach and district curriculum director in Phoenix. Gayle shifted to state-level education after accepting a position as deputy associate superintendent in 2002. Due to her expertise in reading, she focused on literacy policies and programs, such as the Reading First initiative that followed No Child Left Behind (NCLB). Gayle was promoted to associate superintendent in 2008; when John Huppenthal replaced Tom Horne as the elected leader of Arizona schools in 2011, he reorganized the ADE, which added OELAS under her purview. Gayle utilized her expertise in reading to make meaning of the language policies that she was charged to enforce, conceptualizing the ELD model as an 'intensive language intervention' meant to be pull-out and short-term to support students' achievement. In her leadership role, she managed OELAS administrators as they engaged in compliance and professional development efforts with school districts and charter schools. Gayle also described attempts to communicate considerations for the ELD model regarding elementary schools and reading intervention. With the shift in responsibility from the task force to the board, she looked forward to possible revisions to the model, including reduction of hours and integration of content.

Gabby, deputy associate superintendent

Focused specifically on ELs in the larger ADE, Gabby oversaw the operations and personnel of the OELAS as the deputy associate superintendent. She began her career in education in 1995 as an elementary teacher of predominantly ELs in a 'difficult' Phoenix-area district. Due to her passion for language, Gabby opted to receive her ESL endorsement during her undergraduate teacher preparation program, just falling short of the bilingual endorsement due to the writing portion of the Spanish proficiency test. Nonetheless, she spent three of her 11 years of classroom teaching in a bilingual classroom prior to the passage of Proposition 203, which she conceptualized as one of the many issues with bilingual education in Arizona. She recalled her own lack of knowledge of language policies and proficiency levels of students. In 2006, after the passing of House Bill 2064, Gabby moved to the ADE as an OELAS program specialist charged with monitoring districts and charter schools for compliance with new language policy. In this field-based role evaluating practice in the years prior to ELD implementation in 2008–2009, she observed teachers without the knowledge and tools to effectively teach ELs, as well as students who were forgotten and disengaged in general education settings. Using her prior experiences as an underprepared teacher, she welcomed the tools and structures provided by the ELD model, including English language proficiency (ELP) standards and explicit grammar instruction. Through her office's duties of compliance monitoring, professional development and technical assistance, Gabby described the desire to support teachers and leaders in providing effective instruction to ELs.

Institutions of higher education

Teacher preparation has been an essential component of language education policy in Arizona. As described in Chapter 3, state policy required all teachers to receive Structured English Immersion (SEI) endorsements to teach in Arizona schools. ADE and OELAS administrators required that institutions of higher education, specifically teacher education programs, follow state-mandated curricular frameworks to prepare teachers for SEI instruction through 90 clock hours of coursework (ADE, 2005, 2011). In this way, institutions of higher education have held responsibility for implementing language policy in teacher preparation programs. Across the state, three public universities have prepared a large majority of Arizona teachers, partnering with 2-year community colleges to support the teacher pipeline and meet the demand for teachers. Specific to the SEI endorsement, 4-year institutions offered both required courses for the provisional and full endorsements, whereas community colleges typically offered only the first course. Various educators engaged in SEI teacher preparation, including adjunct instructors, clinical faculty members and tenured and tenure-track professors. Two teacher educators who specialized in EL education and taught SEI endorsement coursework participated in this study: Wendy, a community college instructor; and Frank, a tenured university professor.

Wendy, community college instructor

Employed by Desert Community College (DCC) for the past 14 years, 11 years as an adjunct instructor and three years as full-time faculty,

Wendy has balanced responsibilities across the reading and education departments, supporting community college students in their own language development as well as preparing them to support that of K-12 students in future classrooms. Beginning her career in education 32 years ago as a Spanish bilingual teacher in southern Arizona, Wendy moved to the Phoenix area, received her master's degree in reading and shifted into a leadership role as a school principal. Wendy has split her professional career between K-12 and community college education; whereas K-12 teaching and leading took center stage, she found opportunities at community colleges, valuing the gateway that this setting provided to students from diverse backgrounds. At DCC, Wendy has worked primarily with ELs in both reading and education courses, including long-term ELs who attended Arizona schools and international students coming from around the world. She has found that, as learners, many pre-service teachers struggle with skills that they will eventually need to support students, including language-based skills such as grammar and content-based skills such as critical thinking. As the instructor for the first SEI course, the second of which must be taken at a 4-year university, she described her emphasis on language policy compliance supported by effective pedagogy.

Frank, university professor

As a tenured professor at a 4-year university, Frank has taught courses to pre-service and in-service teachers on linguistics and second language teaching for the past 15 years. After completing graduate school in Latin America, he returned to the US and took a tenure-track position shortly before the passage of Proposition 203. Originally an active opponent of the English-only movement and legislation that greatly reduced bilingual education across the state, Frank has shifted to work within the confines of policy to find spaces for educators to appropriate policy via sound practice for ELs. He described the misnomer of *English-only* regarding Arizona policy and his struggle to prepare educators to recognize where native language can be used by students, teachers and leaders within the confines of the law. Although formally situated in the bilingual and multilingual department, his teaching schedule consistently has included Introduction to Linguistics for the optional ESL endorsement and Second Language Teaching, which fulfills the final 45 clock hours for the full SEI endorsement. As a teacher educator focused on ELs, Frank has discovered both pros and cons to the policy requiring all teachers to receive the SEI endorsement. Whereas he has seen value in every teacher having knowledge and skills about ELs, he has discovered the limited scope of essential understandings in the minimal two-course sequence, in contrast to the six courses required for the ESL or bilingual endorsements.

Arizona charter schools

As described in Chapter 2, charter schools have become a fixture in the educational landscape of Arizona. Since the passage of House Bill 2002 in 1994, charter schools have continued to increase in number and student enrollment across two decades. As of 2013, state leaders from the Arizona Charter Schools Association (ACSA) boasted 602 charter schools, making up 30% of the state's public schools and serving 17% of Arizona public school students (ACSA, 2015). Despite a recent uptick in district-run charter schools as public school districts chose to convert schools into charters (ACSA, 2014), 526 of Arizona's charter schools received sponsorship from the state's Charter Board and operated independently of public school districts. Without ties to local school districts, the ACSA has aimed to provide charter schools with a statewide network of support, advocacy and leadership (ACSA, 2014). In addition to the state-level charter network, the ADE has directly overseen the educational policy and practices of non-district-affiliated charter schools. Similar to language policy mandates impacting administrative teams at larger school districts, charter school leaders regularly engaged with state administrators for both compliance and professional development. Wayne, a charter school leader near the Greenwood area, participated in this study.

Wayne, charter school leader

In his seven years as the assistant principal at National Charter School, Wayne has maintained responsibility for EL programming at this K-12 school serving 720 predominantly Latino students across multiple campuses. Wayne spent the entirety of his professional career in charter schools, including six years as a teacher at National prior to moving into administration. Until he created a part-time EL coordinator position in 2013, Wayne maintained all responsibilities for implementing language policy in practice, including coordinating the ELD programs, proctoring the Arizona English Language Learner Assessment (AZELLA), placing ELs in the appropriate settings, maintaining mandated documentation and interacting with OELAS administrators for compliance and training purposes. Whereas Wayne had maintained all roles and responsibilities for ELs, in addition to his other administrative roles as the assistant principal, the 2012 Office of Civil Rights (OCR) legal action and corresponding resolution regarding AZELLA cut scores led to a large increase in the number of students requiring EL services. With 30% of his student body requiring EL services across three program models, including self-contained ELD classrooms for K-5, half-day ELD pull-out for middle school and Individual Language Learner Plans (ILLPs) for high school, Wayne described the complexities of scheduling, supporting teachers and maintaining compliance and communication with OELAS administrators.

State education layers of Arizona language policy

State-level layers and players influenced language policy in practice in local contexts across the state of Arizona. Accorded the enormous power to design the instructional model for all ELs in the state, task force participants recognized their simultaneous executive, legislative and educational roles and responsibilities at the state level, as well as the significant impact that their decisions had on all state and local policy players. ADE administrators conceptualized their role as the intermediary between the task force and local contexts, ensuring compliant implementation of language policy in school districts and charter schools. Despite the state language policy and corresponding ADE guidelines for the SEI endorsement, ADE leaders described less influence over the policy work conducted in higher education, which was mirrored by teacher educators who did not speak of compliance mandates but rather described agency in teaching SEI coursework. Unique to charter schools, Wayne was situated similarly to district administrators, such as Cynthia in the Jackson Elementary School District (JESD), dealing directly with ADE for compliance monitoring and teacher training. Whether designing the ELD model, monitoring for compliance, training teachers at universities or supporting practice in charter schools, state players influenced EL education through daily actions and interactions with policy.

State Policy Players' Past Experiences in Arizona Education

Building out from local educators at the center of language policy, state-level players engage in policy work across multiple layers of policy (Ricento & Hornberger, 1996). To understand the multilayered and multifaceted nature of language policy in practice, one must consider the metaphorical onion's growth over time. When an onion grows, its layers move outward as new layers begin to grow at the center; within education, this growth is reflected when policy players begin as classroom teachers and move outward as school, district and state leaders. In this study, state education players began their careers in Arizona education prior to the passage of Proposition 203, which led to personal experiences and historical perspectives on EL education through various eras of language policy, including bilingual education, SEI and ELD. See Table 6.2 for an overview of state players' historical trajectories in Arizona education. Distinct from the novice teachers described in Chapter 4, state players had ample experience with ELs spanning decades in Arizona education, which they utilized to make meaning of their daily language policy work in the current context of the 4-hour block (see Table 6.2). In this section, I explore state players' past perspectives and experiences, organized sequentially by Arizona language policy: bilingual education and the English-only movement, Proposition 203 and SEI and House Bill 2064 and ELD.

Table 6.2 State education players' professional trajectories

	Pre-2000 bilingual education	2000 Proposition 203	2006 House Bill 2064	2008 ELD implementation
Alex	Economist		EL Task Force leader	
Pat	Teacher	Writer and activist	EL Task Force member	
Gayle	Teacher	District leader	State administrator	
Gabby		Teacher	State administrator	
Frank	Student		University professor of bilingual education	
Wendy	Teacher	School leader	Community college instructor	
Wayne	Student		Teacher	School leader

Bilingual education and the English-only movement

Prior to the passage of Proposition 203 in 2000, schools across Arizona housed bilingual programs that utilized native language instruction to educate ELs. Five of the seven state education players who participated in this study engaged in K-12 educational practice during this epoch. Gabby taught ELs as a bilingual and ESL elementary teacher, whereas Pat taught German and Latin as a foreign language in secondary settings. Wendy began her career as a bilingual teacher before shifting into school leadership in bilingual schools, much like Gayle's teaching and leading in non-bilingual settings with an emphasis on reading intervention. As a young professor of bilingual education, Frank engaged in professional preparation and advocacy for bilingual education, whereas Pat joined the English for the Children initiative and advocated to end native language instruction. In this sub-section, I focus on the experiences of three former K-12 language-specific educators, including Gabby's bilingual teaching, Wendy's bilingual teaching and leading and Pat's foreign language teaching. Eventually shifting to different positions within Arizona state education, including state administration, higher education and the EL Taskforce, players' experiences with bilingual education influenced current perspectives on language policy in practice.

Gabby, bilingual teacher

As a pre-service teacher at a 4-year Arizona university, Gabby enrolled as an undergraduate elementary education major, minoring in ESL and bilingual education. Training to be a teacher in the early 1990s, Gabby and other teacher candidates opted to add ESL and bilingual endorsements to their teaching certifications. Despite having completed both ESL and bilingual course requirements at university, Gabby was unable to pass the written portion of the Spanish proficiency test to obtain her bilingual endorsement. After three failed attempts, she recognized her Spanish deficiencies as a non-native speaker; however, she secured a job as a bilingual teacher for her first three years in the profession on an emergency certificate. Gabby reflected,

> In all honesty, looking back, I probably had no business teaching in a bilingual classroom. I was not at the fluency in Spanish that I had the capability to teach another [person] in that language. I could certainly read stories, which is what I did. I fulfilled those [teaching] requirements to the ability that I could, but I also think that some of the detriment of bilingual education is they put people like me who had [only] enough Spanish to get by. I don't think that's the person who should be teaching someone, teaching [in] that language.

As a novice teacher who spoke 'enough Spanish to get by', she took the job out of college with emergency credentials, desperately wanting a job working with ELs in the Phoenix area. She went on to describe herself as 'part of the problem' with bilingual education in Arizona, as she recalled utilizing primarily English and not impacting students' native language development.

Extending from her experiences as an underprepared bilingual teacher, Gabby made meaning of past language policy in practice by raising broader issues regarding bilingual teacher and program quality. From her perspective, bilingual education failed primarily because of the teachers in bilingual classrooms. Without strong bilingual and biliterate teachers, Gabby recognized the corresponding impact on students' language development. Using herself as an example of teachers 'who had no business teaching in bilingual education', she connected to ELs' experiences: 'What I saw in my experience were students who struggled and struggled, and by middle school were so frustrated because they weren't even speaking English in middle school, and they gave up'. Although she saw teaching as the primary lever for programmatic failure, Gabby also described the lack of structures to consistently move students through bilingual programs. She explained,

> We had kids who were told, 'Don't worry. When they're ready, they'll speak English'. I really did hear those things, 'when they're ready'. I guess I'm wondering how many kids really came to you as a teacher and said, 'Teacher, I'm ready to start speaking English. I feel I have enough vocabulary, and I've listened enough, and I'm ready now to start doing this'. They don't do that.

Observing unqualified and underprepared teachers in bilingual classrooms, paired with scant programmatic structures for language development, Gabby utilized her prior experiences to frame current perspectives on language policy in practice as the OELAS leader. Whereas she explicitly stated the value of bilingualism and desire for kids to be bilingual, Gabby asserted that Arizona did not have the capacity to offer bilingual education that fostered bilingualism and biliteracy: 'It's not about whether kids should be bilingual or not. Absolutely. The problem was we tried that [bilingual education], and it didn't work. It did not work at our state'.

Wendy, bilingual teacher and leader

Like Gabby, Wendy began her career in education as a bilingual teacher with an emergency certificate. With her undergraduate major in Spanish and minor in English, she secured a bilingual teaching job following college graduation. As a native speaker of English, Wendy looked back retrospectively and questioned her Spanish proficiency as a novice teacher charged to provide bilingual content instruction to Spanish-dominant students. Using prior experiences to guide her current practice in facilitating SEI endorsement coursework to pre-service teachers at the community college, she explained, 'What I tell my students is that there were no guidelines for how to do bilingual [education]. Nobody checked my [Spanish] language proficiency, nobody'.

In addition to her experiences as a bilingual teacher, Wendy considered bilingual education through the lens of a school principal, reflecting on the lack of resources provided to support high-quality bilingual education. She recalled no clear standardized policy for bilingual education across the state, which led to local difficulties in describing bilingual program goals and structures to parents and community members. Recounting her experiences as a school leader, Wendy explained,

> I had bilingual teams, ESL teams, and English teams [of teachers] in my middle school, but there weren't guidelines on, 'Well, wait a minute. How do you move someone from one [language] track to the next? How do you scaffold their [students'] language growth?'

In addition to the lack of resources for tracking students' language progress and scaffolding language development in and across bilingual classrooms, she also experienced a dearth in quality bilingual teachers. Wendy asserted, 'I had English [language] teachers who could barely speak English, but they were exceedingly proficient in Spanish'. In classroom settings where there were no clear allocations for English and Spanish language use, Wendy found that Spanish-dominant teachers favored using Spanish in daily practice, whereas English-dominant teachers prioritized English as the medium of instruction.

Wendy's experiences with bilingual education continued beyond the bilingual epoch prior to 2000. As a community college instructor who often partnered with schools and districts, she supported a suburban

Phoenix district in designing and implementing a dual-language immersion program. With bilingual education eliminated as an educational option for ELs with Proposition 203, state policy continued to allow for bilingual education for English-proficient students. Wendy described her recent work on the suburban dual-language program:

> The rules are very, very specific, [and] very clear. We have assessments in place now to make sure that [students'] language proficiency and growth in reading and writing is occurring in both [Spanish and English] languages. I think we're more explicit now, and I don't think there's a problem with that. I think it helps us, without sounding too heavy handed, it gives us some quality control and I think we owe that to our students.

In addition to utilizing her prior experiences with inconsistent structures for bilingual education, she also drew from her knowledge of effective bilingual programs. Overall, Wendy recognized both the strengths and weaknesses in bilingual education and utilized prior knowledge and experiences to shape her practice in working with future teachers and school district partners.

Pat, teacher of English as a second language

Moving around the Phoenix metropolitan area to different school contexts across her career, Pat's experiences centered on language teaching across four secondary school settings, including roles in reading, ESL, German and Latin classrooms. As a non-Spanish-speaker working with predominantly Spanish-speaking ELs, she described the need for high expectations for ELs in using English across listening, speaking, reading and writing; however, she did not regularly see this occurring in classrooms outside her own. In one high school, Pat described the overall culture of low expectations in the ESL department.

> I was very disgusted with everything because my [EL] kids and their classes were too easy... Now those [mainstream] kids were being pushed [academically], there was rigor. But in the ESL department, they were having lots of parties and movies, and this just did not go over well with me.

She reflected on her students in this particular context, all Spanish-speaking ELs who had been in bilingual programs and yet had not attained English proficiency on entering high school. To remedy this, Pat found success in teaching English skills to push forward students' language development, such as teaching phonics for students who struggled with pronunciation and grammar to those who struggled with writing. By explicitly teaching verbs and prepositions in ways that were engaging to students, she recalled students' increased language acquisition and school engagement.

Whereas Pat recognized the need for explicit teaching of English grammar, she valued a more implicit way to teach vocabulary by tapping into the many cognates – words that look and sound the same across languages – used in secondary content areas. Pat recounted, 'I sat in on a class being taught in Spanish in science and I was amazed how much I could understand… I became a big believer in using the content [to teach language]'. Pat's experiences confirmed her value of immersion education where the learner is immersed in the target language, similar to the schooling of her daughter during their time in Germany. Nevertheless, schools utilized native language in a way that she found detrimental to English development.

> We also brought in more bilingual [classes], and it was a problem. The kids weren't learning English as they should. In some ways, it was good in that they were offered the higher-level classes that they couldn't have taken otherwise. It was a mixed bag but to the majority of the kids, it just seemed like everything was now on Spanish, there wasn't enough English…. the only English they had was with me [in ESL class].

Recalling schooling with the majority of content area instruction in Spanish, paired with low expectations for learning English in ESL classrooms outside of her own, Pat found bilingual education to be ineffective at producing bilingual students.

These observations and experiences led Pat to get involved in the English for the Children movement, which ultimately restricted bilingual programs for ELs. After describing what she perceived to be an educational system for ELs in Phoenix-area high schools that was ineffective overall, she explained,

> I left [teaching], and that's when I started writing. I became involved in the movement to get rid of bilingual [education]. My problem with what I saw [in schools] wasn't as much bilingual as just poor teaching. I can see how the native language can be used in a very helpful way, but it wasn't being done that way.

Pat described her recognition of bilingual education as a sound approach to support bilingualism but one that was inappropriate for ELs who needed to master English before entering bilingual programs. Using her prior experiences in Arizona schools to frame bilingual education as ineffective for ELs, she worked with both educators and non-educators to push the campaign to change state language policy, which eventually led to the passage of Proposition 203.

Overall, former classroom teachers turned state education players utilized prior language teaching experiences to make meaning of current language policy mandates. Recalling their past careers as K-12 teachers and leaders, participants rationalized the shift away from bilingual education, describing what they identified as poor implementation of policies and programs in practice. Specifically, they saw teaching as the primary issue with bilingual education, as teachers did not receive preparation, tools or guidance to effectively support students' language development. Whereas all state education players explicitly stated the value of bilingualism, they perceived bilingual education as a failure in Arizona, which therefore prompted restrictive legislation, which is described in the next sub-section.

Proposition 203 and Structured English Immersion

As described in Chapter 2, the English for the Children movement proved successful, and Proposition 203 passed in 2000 to vastly limit bilingual programming for ELs. To skirt submersion in monolingual settings, Arizona policy defined SEI as the approach to EL teaching and learning. During this epoch, when ELs received sheltered instruction alongside English-proficient peers, five study participants engaged in educational policy in practice. Having recently entered the profession, Wayne was a classroom teacher of ELs at a Greenwood-area charter school. Wendy persevered as a K-12 school leader, adding the role as community college adjunct instructor of SEI coursework. Gayle and Gabby both shifted from the K-12 setting to the ADE, with Gayle overseeing state reading initiatives and Gabby serving as an OELAS compliance manager. Frank continued as a professor of bilingual education but morphed to focus more on state-required SEI coursework. In this sub-section, I focus on players' prior experiences with SEI from three perspectives: those of Frank as a university professor, Gabby as a compliance manager and Wayne as a charter school educator.

Frank, university professor

Moving to Arizona to take a tenure-track faculty position in bilingual education, Frank arrived on the educational scene in the final months before the eventual passing of Proposition 203. Whereas Pat threw her support behind the English-only movement, Frank maintained his commitment to bilingualism based on his teaching and graduate studies in Mexico. He described himself as a 'proponent of bilingual education' who advocated against the English-only movement through participation in statewide committees of university faculty and local educators. He explained,

> Language teachers in general just didn't like it [Proposition 203] at all –
> politicians meddling again in something that should be an educational
> issue. I mean, it's one thing if they try to tell you how to teach math,

right? That was the argument, and we tried to pick it apart. But we didn't win. The Proposition passed. It wasn't overwhelming, but it did pass, and so it became the law. We've been living with it ever since, and it's changed a lot of things. How we do our work here [at the university]. How teachers do their work at school. How they just configure everything.

From the perspective of this university faculty member and expert in bilingual education, Proposition 203 significantly shifted his practice in preparing teachers and supporting schools.

Despite recognizing the research demonstrating the efficacy of specific language immersion programs, Frank described Arizona's SEI approach as the opposite – ineffective and inefficient for EL education. He described the prototypical classroom in the SEI approach: (a) labeled EL students being integrated into mainstream classrooms, (b) general education teachers being asked to differentiate for ELs while simultaneously teaching all students and (c) ESL coordinators and coaches occasionally working with ELs at the back of the classroom. Frank critically reflected,

How much actual differentiated instruction do those ELL kids actually get? We were seeing around the state that they weren't getting any instruction. That is hard to do as a classroom teacher. That is a really hard thing to do. It is. I work in the classroom all the time. I know how hard that is. A lot of times those students are just getting bored.

Recognizing the challenges presented to teachers through this approach, his regular classroom observations resulted in a straightforward hypothesis on this epoch of Arizona education: 'What that [SEI] turned out to be was just the old submersion'.

Frank's first-hand experiences with the challenges of the SEI approach provided perspective on the eventual ELD model that followed. He asserted,

Whatever you think about the 4-hour block, it was a response to that problem [submersion through SEI]. Whether you're for or against it [ELD model], it was an attempt, the way I see it, to solve that problem. It may not be the best solution. That's what it was a reaction against .... The old system [SEI] was just totally broken. It just wasn't working.

Despite his continued belief in and advocacy for bilingual education as the most effective approach to educate ELs, his prior experiences with the nebulous and unregulated SEI approach allowed him to rationalize the restrictive 4-hour model.

Gabby, compliance auditor

After leaving the classroom, which included teaching in both bilingual and EL elementary settings, Gabby shifted to the state education layer of language policy when she took a job at the ADE. Through her position as OELAS compliance auditor, she was charged with observing practice in classrooms, schools and districts to ensure compliance with Proposition 203 mandates and SEI instruction. Drawing from her experiences in classrooms and conversations with teachers, Gabby reflected on the perceived inefficacy of SEI as an approach to teaching ELs. Similar to her perspectives on bilingual education based on her personal classroom experiences, she attributed the lack of effectiveness to underprepared teachers and unclear programmatic structures.

Using SEI as an inclusion model, wherein ELs learned content alongside English-proficient students, Gabby found that teachers lacked the knowledge and skills to adequately support ELs' needs simultaneously to those of other students. She recalled observations in upper-elementary, middle-school and high-school classrooms, where ELs sat in the back of classrooms unengaged in learning. Unlike the active learning she observed in most primary classrooms, Gabby attributed the increased focus on content-area academics to teachers' struggles to integrate ELs. She recounted her conversations with classroom teachers.

> We'd have teachers who'd say, 'I don't know what I'm supposed to do'. They would really verbalize to us, 'What am I supposed to do? I don't know that [students' native] language. I can't'. Typically, it was [teachers saying], 'We buddy them up'. [I would ask,] 'So what strategies do you use?' 'Oh, I use José, who's bilingual, and he tells them what to do'.

In this way, Gabby's observations of and conversations with underprepared teachers melded into her perspective that ELs' needs were not being met in SEI classrooms.

Gabby asserted that teachers' supposed inability to effectively support ELs often stemmed from inadequate tools and structures to label and track students' progress and language proficiency. Because the SEI approach was characterized by EL placement in general education classrooms with English-proficient peers, she found that teachers rarely knew of the specific language needs and levels of students. Additionally, she learned that teachers often did not even know which students were labeled as ELs. Gabby told the story of what she remembered as a regular conversation with classroom teachers during her compliance visits:

> So I'd say [to teachers], 'Great, so just tell me about your students. Tell me how things are going'. Rarely could they even identify exactly who [were ELs], because I always knew their numbers [of EL students]

were different. But then furthermore, they would use references to students like, 'She's really high. He is really low', which indicated to me they had no knowledge of the child's [English language] proficiency level at all.

From her perspective, teachers needed explicit knowledge of students' language proficiency level and label to provide needed scaffolds and supports. Without knowledge of students' ELP, or a wide repertoire of strategies to support language learning in content instruction, Gabby believed that ELs' needs were not met in the SEI approach that followed Proposition 203.

Wayne, charter school teacher and leader

Following the passage of Proposition 203 in 2000, charter schools utilized SEI for approximately eight years, which encompassed Wayne's six years of classroom teaching and initial two years as a school leader. Whereas other state players emphasized the disadvantages of the nebulous SEI approach to teaching ELs in general education settings, Wayne drew from his teaching and leading to recollect both positives and negatives in this epoch of Arizona education.

As a classroom teacher, Wayne received his SEI endorsement and worked with his colleagues to implement the Sheltered Instruction Observation Protocol (SIOP) model, an operationalized version of sheltered instruction that provided planning templates and strategies for teaching language simultaneous to content (Echevarría *et al.*, 2013). He recalled,

All teachers had to take SEI [courses]. Every classroom was supposed to implement [SEI]. We did the SIOP model. I think that was great. We had primary content-level objectives with your secondary language objectives. I think those all are great practices.

Despite recognizing the value of certain pedagogical practices for all students, such as writing language objectives to guide instruction, Wayne critiqued the inclusion of ELs in general education classrooms. He asserted, 'With that whole inclusion SEI model, I feel that students were not really getting what they needed'. More specifically, he felt that ELs did not receive the additional language scaffolds and supports that they needed to achieve, specifically 'for those kids who are considered anywhere intermediate to basic and pre-emergent'.

When Wayne shifted into a leadership position at the charter school, with a large portion of his responsibilities focused on EL assessment and instruction, he continued to question the SEI approach. Situated at a predominantly Latino school, Wayne described his student population as recent Mexican immigrants prior to Arizona's controversial immigration policy shift in 2010. When newcomers would arrive during the SEI epoch, he provided an example of the challenging predicaments, specifically for middle-school students.

> An 8th grader would come and they wouldn't know any English. I'd send her, 'Sit in your class, your 8th grade class' and you say, 'You have very little time between now and next year [in high school] when you need to start earning credits and you need to pass every class individually'.

Wayne observed ELs struggling to grasp academic content in a language that they did not yet understand and teachers trying to accommodate students so that they could pass their classes to be able to attend high school. Overall, Wayne's prior experiences with SEI influenced his perspectives on current policy in practice. Drawing from the shortcomings of the approach whereby ELs learned content alongside their English-proficient peers, Wayne shared, 'I don't think we necessarily need to go back, in my opinion, and reconsider the mode of instruction, in other words, inclusion, SEI... I think the pullout ELL model [ELD] can work'.

In summary, state education players retrospectively considered their experiences with SEI and recognized its shortcomings as an approach to teaching ELs. Similar to players' perceptions of bilingual education, they described a nebulous and inconsistent approach to instruction that resulted in little to no supports for ELs. Participants utilized prior experiences with SEI to make meaning of current language policy, specifically by juxtaposing the nebulous SEI approach with the explicit ELD model. Whereas players did not agree with all facets of the more restrictive model, they recognized the shortfalls of the previous approach that led to House Bill 2064 and the ELD model, which are discussed in the next sub-section.

House Bill 2064 and English Language Development

State lawmakers mandated a more specific approach to EL education with the passage of House Bill 2064 and the subsequent creation of the EL Task Force. Immediately following the passage of House Bill 2064 in 2006, the state shifted away from the previous SEI approach, as the task force designed the 4-hour ELD model and the ADE enforced programmatic pilots in select Arizona districts, followed by implementation across the state. Whereas school, district and teacher educators such as Wayne, Wendy and Frank continued with SEI prior to ELD implementation in 2008–2009, task force members and ADE administrators began the shift from SEI to ELD. In this sub-section, I focus on the experiences of three state education players engaged in early policy work related to House Bill 2064 and ELD, including Alex's leadership of the task force charged to design the ELD program model and Gayle and Gabby's supervision of the ELD pilot and implementation in Arizona schools.

Alex, program designer

As an appointed member and elected leader of the EL Task Force that formed following House Bill 2064, Alex brought decades of experience as an economist focused on public policy. He described his role as guiding the process of program design as educators and non-educators on the task force came together to define the ELD model within 'the statutory parameters we were given, [such as] not normally intended to exceed one year, which absolutely no one said was possible'. Conceptualizing one year as a 'goal, not a metric', Alex recalled the task force's decision-making process to first extend the 4-hour requirement to all ELs, rather than solely for first-year ELs as written in House Bill 2064, and then provide standardized structures to what became designated as the ELD model.

In addition to the extended time dedicated to English language instruction, Alex recounted the task force's decision to mandate discrete skill-based language instruction within the 4-hour ELD block.

> We had a lot of conversations about whole language versus discrete skills. In my mind at least, whole language sounded more like art, and discrete skill sounded more like science. It is easier to replicate science, boring as it is, than it is to replicate art. When I looked at the number of students and the number of teachers and the number of districts and all, the more methodologically boring but consistent approach seemed like a better approach to accomplishing the goal. Maybe not as rich, maybe not as artful, maybe not as clever, but more doable, more replicable, more scalable. That seemed like a better approach. I came to think it was actually a better learning technique.

In addition to the four hours of emphasis on discrete skills of the English language, the task force decided to layout specific time blocks for each skill, including grammar, vocabulary, conversation, reading and writing. Building on the desire for the program to be replicable and scalable across the state, Alex described the value of uniformity: 'You could take a student, drop them in the middle of an intermediate third-grade class, and they'd feel at home'.

Gabby and Gayle, English Language Development program implementers

Following the initial program design by the task force, ADE administrators quickly began work to transition school districts and charter schools to implement the impending 4-hour model. Gabby described her first year as an OELAS administrator in 2006:

> Even though we knew the [ELD] models weren't in place, we knew there was a task force working, and we were communicating, 'It's going to be four hours'. Even in that year, we did some work to educate the

districts. Even though we didn't know what the model would look like, we could guarantee them that, 'You will spend four hours teaching them English'.

In what they deemed the 'early implementer' districts and schools, Gabby described the ADE's work with local players to reorganize classroom grouping to meet the requirements of the ELD model that would separate students based on language proficiency.

Drawing from her personal experiences of learning Spanish as a foreign language, Gabby described her 'light bulb' moment in the early design and implementation phases of the task force's ELD model.

> The notions of ELD, and the fact that we really need to teach kids English, we just don't necessarily teach [content] in English, but we really do need to teach them English [skills], was a concept that was like a light bulb went off for me. Duh! Someone had to teach you concepts in Spanish to be able to be successful. Why would we think it's different for kids? Yes, they're younger. Yes, they may acquire [language] faster, but with the same strategies that I was given to learn a foreign language, why would we not use those same strategies to support the learning and facilitate learning of English for these students?

Building on prior negative perceptions of and experiences with bilingual and SEI education, Gabby conceptualized the new ELD model as the correct approach to teaching ELs, providing the needed attention on ELs' needs by separating them from peers to teach language skills.

Just as Gabby drew from prior experiences to support ELD implementation, Gayle utilized her previous professional experiences with reading instruction at the classroom, school, district and state levels of Arizona education. In her administrative role overseeing the OELAS department, Gayle communicated her interpretation of the ELD model:

> How I interpreted the SEI model was intensive language intervention. You can see I'm coming from a Reading First perspective. But before that, I was a curriculum director in a K-8 district. Before that, I was a literacy coach in the district, and before that, a primary teacher. All of that experience was pulled into this [interpretation].

In the early phases of implementation, Gayle found that her interpretation of language policy contrasted with that of Gabby and EL experts in the OELAS.

> They saw that [ELD classroom] as home base for an English language learner. I said, no, it's not home base. It's an intensive language

intervention. Arizona's model is language first, and then content... To me, that's intensive language intervention. I saw the 4-hour block as exactly that. The legislation does [stipulate] really specific 'at least for one year', meaning it's meant to be short-term. It's that intensive, so it's short-term. Then, let's see what kind of an impact we could have.

Nevertheless, with Gabby and her team supporting implementation in practice, local players separated ELs from English-proficient students for the entire school day rather than according to Gayle's interpretation as a short-term, 4-hour intervention. Apart from varying interpretations of initial implementation for classroom organization, Gabby and Gayle agreed on the value of the singular and clearly defined program model to lessen the complications of monitoring EL education in thousands of schools across the state.

Overall, state education players consistently drew from varied histories and experiences to shape perspectives on current language policy in practice. By reflecting on the perceived shortcomings of bilingual education and SEI observed and experienced in classrooms and schools, players rationalized the trajectory of educational events that resulted in the ELD model. These state-level participants made meaning of the current context of EL education through policy antecedents: bilingual education did not work in their less-than-ideal classroom contexts, so an English-only approach across the state was justified; the nebulous SEI approach to the English-only approach did not work, so the restrictive 4-hour model was the response. State education players viewed 'what worked' based on the perceived structures in place to guide practice: without structures to guide teaching in bilingual and SEI settings, the context for learning was perceived to be poor. Connected to the swinging pendulum of Arizona language policy, the resulting ELD model went into effect in 2008–2009; the next section describes emergent issues in ELD policy in practice from state players' perspectives and experiences after 5 years of implementation.

Macro-Level Players' Perceptions of Current Policy in Practice

After growing in the context of Arizona education for decades, layers and players harvested the metaphorical language policy onion in 2008 on the formal implementation of ELD. Since then, Arizona language policy has remained stagnant, demonstrating scant shifts in policy since the original implementation. Meanwhile, local schools and districts have struggled with the implications of the ELD model, including the repercussions of separating ELs from mainstream peers for the 4-hour block and retaining quality teachers in the complex and often challenging context of ELD classrooms. Whereas local players emphasized these challenges, state players differed in perceptions and urgency related to language policy in practice. In this section, I use themes emergent from the JESD to consider how state players recognized and responded to local issues with policy implementation. Focused on topics related to students and teachers, I consider the backgrounded plane of local policy in practice, describing the needs of ELs from the perspectives of ELD teachers, school leaders and district administrators. I then connect to the foregrounded plane of state education to investigate the corresponding shifts or stagnancy of state-level players across five years of ELD policy in practice.

Separating students by language proficiency: Help or hindrance?

Emergent across layers of language policy, players considered the implications of separating students by English proficiency. As discussed in Chapter 3, after AZELLA scores ascribed EL labels, students were separated from English-proficient peers and placed in ELD classrooms for four hours of skill-based language instruction. Across layers, players varied significantly in their perceptions of the efficacy of this policy mandate. Framing the issue through consideration of 'what's best for kids', teachers, leaders, administrators and teacher educators differed in what they perceived as either the negative or positive ramifications of EL and English-proficient student separation.

Local players recognized the disadvantages of separating ELs from peers. Greenwood players in classrooms and schools described the negative implications for students, asserted separation as the primary issue with the ELD model and connected all other practice-based challenges to this specific mandate of the larger language policy. Classroom teachers primarily focused on the negative implications for students, describing firsthand accounts of the social and emotional repercussions of ELs being segregated from peers. Paula, the middle-school ELD teacher with all labeled ELs across sixth, seventh and eighth grades at Mountainside School, utilized stories to depict the social 'isolation' that resulted in her early adolescent students feeling like 'outcasts'. Tammie, who spent her first year teaching ELs spanning ELP levels across third and fourth grades at Longview School, recalled her students' self-ascribed label as the 'stupid class'. Utilizing a school-wide lens, school leaders used words like 'discriminatory', 'segregation' and 'sequestered' to explain the social impact of the mandate on students.

In addition to concerns for students, local players described the mandate as negative for ELD teachers. Teachers focused on the complexities of teaching in the isolated context, describing how the diversity within the EL label, including students' native languages, grade levels and proficiency levels, exacerbated the challenges of discrete skill-based instruction. JESD school and district leaders concentrated on the negative implications of segregation for teachers, such as the dearth in content area teaching, recognizing the direct connection to the challenges of teacher attrition. Situated in a charter school, Wayne concurred with public school leaders that student segregation instigated challenges to teaching and teachers in ELD classrooms; however, at a school with 98.5% Latino students, he did not see the same negative social impact on labeled ELs as described by Paula, Tammie and Annie. All local players in Greenwood-area classrooms, schools and districts converged around the same assertion: homogenous grouping by English proficiency made teaching more complex and difficult.

Whereas local players communicated challenging implications for students and teachers, state players lauded the separation of students as positive, specifically describing student grouping by language proficiency as the primary factor that made the ELD model work. From the perspectives of ADE administrators and task force members, homogenous grouping simplified the practice of teaching, making classrooms less complex and easier to manage. Alex, chairman of the EL Task Force, highlighted the separation of the ELs from peers as the driving force behind the model. He described the importance of 'grouping by proficiency and the impact it had on our curriculum and pedagogy, curriculum being discrete skills, and pedagogy being "I've got all the same kids in my room." That is probably what holds the whole thing [ELD] together'. Because teachers typically split general education classrooms into homogenous groups to differentiate instruction, such as the use of leveled reading groups, Alex explained the task force members' decision to 'keep the group as homogenous as you can, given your limitations' to simplify the pedagogical context for teachers. Through his lens, ELP was the sole variable of import, making all ELs 'the same kids' due to the ascribed label.

Similar to its perceived centrality to policy design, Gabby asserted the efficacy of student grouping by language proficiency in the implementation of ELD policy in practice, as she perceived the separation as easing the demands of classroom teaching. Similar to Alex's push for homogenous classrooms based on AZELLA scores, Gabby described how the ELD approach 'narrowed the gap' between students' abilities in classrooms:

> Let's narrow the gap. You have kids who don't speak a word of English at the pre-emergent level all the way to a gifted mainstream student in your [general education] class.... What we did for [ELD] teachers was narrow the gap. We've narrowed the gap.

Although she concurred with the task force's design of this policy facet, Gabby recognized other players' push-back regarding student segregation based on ELP level; however, she utilized her own experiences to rationalize the state's approach to policy implementation through compliance monitoring efforts. She expounded, 'The scrutiny regarding our grouping of students, but I see from my [professional] history, that now I walk into a classroom, and teachers can rattle that information [English proficiency levels]. They know exactly who's who'. Despite knowing 'who's who' with regard to AZELLA scores in the homogenous ELD classroom, Gabby coached educators to teach all ELs at the high-intermediate level with the goal being to exit students quickly from ELD.

Whereas Alex and Gabby defended the separation of ELs, teacher educators took the middle ground. Wendy and Frank asserted that separating students by ELP should be done when necessary, using strategic and flexible grouping as a pedagogical approach for both heterogeneous and homogenous grouping depending on learning objectives. Wendy understood the need to target ELD in students' first year in school, but perceived ongoing effective teaching as heterogeneous grouping to support the teaching of content. Frank questioned the settings that best support student learning.

> Of all content that we're covering the 4-hour block, how much of it can we do together with native speakers of English? Is there any of this [instruction] that we can do better if we can do it together when they speak the language in an integrated setting? Is there some content that can be more effectively or more efficiently delivered, or implemented, when I'm just working with my second language learners?

Frank characterized his approach to the issue as pedagogical rather than ideological, using the juxtaposition between prior and current language policies: 'Sometimes the 4-hour block is characterized as segregation. I don't know if that's really helpful to move the discussion along. It's a hard question because the other model [SEI] wasn't working'.

In addition to the pedagogical considerations described by teacher educators, one participant raised concern about political forces driving EL segregation in ELD classrooms. Pat explained her perceptions of the mandate through the task force responsibilities of model design and ongoing monitoring. She asserted her disagreement with student segregation first during the design of the ELD model; however, despite her desire to utilize a more integrated model, task force members who 'didn't understand language learning' sided with Alex, who pushed homogenous grouping. Pat explained why heterogeneous classrooms allowed teachers flexibility with grouping using student attributes other than language proficiency.

> If you have a large number of kids... you can put them in groups that are exactly right. The more kids you have, the more you can do that and just really zero in on their needs. From what the other program directors told me before the models, the English learners didn't end up in the same reading groups at all.

After the design of the ELD model, the task force shifted responsibility to the ongoing monitoring of policy implementation, hearing from local educators to adjust the model accordingly. Pat recalled educators' descriptions of the challenges of homogenous classrooms, as well as her own observations of negative implications when she visited schools. Nevertheless, the task force refused to change the model, which Pat presumed to be due to political pressures.

Whereas local players converged on the challenges caused by separating students into classrooms based on English proficiency as measured by AZELLA scores, state education players differed in perceptions in relation to policy, practice, and politics. Nonetheless, across the five years of ELD policy implementation, the mandate regarding student grouping in ELD classrooms remained stagnant. Pat pointed the finger at the politically connected Alex as the primary obstacle to change, despite her advocacy and the local players' pleas at ongoing task force meetings. From his perspective as chairman, Alex recalled the tumultuous second term of the task force, when new and existing appointees engaged in political infighting that ultimately prohibited any shifts in policy. Despite the challenges of student segregation faced in classrooms and schools, the nine-member task force maintained the ELD model as originally written, leading to stagnancy in language policy.

Preparing and supporting teachers: What makes a high-quality teacher?

Local and state education players framed perceptions of language policy in practice based on what they perceived as 'what's best for kids'. What players conceived as being as sound practice for students directly connected to perceptions of good teaching, or what teachers must know and do to provide 'what's best for kids'. As described in Chapter 3, the classroom teacher is of primary importance in English-medium policy and instruction, as the well-prepared teacher is the only difference between immersion and submersion, which is illegal per federal law. Findings demonstrated players' agreement that high-quality, master and expert teachers must teach in ELD classrooms; however, they differed around what knowledge and skills constituted a master teacher in the context of the 4-hour block.

Whereas local players recognized the dynamic knowledge and skills needed to reconcile the complexities of the ELD context, ADE administrators and EL Task Force members perceived ELD teachers as needing only basic knowledge and skills in contrast to the more extensive repertoires required for mainstream classroom teachers. As portrayed through the perspectives of Gabby and Alex, state leaders believed that separating students simplified teaching, which thus simplified teacher preparation and training. Gayle asserted that the model placed a master teacher in front of every EL; however, a master ELD teacher varied in the depth and breadth of knowledge and skills from other teachers.

SEI teachers have been afforded the opportunity to concentrate their own professional development in one critical area, whereas for most elementary teachers, you're expected to be an expert in literacy, in mathematics, and in science, and in social studies, and don't forget about technology. How about classroom management? What about the special ed[ucation] student at the back of your room? That's a lot of learning for a teacher.

Drawing on her experiences as an elementary teacher and instructional coach, Gayle asserted the distinction in needed knowledge and skills between ELD and general education teachers. She understood that in contrast to elementary teachers needing varied expertise across content and pedagogical knowledge and skills, ELD teachers required a limited teaching repertoire focused solely on teaching discrete English skills.

Having the perception that ELD simplified teachers' practice, players magnified the importance of ELD tools in mediating instruction. ADE administrators and task force members perceived quality ELD classroom teaching as teachers' appropriate use of policy-based tools provided by the ADE, such as the Discrete Skills Inventory (DSI) and ELP standards described in Chapter 3. Gabby highlighted the helpful nature of ELP standards, telling teachers what to do in classrooms by teaching to the high-intermediate proficiency level and following the DSI. Alex lauded the task force's addition of the DSI to explicitly prescribe ELD teachers' practice: 'Because we [task force members] were driven by the "what do I do on Tuesday afternoon" process and talking to teachers'. Whereas these players perceived formal tools as helpful to guide ELD teaching, local players found the opposite. Wayne described the ELP standards as bulky and vague, lacking the level of precision to guide teachers' practice. JESD educators concurred with Wayne's assessment of the standards as cumbersome and unhelpful, going beyond this to describe creative uses of ADE tools and standards to appear in compliance with policy mandates.

With state leaders distinguishing an expert ELD teacher as using policy-based standards and tools to guide teaching, it is no surprise that they also perceived these same tools as central to teacher preparation and training. ADE administrators and task force members described the design and implementation of teacher training centered particularly on the DSI. This inventory of grammatical rules, once a separate document but then merged into the ELP standards, aimed to provide a 'logical and linear ordering of English language concepts and skills to assist teachers in the design, development, and implementation of ELD instruction' (ADE, 2008). Pat remained steadfast in her assertion that grammar was the most impactful component of the ELD model, describing how the emphasis on grammar guided policy design: 'We wanted to be sure all the teachers learn the grammar and taught grammar in a reasonable way'. Gabby reinforced the importance of grammar to support policy implementation; however, she saw this as the primary area of need in ELD teacher preparation. She explained, 'Grammar training, that's where the need is. When we go out and work with teachers and we talk with teachers and when we monitor [for compliance], we see those [teaching grammar] are the weakest spots, and so we targeted our trainings to those'. Nevertheless, other state players found the state's grammar training as unhelpful, including Wendy as a teacher educator and Wayne as a charter school leader. Wayne, who relies on the ADE for all teacher training, described sessions as 'very spotty... not really rigorous... not high quality'.

Whereas ADE training focused on explicit grammar teaching, teacher education espoused the content-based approached to teaching ELs, as guided by the ADE curricular framework for the SEI endorsement described in Chapter 3. As a state administrator, Gabby described the challenges of preparing the majority of Arizona teachers, as the ADE had little control over individual SEI endorsement classes at community colleges and universities. Drawing on conversations with teachers, she concluded that programs were not preparing teachers for the skill-based context of ELD and reflected on the subsequent onus placed on OELAS compliance managers and teacher trainers. She stated, 'We know it [lack of teacher preparation] exists, and so we do the best we can to support it, but again, there are a lot more teachers than there are us [OELAS administrators]'. Although Gabby inferred that teacher educators often disagreed with the model and therefore did not prepare teachers accordingly, Alex revealed that a sub-set of higher educators supported ELD but did so in secret in dialogue with the task force so as to not upset their colleagues. Despite the different ideologies and approaches to teacher training between the ADE and higher education, Wayne found both tracks contributed to poor teacher preparation: 'There are more ELL teachers out there really than there are trained ELL teachers. These people, they may be certified teachers. They may be good teachers, high quality teachers, but they haven't received proper training'.

Because language policy required all Arizona teachers to receive the SEI endorsement, both community colleges and 4-year universities include one or both state-mandated courses in programs of study for teacher certification. Wendy taught the first SEI endorsement course at DCC, where she utilized the ADE curricular framework to design her class focused primarily on sheltered instruction, or teaching academic content simultaneous with supporting ELs' language development. With the curricular framework calling for 24 of the 45 clock hours to focus on sheltered instructional strategies, Wendy modeled strategies for teaching academic content using the four domains of language, including Socratic seminar, Cornell notes, graphic organizers, elbow partners, Think-Write-Share and small-group presentations. In addition to drawing from the curricular framework, she utilized her expertise as a former teacher and leader to prepare teachers for 21st-century classrooms, including explicit connections to Common Core Standards (CCS), critical thinking, communication and technology. Nevertheless, she described the challenges of preparing her students as future EL teachers: 'One of our biggest challenges is the efficacy of teachers who are not yet convinced that they can do it – that they can teach academics in a highly interactive engaging way and not dumb it down for students'. Further, in line with the state leaders, Wendy recognized that 'students stink at grammar'.

With pre-service teachers moving between community colleges and 4-year universities to complete requirements for Arizona teaching certification, some students overlapped across settings, taking one community college and one university course to fulfill state mandates. Frank taught both the first and second SEI endorsement courses to pre-service teachers, purposively planning coursework to emphasize teachers' agency and appropriation of policy to mediate effective EL practice. He explicated his use of the language policy itself to prepare teachers as agents of policy:

> People on both sides exaggerate the scope of the restriction. Example, it's [the policy] not really English-only. That would be a bad way to say it. We always have to explain to teachers that all things it [policy] doesn't prohibit. It doesn't prohibit, for instance, children from speaking another language in school. It does not do that. Children can speak anything they want in school. They can speak Spanish at the playground. They can speak it at lunch. They can even speak Spanish during instructional time. There is nothing in the law that prohibits children, the students themselves, from using Spanish. It doesn't. It's very strict for the teachers, but not the student. You'll get the nervous administrators telling the teachers that they don't want to hear any Spanish in the school because it's against the law. That's not true.

Frank, a bilingual educator at heart, maintained his commitment to students' native language use when working with pre-service teachers in SEI endorsement coursework. In line with the ADE curricular frameworks that mandated teacher knowledge and use of language policies and guidelines, Frank encouraged teachers to read between the lines of the policies to promote what he perceived as effective instruction for ELs.

As described in Chapter 4, classroom teachers consistently reflected on the poor and misaligned preparation prior to entering the ELD classroom. All teachers, including Paula, Tammie and Annie, lamented that the focus of the SEI coursework was unaligned with their realities in ELD classrooms. Similar to the course content defined by Wendy, teachers recalled learning about sheltered instruction in general education classrooms rather than skill-based blocks of conversation, grammar, vocabulary, reading and writing as mandated in their classrooms. Whereas Gabby attributed lack of alignment to teacher educators who disagreed with the ELD model, Wendy's description of her course demonstrated alignment to the ADE curricular framework, as well as what she perceived as good practice in EL instruction. Similar to the content described by Frank, Paula and Annie reflected on policy-focused university courses in their master's and teaching certification programs. Paula, a first-year teacher with scant preparation prior to entering the ELD classroom through Teach for America (TFA), found learning about policy to be unhelpful; however, Annie came to embrace the policy content from her prior university course, using her knowledge to appropriate policy in her ELD classrooms to support student learning and foster native language use.

Five years after the initial implementation of the ELD model, Arizona teacher preparation has continued to be characterized by staunch misalignment. With ADE training focused primarily on teaching discrete skills and tools and the SEI endorsement courses in higher education geared toward teaching academic content in general education settings, the ADE and institutes of higher education have diverged greatly in approaching teacher education. Additionally, teachers converged around the realization that teacher preparation did not align with daily realities and complexities of ELD classrooms. Connecting back to findings at the local level, the misaligned preparation between layers has fueled teacher attrition in the JESD. Despite emerging as the primary issue cited by school and district leaders, state education players did not have teacher attrition anywhere on their radar. They maintained insistence on having a master teacher in every ELD classroom but failed to acknowledge the stagnant reality that underprepared teachers like Paula, Tammie and Annie have continuously been placed for short-term stints teaching the high-need student population of ELs.

Discussion: Language Policy (P)layers in State Education

This chapter foregrounded state education layers, focused on the perspectives and experiences of players engaged in language policy work traversing the state of Arizona. This macro level of policy included a smaller network of players with large reach across the state, including task force members who designed and monitored the ELD models and mandates, ADE administrators who implemented and monitored school districts and charter schools for policy compliance and teacher educators who prepared teachers through SEI coursework. With participants representing various layers within state education, findings indicated the pertinence of state-level players' socio-historical lenses, as multiple years and experiences in Arizona education shaped current perceptions of policy in practice. Drawing from past policy roles as teachers and leaders of ELs, state players rationalized shifts to restrictive language policy by using historical trends of what they perceived as being ineffective in prior approaches to EL education. For players who found bilingual education to be ineffective, SEI ensured that ELs learned English. For players who found inclusive SEI to be ineffective, the restrictive ELD model provided more structure and attention to language learning. These longitudinal lenses, shaped by past experience and personal perceptions of EL education, impacted how state players appropriated language policy in practice. Due to the power and positionality of these players, notably all White and native-English-speaking, findings demonstrated the *amplification of appropriation*, as the policy decisions of this small network of educators more broadly influenced facets of EL education across Arizona.

In addition to the exploration of the foregrounded layer of state education, connection to backgrounded layers revealed misalignment between state and local players' experiences and perceptions of language policy in practice. Whereas local players struggled with the negative implications of separating students into classrooms by ELP levels, such as social and emotional repercussions for students and pedagogical challenges for teachers, state players considered homogenous grouping as valuable; Alex, Gabby and Gayle in particular lauded this mandate as integral to successful implementation of the ELD model. Similarly, state and local layers diverged in their perspectives and experiences on teachers and teaching. In Greenwood, teachers recognized the lack of preparation and misalignment of SEI coursework when compared to the realities of ELD teaching; further, administrators struggled to retain teachers in ELD classrooms as the challenging context and lack of appropriate training led to a revolving door of underprepared teachers. At the state level, administrators asserted that ELD classrooms employed expert language teachers who utilized policy-based standards and tools to guide effective practice with ELs. Whereas these misaligned perceptions of policy in practice might be attributed to state players' disconnect from local settings, insight from the EL Task Force member indicated the awareness of specific challenges in the ELD model but a refusal or inability to change the policy due to the political pressures and infighting of task force membership.

The explicit connection between education and legislation emerged in these findings on the foregrounded layer of state education, particularly when considering the power and positionality of the politically connected task force members. Appointed by state officials and charged to rewrite legislation guiding the education of ELs, the nine-member task force made policy decisions that impacted all other policy players, including local educators and state legislators. Whereas the task force participants described exertion of executive and legislative power in policy appropriation, they also deflected responsibility for certain decisions onto House Bill 2064 and the state legislators who passed it. In the next and final findings chapter, I foreground the state government layers, including the legislators, lobbyists and community leaders who worked outside the educational sphere to impact language policy in practice.

7 Legislators and Lobbyists: Power, Politics and Policy in Arizona

In this final findings chapter, I foreground the state government layer of language policy in practice. Focused specifically on Arizona state legislators and community leaders at the macro level, findings indicated that these players engaged in policy work on multiple fronts in addition to language policy. In this way, I investigate the state government layer by exploring the interactive policy network across this macro-level layer, as well as the multiple policies prioritized by various players. I organize the state government findings into three sections focused on (a) the networks of politics and power, (b) shared spotlight on broad social and educational policies and (c) players' policy priorities and advocacy efforts.

Politics, Power and Policy: The Network of State Legislative Players

Emergent from this study's findings, a centralized and powerful network of policy players in both state government and community contexts consistently collaborated around issues of English learner (EL) education. In this section, I introduce the network of players influencing Arizona language policy by profiling the state legislators and community leaders who participated in the study. See Table 7.1 for details on state government participants.

The Arizona state legislature and legislators

State governance in Arizona is organized into two legislative bodies, the Senate and the House of Representatives. Elected from across the Grand Canyon state, the 30 senators and 60 representatives are elected for 2-year terms with legislative sessions in the first four months of the calendar year. On each side of the legislature, Education Committees bring together approximately eight legislators with varied personal and professional experiences inside and outside of education. Appointed to committees after individual discussions with the President of the Senate or Speaker of the House, many lawmakers with prior careers in education find themselves

Table 7.1 Study participants in state government layer

Pseudonym	Position	Gender	Ethnicity	Language abilities
Ray	Senator	Male	White	English
Don	Senator	Male	Native American	Navajo, English
Rex	Representative	Male	White	English, Spanish
Dua	Representative	Female	Latina	Spanish, English
Louis	Legal advocate	Male	White	English
Chris	Education advocate	Male	White	English
Bill	Business advocate	Male	White	English
Esther	Education advocate	Female	White	English, Spanish
Hector	Latino advocate	Male	Latino	Spanish, English

on the Education Committee, where they draft bills and collaborate with others around educational issues. Four state legislators participated in this study, with Republican and Democratic representation from both the Senate and House. Mirroring the Republican-controlled state legislature, I begin by introducing the Republican participants, followed by the Democratic participants, in first the Senate and then the House.

State Senator Ray

Senator Ray, a White male legislator from the Republican Party, represented a predominantly White constituency in rural Arizona where he contributed three decades to the local school district as a teacher, school leader and district leader in both elementary and secondary settings. After retiring, he saw that the state's education system needed fixing, so he ran for office and quickly found himself on the Senate's Education Committee. Shaped by his former position of district superintendent, Senator Ray insisted on the need for local control in Arizona education, where local educators made decisions about and carried out policy in practice to match the needs and contexts of their communities. He extended this perspective to language policy, asserting that the English Language Development (ELD) model should provide flexibility for districts dependent on the student demographics and other factors. Further, the Senator disagreed with the state mandate that all Arizona teachers received Structured English Immersion (SEI) endorsements, drawing from his prior experiences teaching and leading in a rural area without a significant EL population.

State Senator Don

Senator Don, a Native American male legislator from the Democratic Party, represented a predominantly Native American constituency in rural

Arizona, a reservation community where he grew up surrounded by family, heritage and tradition. A young lawmaker with an MBA and experience in industry, he chose to run for office to better advocate for the economic well-being of his community through education and other policy initiatives. As a member of the Senate's Education Committee, Senator Don described his focus on challenges specific to education within his constituency, including teacher retention, charter schools and student achievement gaps between Native and non-Native students in Arizona, as well as the opportunities represented by a recent bill focused on language revitalization. Specific to the state's restrictive language policies, he considered the practical effects on medium of instruction in Native American schools as well as the broader impact on all Arizona students. From Senator Don's perspective, bilingualism and language education needed to take on integral roles to better prepare an effective and competitive workforce for the global economy.

State Representative Rex

Representative Rex, a White male legislator from the Republican Party, represented a predominantly White constituency in suburban Arizona after a three-decade-long career teaching high school. After getting involved in local politics within his community, he ran for the House of Representatives and joined others with education backgrounds on the Education Committee. Aligned with his local leadership experience, he emphasized the need for local control in education, proving municipalities control over policy decision-making rather than taking on a problem facing one community and mandating the solution across the state. Specific to language policy, Representative Rex agreed with the premise of the ELD model, drawing on his experiences with one Guatemalan immigrant student who needed targeted support to become fluent in English and then succeed inside and outside the classroom. Nevertheless, he admitted overall lack of awareness about the current state of EL education in Arizona, recognizing the need to build general awareness across the state legislature before being able to play a role in fixing issues with the ELD model.

State Representative Dua

Representative Dua, a Latina legislator from the Democratic Party, represented a predominantly Latino and African American constituency in urban Arizona where she was born, raised, attended school and worked as a classroom teacher and school leader. After sitting on the school board within her community, she shifted her sights to state leadership, being elected and appointed to the Education Committee of the State House of Representatives. Within her legislative role, she has prioritized various educational initiatives perceived to support the narrowing of the academic achievement gap between Latino, EL and low-income students and their mainstream peers. In this way, Representative Dua insisted upon Common

Core Standards (CCS) implementation and school funding focused on equity for low-income students. With a specific lens on language policy, she considered implications for students in ELD classrooms within the broader scope of CCS and corresponding standardized assessments.

The community context of leaders and lobbyists

In addition to the elected officials in the state legislature, the state government layer of language policy in practice in Arizona also included a network of statewide community organizations that employed non-elected officials to organize, advocate and lobby for education in various ways. With education directly linked to various facets of the state's infrastructure, community organizations and organizers connected to state governance through foci on education, business, law and Latinos. Five participants from the community sector participated in this study, representing a range of organizations committed to Arizona education. In this sub-section, I introduce the community-based participants, organized by their approach to impacting policy change at the federal, state and local levels.

Louis, legal advocate

Louis, a White male attorney, worked at a public-interest Arizona law firm focused on educational policy for the two decades. Describing the state legislature as 'rather hopeless', he has utilized legal channels to advocate for changes in Arizona education through the Office of Civil Rights, the Department of Justice and the Supreme Court. Having worked in the past on school finance litigation, including the extensive *Flores v. Arizona* lawsuit described in Chapter 2, Louis recently challenged the ELD 4-hour block through litigation focused on two premises: the segregation of students and lack of content area instruction. Drawing from the federal EEOA (1974), he asserted confidence in his litigation focused on ELs receiving the same access to content area teaching and learning as their English-proficient peers. A well-known player across language policy layers, Louis utilized his deep and extensive knowledge of the EL education scene in Arizona to describe the political and ideological challenges to implementing sound educational practice with ELs.

Chris, education lobbyist

Chris, a White male educational advocate, directed the state affiliate of a national organization focused on engaging parents, educators and community members to improve education through policy, investment and political involvement. A former Arizona teacher and Teach for America (TFA) alumnus, he described the work of his organization as impacting educational change from the macro level through legislative lobbying and the micro level through parent awareness and advocacy. At the macro level, Chris lobbied the state legislature, working with Senate and House Education Committees to support bills and priorities that the organization found important, such as the CCS. At the micro level, the organization worked to prepare parents from low-income and marginalized backgrounds to take active roles in education rather than be positioned as policy targets in Arizona's 'compliance culture'. To support the work, Chris engaged in conversations across policy layers, such as the story from an urban elementary school where 75% of fifth-grade ELs had been in the content-devoid ELD classroom since kindergarten. He used his political connections to share these practice-based language policy challenges with lawmakers.

Bill, business lobbyist

Bill, a White male business leader and lobbyist, coordinated efforts across the state with government and education entities to improve Arizona's industry and commerce. A Phoenix-area businessman married to a lifelong EL educator, he described the merging of his professional and personal lives to recognize the direct connection between educational policies and workforce development. Through his role chairing a statewide committee ensuring the interests of business and commerce, his organization regularly engaged in lobbying with state legislators on related issues of policy. In addition to frequent collaboration with state legislators, particularly from the Republican Party due to the organization's emphasis on business, he also regularly collaborated with Esther, Chris and other state educational advocates. Specific to language policy, Bill asserted the inefficacy of the ELD model for preparing a strong state workforce, as poor pedagogy and monolingual instruction in classrooms produced non-bilingual workers incapable of communicating in the bilingual context of Arizona industry. He utilized his state-level position to advocate for instructional settings that fostered bilingualism and rigorous content instruction.

Esther, education advocate

Esther, a White female educational advocate, directed an organization that fostered collaboration among Arizona education and business leaders to improve the state's workforce development. A former bilingual classroom teacher in a low-income Phoenix-area community, she entered policy work when she burned out of teaching, aiming to continue her passion for education through community advocacy efforts. Unlike other community-based participants, Esther's organization did not engage in lobbying but rather aimed to educate legislators and stakeholders on educational issues related to economic development, including school funding and student achievement. Specific to language policy, she drew from her prior experiences and those of her daughter, an ELD teacher at a local charter school, to describe the negative repercussions of the ELD model for ELs needing bilingual abilities and content knowledge and skills to succeed in Arizona's workforce. To foster change in language policy in practice, Esther asserted the need for stakeholders to collaboratively build awareness and advocacy.

Hector, Latino advocate

Hector, a Latino community advocate, led a state-wide organization focused on fostering positive change for Latinos, including efforts to provide parents with a voice in local education. In addition to efforts on immigration policy, he oversaw various educational initiatives, including early childhood programs, elementary and secondary charter schools and higher education scholarships. Through the organization's network of charter schools implementing culturally and linguistically relevant curricula, he asserted the importance of parental awareness and choice in Arizona schooling. With what he perceived as public schools' rote implementation of language policy through the 4-hour block, Hector described his charter schools' pushback against the one-size-fits-all model. Connecting to his own experiences as an immigrant and EL student in Arizona schools, he explained that student segregation served no clear purpose or benefit to children. By empowering parents through school choice, his organization aimed to put pressure on public school districts to reconsider practices and offerings for Latino EL students, parents and families.

The Broad Policy Scope of State Government Players

In this network of state legislators and community leaders at the state-government layer, players engaged with multiple issues and policies influencing Arizona's social, economic and educational realities. Unlike the EL-specific players within local and state education layers, these leaders worked on multiple facets of Arizona policy. In this section, I explore language policy within the larger social issues and varied educational policies influencing EL education. Findings indicated that state government players situated their experiences and perspectives on EL education within social issues, educational policies and language policies.

Considering the social context of Arizona education

Distinct from local and state education layers of language policy, players in state government consistently situated language education policy in the broader social context of Arizona, including the pertinent and interconnected issues of the economy, poverty and immigration. Juxtaposed with the micro-level perspectives taken by local policy players, such as the day-to-day challenges within the context of Greenwood classrooms and schools, state players utilized macro-level lenses that explicitly and implicitly connected to state-level politics and power, such as legislators' political affiliations and community leaders' business interests. State leaders drew from policy reports, statistics and personal and professional histories to make meaning of the interplay of social influences on language policy in Arizona.

Emerging as the overarching social theme across state government, players explicitly discussed education using economic lenses. From the macro-level perspective of Arizona society, policy players recognized the inherent link between student performance and achievement in K-12 schools and workforce and economic development. Democratic Senator Don explained, 'Education is the foundation for a continued economic success of the state and of the country. For us as legislators, our job is to continue to grow our economy. That's what makes the world go round, fundamentally'. Similarly, Esther described the work of her organization as 'focused on three big things. One is student performance; we want all students to perform because of the inextricable link between student performance and economic development [and] workforce preparation'. Both lawmakers and community leaders prioritized education as connected to the economic well-being of the state; an enhanced Arizona economy required a better developed workforce, which was directly dependent on student development, performance and achievement in the K-12 educational context.

Within this general connection between education and economics, state government players described efforts to prioritize specific subsets of Arizona students to better improve the workforce and economy. Community leaders and Democratic lawmakers cited the significant populations of traditionally marginalized sub-groups that often overlapped with students labeled as ELs, including low income, people of color, Native Americans and Latinos. Chris and Esther, both former Phoenix-area teachers in low-income Latino communities, described their perspectives on the need to concentrate on the educational attainment of students living in poverty. Esther explained,

> For our small businesses, it is totally about the pipeline [of workers]. So, what are we doing about our minority students to meet their needs? This so core to economic development that, in fact, it's got to be framed that way, particularly in a state that has so many other issues around kids of color. I submit that most of your average person in Arizona doesn't realize that 25% or more of our children live in poverty. I think there are people who are in power who don't know that. And, frankly, if they do know it, they don't care. And secondly, if they do know it, it's not their kids, so, therefore, it's not a big deal. But if you're a business owner, you better be caring about it.

In her leadership capacity at an organization focused on workforce development through educational and economic collaboration, Esther communicated how the consistently low educational expectations for Arizona students living in poverty and students of color, including ELs, led to diminished access to higher education. Working at an organization focused on improving education in low-income communities, Chris also honed in on higher education as connected to poverty and ELs: 'The students who typically don't graduate from college or go to college are those who grow up in low-income communities. If you look at English language learners, they typically overlap pretty heavily with low-income communities'. Drawing on prior experiences, these community leaders situated their perspectives on education and language policy within the social realities of Arizona children living in poverty.

Among the economic and educational considerations for the wider sub-groups of students of color and those living in poverty, one lawmaker specifically deliberated social influences on Native American communities. As described in Chapter 1, Arizona has historically been home to hundreds of tribes and currently has four times more Native American citizens proportionally than the rest of the US (Milem *et al.*, 2013). Representing a predominantly Native American district, Senator Don considered the education and language policies from this particular perspective in the larger population of Arizona.

> Demographically, I think that student achievement is one of the greatest areas that we have to work on for Native American communities, which directly affects the ability for these students to even go on to post-secondary education. We also struggle with these [college] graduation rates for Native American communities, tribal communities. One of the lowest graduation rates in the state and even in the country. We look at graduation rates among Native American students, among any sub-group in Arizona, 65% of Native American students graduate within four years. That was based on 2012 data, compared to 77% for all students across the state and 84% for white students. We're not even close… It [student achievement] directly attributes to not only the current generation, future generations of that community demographically, economically. I think the tribes today are well on the way to becoming more successful economically, socially, but yet I think that we've got a long ways to go.

Like community organizers Esther and John, Senator Don linked K-12 student achievement, post-secondary attainment and economic and social well-being. Beyond tribal communities, he also recognized the need to improve education, specifically language education, to better prepare Arizona students for the global economy. He described his support for a Senate-sponsored bill 'premised on economic development and allowing kids to learn other world languages because our economy is hinged now on a global economy'.

> With the power of two [languages], students are better able to prepare
> to meet the global world and the global society that we live in. They
> are able to better meet the life challenges of enhanced cognitive
> skills, successful cross-cultural communication, [and] more career
> opportunities.

Whereas the bill originally focused on foreign languages deemed critical
to the economy like Chinese and Japanese, Senator Don amended the
bill to include Native American languages, recognizing the link between
linguistic and cognitive development and the corresponding value to both
the individual student and wider tribal community.

State players, particularly those from Latino backgrounds, also
demonstrated specific interest in Latino communities. Similar to the large
proportion of Native American citizens, Arizona has maintained double
the number of Latinos as compared to the larger US, with Latinos recently
surpassing Whites as the largest student sub-group in Arizona schools
(Milem *et al.*, 2013). Similar to Senator Don's elevated interest in his tribal
constituency, Democratic Representative Dua described her perspective on
student achievement in Arizona from the lens of the large and growing
Latino population.

> There's a lot of work to do in education. I think here at the legislature
> we have to really first have a discussion about the gap, the education
> [achievement] gap of Latino [and] non-Latino. There's a huge gap there.
> The demographics have changed, and there just is not a lot of discussion
> about the demographics of our Latinos that are here, and the poverty
> that is here, in Arizona. Because I truly believe if we concentrate on
> our ELL population, which happens to be our Latino demographics that
> have grown here, that would be the beginning to closing this [student
> achievement] gap.

Representative Dua, a former Phoenix-area teacher in a largely Latino
community, asserted the need for state government players to prioritize
Latinos in the broader dialogue in Arizona education. Hector, an advocate
and leader within the Latino community, stressed the prioritization of the
Latino population as essential for the state's economy.

> We realize and believe that because of the numbers, just the sheer
> numbers [of Latinos in Arizona], as the Hispanic community prospers
> and as we move up the economic ladder, we're all the same. If we don't
> invest and people don't invest in that segment, then Arizona will start
> to become a state of more economic deficiencies. We'll probably be more
> with Louisiana, Mississippi or the states that are having challenges in
> attracting companies and especially companies that pay higher wages and

require higher skills. I believe that's the way we'll be viewed, as a state with deficiencies. Again, I think that it's extremely critical that education is viewed as an investment that not only benefits the Latino community and all communities of color, but really an investment in Arizona.

Additionally, Hector called for multicultural and multilingual education to better prepare students for the global economy, particularly Spanish due to our relationship with Mexico and Latin America. Like other state players described above, Latino participants made explicit connections between education, language and economic development.

State-level business leaders identified the importance of language in preparing Arizona's future workforce, particularly the need to develop students' bilingualism in Spanish and English. Bill, a Phoenix-area businessman and state business leader, described the interconnectedness of language, economics and immigration. He asserted the 'dominant opinion' among the business community:

> The business community perspective from the beginning has been, first of all, immigration is a good thing. We have the work for them to do. They are not displacing, it's not like they are displacing others who are already doing those jobs. [Being] bilingual is good. We're a border state. Our economic growth potential rests more with Mexico than it does with Utah. Our southern border is more important than our northern border. If we can embrace that and work with Mexico to grow that, that's good for everybody.

As a long-time leader in the business community, Bill perceived a positive correlation between immigration and economic prosperity. Whereas many Arizonans had backlashed against the growth in the Spanish-speaking population, the business community embraced the shift due to positive impact on business, including Spanish-medium 'small business energy' and 'entrepreneurial environment' in Latino neighborhoods, as well as increased supply and demand for bilingual employees in both retail businesses and industries. Nonetheless, his perspectives differed from 'what was politically popular at the time' regarding both immigration and language policy, which he perceived as interconnected. Despite the need for bilingual workers, Bill described the ideology driving Arizona language policy: 'That [English] immersion movement, there a large part of what's become the train of thought is: "They moved here, if they want to be here, by God, they better speak English, and they better get with it right now"'. An opponent of Senate Bill 1070, the anti-immigration legislation detailed in Chapter 1, Bill depicted the hefty economic price that the state has paid since 2010 as immigrant families have moved out of Arizona into other states to settle, work and pay taxes.

Despite the value of bilingualism discerned by the Democratic lawmakers and community leaders, conservative monolingual ideologies prevailed in 2000 with the passage of Proposition 203. Further, the passage of House Bill 2064 in 2006 further restricted EL education with the shift to the ELD block. In contrast to the experiences and perspectives of the state government players described above, Alex, the chairman of the EL Task Force, described his perceptions of the interplay of language, education and the economy.

> The bottom line is it [English] is still the language of commerce. It will be for anybody whose alive today, so 50 years. It may change someday but it's going to be a long time. Heck, the biggest risk most of these other countries have is that their languages are going to become obsolete by virtue of the dominance of English in their culture. I have friends of my daughter who practice their native languages with their parents to preserve them in their lives but they live in America now. Particularly they come from a lower immigrant population so they don't have a lot, [they] maybe talk to their grandmother and their mom and maybe their aunt, and that might be all that's close to them. I'm more worried about the other thing happening, not them [speaking another language to family], learning English at a functional level for the purposes of commerce.

In contrast to other players' recognition of the significance of multilingualism in state and global economies, Alex perceived English to be the sole language of import. With the task force wielding unprecedented executive and legislative power, monolingual ideologies and policies persisted in state policy regulations. In this way, regarding the interplay of language, education and immigration, Bill contended, 'Unfortunately, I think the kids and the English language learners have, at times, been pawns in that conversation'.

Situating English learners in the broader educational arena

In addition to framing EL issues in Arizona's social context, state players utilized broad educational policies to situate language policy in the wider political arena. In this way, these macro-level policy players discussed policies impacting all students across the state, such as educational funding, charter schools, early childhood education and the CCS, weaving general policy considerations into the dialogue on specific impacting ELs. Findings across the state government layer indicate that these broader educational issues persisted at the forefront of Arizona's priorities and legislation, whereas ELD policy did not. In particular, state legislators and community leaders prioritized educational funding and the CCS.

Educational funding in the Arizona state budget

Directly connected to the socioeconomic issues described in the previous section, the funding of Arizona education emerged as a common theme at the state government layer. Representative Rex connected economic conditions with the state budget and educational funding: 'From the height of the economy, we [have] cut three billion dollars out of the state budget. Three billion! That's huge. Because education is a huge part of the budget, it took a major hit'. Whereas funding did not surface as an issue in local and state education players' perspectives and experiences, all the state government players, apart from Hector, discussed school finance at length, whether situated broadly in general educational policy or connected specifically to EL education and language policy. A predominant policy issue at the legislature that Chris described as having 'about a thousand hands in the cookie jar', state lawmakers concurred about problems inherent in the school finance system but differed in solutions to benefit their own constituents. Senator Ray asserted,

> The biggest problem we have in the state of Arizona is our antiquated funding formula of how we fund K-12 education... That [changing funding formulas for schools] has some risk with it when you start taking from those that have and moving it over to those who have not.

Located in the state that players purported as the last in per-pupil funding in the US, participants in this study split along party lines, with Republicans discussing school choice and charter schools and Democrats prioritizing high-need districts and student populations.

Republican lawmakers concentrated on legislation to shift the school funding formula to a per-pupil basis to allow for uniformity and equality in taxpayer monies received by public and charter schools. Highlighting school finance as his primary focus and priority for the 2014 legislative session, Senator Ray rationalized his proposed shift in the funding formula.

> Instead of it being collected and held at the district level, [funding should] be moved into the state so that we can start doing it out on a per student basis, start to remove some of the regulations that we have on the traditional districts. To have it more like the charter schools so that we can see a more uniform funding mechanism. Then, I think you start to get a true picture of really who's doing the best job. You have a hard time doing comparisons when this one's regulated this way and this one is not regulated that way.

With public school districts drawing funds from property taxes and charter schools receiving funds from a general fund without support from local taxation, he perceived the solution to uniformly distribute funds to both public and charter schools based on student enrollment. Representative Rex echoed the desire to equally support public and charter schools, stating his alignment with his party on the issue of school choice but his continued personal commitment to public schools. He wrestled with this dual commitment as connected to the broader issue of school finance between public and charter schools:

> We have made some tough choices [in public schools]. We thinned and narrowed, and not always to kids' benefit. Class size has gone up in a lot of districts, in our district [it] went up. We closed two schools, we've lost 65 teachers, and class sizes went up... My party is for school choice, and I support that. Let me say that choice has additional expense, as does accountability. It's all expenses. It's how far do we go with those kind of expenses? I will sit on my porch and I see three school buses drive by... So it's additional cost, so at what point you start to see the diminishing returns on those expenses?

A former public school teacher in the same district that he represented as a state lawmaker, Representative Rex remained connected and committed to public schools in his constituency, which he negotiated with his party's stance on school choice and corresponding school funding.

Reflecting the divide in the state's political landscape, left-leaning participants suggested a different direction to solve the woes of educational funding in Arizona. Esther attacked the Republican-led legislature, stating, 'We have got people in leadership who perceive the only remedy to dealing with education is to provide charter schools or private schools as an option, which is ignoring the issue. And I think that is going to fail us'. Concurring with that sentiment, Democratic lawmakers emphasized the need to reform school funding to prioritize public schools in marginalized and low-income communities. Senator Don and Representative Dua critiqued performance-based funding, whereby schools and districts received more funds for students' high standardized test scores, explaining challenges posed to their predominantly low-income, Native American and Latino constituencies. After describing the challenges of mainstream tests of student achievement with Native American students on the reservation, Senator Don asserted, 'Rural schools, or even tribal schools, have more difficulty by nature of ruralness or quality of educators or capacity, but you also have the... struggle to do a lot more with a lot less'. Echoing the need to support underperforming schools, Representative Dua argued for the need to fund early childhood education in low-income communities as a strategy to level the playing field with children living in wealthier regions; she affirmed, 'We really have to start providing resources for all students'.

Whereas school funding as a broad policy issue emerged frequently within the state government layer, only two participants discussed EL funding and the well-known *Flores* lawsuit. As described in Chapter 2, the *Flores* case originated in 1992 in Nogales, Arizona and focused on the lack of district and state funding for EL education. When critiquing how ELD policy deterred from local control of education, Senator Ray connected to the *Flores* case.

> They [districts] were doing [their own EL programs] up before the state had to take it over because of another lawsuit. The lawsuit was basically because you're not spending enough money in the ELL instruction. We don't do very well in the education process when we have to legislate by decree of the judges.

Whereas Senator Ray perceived the lawsuit as an overstep of the judicial system into the legislative process, Louis, an active advocate and attorney involved in the *Flores* litigation, perceived the state legislature as the source of the problem.

> After the first [Flores case] judgment was issued in 2000 indicating, declaring that the state had not adequately funded ELL programs, the legislature pretty much did nothing. I went back to court a number of times to attempt to force the state [legislature] to comply with the judgment and provide adequate funding... When they didn't do anything after that [a multi-year cost study], I went back to court again, [and] ultimately the court imposed 20 million in fines on the state, which caused the state legislature to intervene in the case.

Louis, an attorney by trade, remained staunchly at odds with Senator Ray, a former teacher and district leader, on the issue. The senator recalled the series of language policy events following the state legislative action on the *Flores* case.

> So, the state comes in and says, 'Naw, we don't care what you're [local educators] doing. We want you to do this [ELD] because we say so'. Not necessarily a proven program, not necessarily, but we sit down in the think tank [EL Task Force] and this is what we come up with, and we run it through the court system, and the court says, 'Yeah, okay, let's do it'. It's not good policy.

In addition to the *Flores* case, which influenced language policy work at the state government layer for two decades, Louis brought other legal actions against the state of Arizona, which will be discussed in upcoming sections.

Arizona's college and career readiness standards

At the forefront of educational policy at the state legislature, the CCS appeared frequently in the data at the state government layer. Similar to the national debate over these New Standards being implemented across the country, including both the CCS and the Next Generation Science Standards, Arizona lawmakers and constituents remained divided on the shift in standards guiding classroom instruction in English language arts, mathematics and science. Recognizing this political divide between the left and right, Bill framed the issue in the context of Arizona's prevalent right-wing ideologies:

> Until it hit the national hard-right agenda, it [CCS] wasn't much of an issue here, but as it nationally started to ramp up it got the attention of our local tea party faction and, of course, there's a certain segment of that [conservative group], and the left has its own version of this, they [conservatives] don't believe anything that they haven't heard Glen Beck say. If he says it, they don't question any of it. There's a lot of misinformation [about CCS] out there.

With both liberal and conservative factions taking issue with facets of the CCS as aligned with national debates on the policy issue, Arizona state leaders changed the name to the *Arizona College and Career Readiness Standards*. Representative Rex and Bill explained the Governor and Superintendent of Public Instruction's joint attempt to avoid controversy and confuse opponents of the originally named *Common Core Standards*.

Regardless of nomenclature, this contemporary educational issue emerged across participants in this study. Whereas local and state education players negotiated CCS implementation in ELD practice, state government players considered legislative action through bills brought to the Senate and House, typically drafted and sponsored by one of the two Education Committees. With both the Republican and Democratic parties taking different positions on the New Standards, lawmakers brought various bills to vote to shape CCS implementation in Arizona. A proponent of the New Standards, Chris explained the current context in the state legislature:

> There were six bills [related to CCS] that were composed this year. One of the bills was killed yesterday. There are two [bills] that didn't make it out of the Senate Education Committee. They were not dead. They just didn't get to them so they could be rolled into other bills. There are three others that are live at the moment. It's understood that they're likely not going anywhere because there's enough Republican opposition to the bills, along with Democratic support of the standards and opposition to the bills. Even if they did make it out of the Senate, the House wouldn't pass them, and even if they

did make it out of the House, the Governor wouldn't sign them. It's for show.

Despite the political divide on the New Standards, which Chris perceived to limit the legislative efficiency on this important issue, Senator Ray utilized his leadership role in the Senate Education Committee to streamline bills that he described as 'counterproductive to each other'. He asserted, 'We've got to sit down and just sponsor the [CCS-related] bills and pick and choose which parts we want where, put where, and then come up with one bill that we will push forward'. These collaborative legislative processes faced challenges in both the Senate and House with lawmakers on the Education Committees divided on issues related to assessment, funding and teacher preparation.

In spite of the continued public debate over the CCS, both state legislators and community leaders recognized that the standards had already been adopted and implemented, leading them to move on to focus on the related issues of assessment and funding. Bill explained, 'This is the thing a lot of the people were supposedly opposed to and [what] they don't understand, it's [CCS] fully implemented. All we're talking about now is the assessment'. Chris echoed, 'The bigger issue is making sure that we have the resources to adopt an assessment with a line through them [CCS], which is going some additional funds this year'. Bill and Chris, who both regularly engaged in lobbying of state legislators as a component of their community leadership positions, understood the important conversations taking place in the Education Committees regarding assessment and funding. Nonetheless, the divide between parties became apparent from the two representatives in this study. Representative Dua, a Democratic lawmaker on the House Education Committee, focused on which nationally recognized assessment consortium might be the best fit for Arizona:

> The biggest challenge is educating our decision makers on what [CCS aligned] assessment is good. Right now, looks like we're leaning really heavily on PARCC [Partnership for Assessment of Readiness for College and Careers]; however, I'm leaning toward Smarter Balance for our ELL students. I brought this message back home [from a conference], and so we'll see how far I can get with that.

Whereas Representative Dua utilized perspectives as a former teacher of ELs to negotiate the best option for an assessment consortium, Representative Rex aligned with his party to challenge the funding of any assessment tied to the CCS. He explained, 'There's an effort to not fund any kind of test to those standards, which were adopted before I was in the Legislature, during my second session of my first term'. With the CCS already adopted and implemented, conservative efforts centered on refusing funding to the required standardized assessment component to evaluate student achievement as tied to the standards.

As both parties geared up for a fight related to assessment and funding, other state government players focused their sights on preparing teachers for the CCS. Chris, Esther and Representative Dua, all former Arizona teachers in low-income areas, supported and recognized the CCS as an opportunity to improve education for underserved populations, particularly ELs. By setting what Chris referred to as a 'higher bar' for all students, players perceived the CCS to provide an opening to negotiate what rigorous instruction looked like in the ELD classroom. In considering ELD policy in practice, Esther specifically highlighted the CCS as a possible lever to promote change:

> And frankly, there's no better time than now to do this [reconsider ELD] because we've got this Common Core, this Common Core looking us in the face. And those kids, our kids [ELs] will not be successful on Common Core if we cannot help teachers learn how to, number one, even do Common Core in the first place, but secondly, providing interventions to help particularly these youngsters deal with the form of Common Core. So, that's got to be done now.

Similar to Esther, Representative Dua negotiated the challenges of ELD teachers who faced mandates for four hours of skill-based English instruction while being held accountable for the New Standards in language arts, mathematics and science. She called on universities to better prepare teachers for this new era of policy in practice, explaining,

> I have a bill right now that is trying to put Common Core rigorous training in our teacher preparation programs in our three universities. Because being a former teacher, I know the most I was out of a classroom was three days for professional development. That's not enough time to learn Common Core Standards and how to teach it. I'm a visionary and I think our aspiring teachers – let's get them prepared so when they come out they are off the ground running. They can go to their schools and already know how to teach these standards.

By integrating the New Standards into extant teacher education programs, possibly through an additional 'certification' in the CCS, Representative Dua's bill aimed to prepare teachers who could better negotiate these more rigorous academic standards with Arizona students.

Representative Dua's perspective on teacher preparation was unique at the state government layer, as most players focused on educational and language policies from macro-level lenses (e.g. funding) or micro-level lenses (e.g. students). In particular, when directly discussing ELD policy in practice, state legislators and community leaders alike shared the perspective focused on student segregation, which is described in the next sub-section.

Critiquing language policy and implications in practice

When speaking specifically to language policy, all state government players, regardless of political affiliation, disagreed with the 4-hour ELD block. Players shared different experiences and perceptions that led to this disapproval of the language policy, including lenses as students, teachers and advocates. Louis, the legal advocate, had the most comprehensive argument against the ELD model, as he had dedicated much of the last two decades to fighting Arizona's language policies through legal means. Other players focused on what they referred to as the 'one-size-fits-all' language policy. Bill, using a macro lens of the demographics across Arizona schools, explained,

> The thing that disappointed me about the change in policy was it stamped one formula on top of every school and every child in Arizona. You've got fifteen new kids from Somalia in one school, which we do [in various districts]. We have some huge refugee populations. It's not the same as the school in the Roosevelt district [in South Phoenix] where 95% of the kids are Spanish monolinguals.

In this study, state legislators and community leaders centered their arguments on issues related to student segregation – both broad across the language policy and specific to the multiple years often spent in the segregated ELD classroom – framed by their own experiences with and in the Arizona education system.

Similar to local and state education layers, student segregation in the ELD model emerged as consistent critique. Unlike the state education layer where various players' perspectives demonstrated the polarizing nature of the issue, state government players all tended to disagree with the separation of ELs into separate ELD classrooms. Whether Democrat or Republican, former teachers turned state legislators concurred that segregating ELs from their peers reflected poor pedagogy that did not support student learning. Senator Ray asserted his discontent with student segregation:

> I think that's [separating ELs] wrong. I think students do best if they're allowed to mingle and be a part of and work with [English-proficient peers], because they make friends. Friends start to work [together] and whatever, and so if you have all of them right here [in ELD classrooms], you miss that ability to make friends and to get involved in the cultural aspect of what I think schools do a pretty good job of doing.

Drawing on his pedagogical knowledge and teaching experience, Senator Ray argued against student segregation due to the value of collaboration and interaction among ELs and English-proficient peers. Representative Dua also connected to prior experiences as an educator.

> It's frustrating because as a former teacher and a former administrator specially my administrative days, it [ELD] is segregation, it really is. Even though the courts have ruled that that it's not, and that was so disappointing because now our Department of Education has this justification. They say we've [Arizona education] been doing a good job, but that's not true. It's not true because they haven't been in the trenches like I have. I've been in the trenches and I've seen these kids segregated. I've seen how valuable it is to have ELL kids with the mainstream kids. They learn so much quicker.

In addition to referencing her own micro-level experiences as a local teacher and leader, she added a macro-level lens as a state legislator in her reference of the ADE's justification of student segregation and the unsuccessful state-level lawsuit described in the previous section.

State government players who were not former educators utilized other personal encounters with Arizona education to make meaning of language policy, specifically Bill's connections to his wife's experiences as a Phoenix-area ESL teacher and Hector's childhood as a Mexican immigrant and EL student. Hector, the leader of a Latino advocacy organization, described his perspective on the ELD policy.

> Right now, this [language policy] is being forced as almost like a one-size-fits-all. Once you have that mandate of the four hours, you don't have a whole lot more time to do really anything after that, right? Are the kids interacting with other kids that are more English dominant? They're clustered based on their English proficiency, especially those that have limited English proficiency. That's what they're seeing, that's what [who] they're interacting [with].

After explaining his perceptions of the primary issues with the language policy, Hector made the direct connection to his personal experiences as a student in Arizona schools.

> I go back to my history and I go back to my exposure. I also spoke Spanish, because that's who my friends were. That's who I associated with. If I'm in a class with other Spanish dominant [students], then that becomes my circle of friends and my social circle. It wasn't until high school that I really needed English, at least in a spoken form. I mean I could read it, I could write it, I would do my homework, but in

terms of being fluent and being comfortable with English, even in high
school I always spoke Spanish.

Similar to the pedagogical argument of Senator Ray that students need
access to a linguistically diverse community of learners, Hector echoed that
contention through personal experiences as a Spanish-speaking student. He
went on to assert, 'Just from my own perception and my own history, I
really equated that [language policy] to segregation'.

Whereas others described detriments of student segregation unilaterally
across language policy, other players specifically critiqued policy in practice
as related to the time ELs spent in ELD settings. Referencing the policy
discourse that EL placement in ELD classrooms was 'not normally intended
to exceed one year' (House Bill [HB] 2064, 2006: 7), Representatives Rex
and Esther conceded the need to target English development in the initial
year in Arizona schools. Both former educators, they connected to their
experiences with ELs to justify this targeted 'intervention'. Representative
Rex explained learning English as the 'first job' of ELs in high schools,
'Whatever content that they [ELs] could get, that's wonderful but they
need to be able to learn a little English to be able to move on and progress,
[to] have more options when they graduate'. Despite his alignment with
the purported intent of the language policy, this Republican lawmaker
acknowledged that the time period ELs spent in ELD classrooms was
typically much longer than one year, thus limiting the efficacy of the model.
Drawing from her expertise as a former bilingual teacher, Esther utilized
research on language development to contradict the policy mandating the
separation of ELs from peers. Nonetheless, after reflecting on the nebulous
SEI approach that preceded the ELD model, she admitted,

> I could see some value in making sure that they [ELs] were getting the
> right interventions in an intensive way and then reintroduced into the
> general population.... If that had been the model that was supported,
> that could have been very good for kids. But what's happened with the
> whole [SEI] program over the last 5 to 10 years is it has been bastardized.
> It has been changed according to the whim of whoever is in leadership.

Like Representative Rex, Esther recognized the contrast between language
policy on paper and in practice, connecting to the power held by the role of
the State Superintendent.

In addition to general disdain for the long-term segregation of ELs,
Chris provided a specific example of the negative implications of policy
in practice. In his role as leader of an educational advocacy organization,
he regularly communicated with educators and participated in various
educational policy outlets. Chris recalled a public meeting of the State
Board of Education in 2013, shortly after the passage of House Bill 2425,

which shifted the oversight of the ELD model from the task force to the State Board. In this meeting, a school leader spoke about the repercussions of the ELD model, describing the fifth-grade ELD classroom at his school. Chris recounted, 'He [the school leader] asked how many students had been at that school since kindergarten, and 75% of the kids raised their hands'. He went on to make meaning of this example:

> The goal [of the language policy] is that students could test out of the program after one year, and here students are five years later and 75% of them haven't tested out. If they've been in that program for five years, then that's the [scant] amount of content they haven't been getting outside [of the four hours].

A former math and science teacher working at an organization focused on closing the achievement gap for low-income students, Chris recognized the long-term segregation and corresponding dearth of content instruction as detrimental. He noted the irony that this particular school district had been highlighted as one of the two districts in complete compliance with language policy per the ADE. In other words, 'following the [ELD] model to a T' as an Office of English Language Acquisition Services (OELAS) 'exemplary district' meant that ELs who entered in kindergarten received little to no content instruction for over five academic years.

Because of these practical realities of ELD implementation, Louis utilized his role as a lawyer and legal advocate to bring suit against the state of Arizona. Recognizing that ELs remained in ELD classrooms for multiple years, he utilized the discourse in House Bill 2064 to argue against the long-term placement:

> The law very clearly states that the [ELD] model only had to be for one year. There's no question about reading the law... What they [ADE administrators] always said and what they testified to in court is, 'Well, if it's good enough for the first year, it must therefore be good enough for years two through infinity', which makes absolutely no sense. It sounds good, but there's no logic to that and, of course, no data anywhere to support any of this stuff.

Because of the misalignment between the law itself, which only required four hours of ELD for first-year ELs, and the resulting implications of long-term ELs in practice, the lawsuit went to trial in 2010. When trying the case, Louis asked a state's witness how long ELs remain in the 4-hour model on average. He recalled,

> They [state leaders] didn't know. They had never looked at the question. I'm not claiming that's the only question, but at a minimum, that's

something you'd want to know. Our law says the goal is to get them [ELs] out in a year. It's the law actually says that, and I'm a responsible administrator of that law. Seems to me like I'd want to know how close we're coming to that goal. They never looked at it.... [the] task force never examined that question, nobody at the [State] Department of Education ever examined that question.

With the state education layer lacking the data to demonstrate the efficacy of the originally written language policy, Louis sought out data from two large school districts with significant EL populations. Data demonstrated that students tested out of the EL label in an average of four years in the ELD model, slightly longer than the time frame in the previous SEI model. Despite the state's lack of hard evidence to support the 4-hour model for all ELs and the data from two sample school districts demonstrating the policy implications in practice, the lawsuit was unsuccessful in changing the ELD policy mandates.

Overall, across the state government layer, players disagreed with language policy, focusing primarily on the issue of student segregation in the ELD model. These state players framed the perceived policy issues with both micro-level experiences (e.g. former teachers) and macro-level perspectives (e.g. research, cross-context comparisons). Despite being positioned in seemingly powerful roles in the legislative branches of state government and wide-reaching and respected community organizations, their arguments seemed to hold little weight in influencing official language policy. Speaking to this reality, Esther posed the question, 'Why is it we've got people who are making these decisions – who don't understand the difference, by the way, between social conversation and academic language – making decisions about this when it is so core to the future of Arizona?' Regardless of the power structure that prioritized first the task force and then the Board of Education in managing ELD policy implementation, state-government players devised ways to appropriate language policy in practice to meet their needs and goals for EL education. Those findings are presented in the next section.

Individual Players' Priorities, Advocacy and Agency

In previous chapters, I shared findings specific to how players at the local and state education layers appropriated language policy in practice to influence the education of ELs in Arizona. Situated at the center of language policy (Ricento & Hornberger, 1996), teachers made decisions in daily practice to shape language policy, such as integrating the required language-skill blocks into more meaningful literacy learning or finding space for native language use to support student learning. School leaders and district administrators at the local layer appropriated policy in practice, including supporting teachers to infuse science and social studies content into the 4-hour ELD block. At the state education layer, whereas EL Task Force members maintained power over the official language policy regulations, other players described agency, such as teacher educators' decisions regarding teacher preparation for the ELD classroom setting. Now shifting focus to appropriation at the state government layer, this section considers how state legislators and community leaders negotiated and appropriated the rigid and restrictive policy regulations in various ways.

Findings indicated the complex and often contradictory role of the state legislator with respect to Arizona language policy. As discussed in previous chapters, House Bill 2064 (2006) gave the EL Task Force unprecedented executive and legislative power, with members maintaining the ultimate control over the ELD model implemented in schools with ELs. Without checks and balances on the unilateral power held by the task force, state legislators – seemingly in a position of power at the macro level – had little control over the official language policy regulations. Nevertheless, education-focused legislators recognized two spaces to impact broader educational policy in practice, including collaborative dialogue and legislative bills. Made up of primarily former educators, state lawmakers on Education Committees described using their roles to educate other legislators on key issues impacting Arizona classrooms. Representative Dua explained,

> My role really, I think, is really creating relationships and taking time with the decision makers here and just sharing my stories with them. Relationships are so important because then you start building the trust and the discussion gets more robust, but to go in there and say this is how it should be and you're wrong, I'm right. It just doesn't work in any piece of legislation around here.

In addition to ongoing dialogue, particularly with non-educators in state government, participants reported efforts to draft and propose bills impacting education, such as the critical languages bill supported by Senator Don, the CCS teacher preparation bill drafted by Representative Dua or the school funding measure introduced by Senator Ray. Nevertheless, when considering the efficacy of both efforts to negotiate policy in via dialogue and bills, lawmakers admitted the challenges of a state legislature typically split along party lines.

Community leaders also recognized the importance of building relationships, maintaining dialogue and supporting legislation on pertinent educational issues. As noted in prior sections, community players like Bill and Esther worked with state leaders to build awareness of educational initiatives supported by their organizations. Drawing on prior experiences and perspectives on bilingual and EL education, their roles as leaders of statewide business and education-focused organizations provided Bill and

Esther with opportunities to dialogue with people in positions of power within state politics, business and education. Bill described his work in leading a statewide working group; he shared, 'The overarching thing is we need to [do] with integrity, support and implement the changes we've already enacted, and Common Core is one of those'. Esther teamed up with lawmakers to engage 'legislator work groups', where advocacy and lobbying took a back seat to educating and promoting open dialogue about relevant policy topics. With an upcoming work group focused on the CCS, she described, 'They [lawmakers] have a chance to talk in a relaxed session and get information without all the posturing and theatrics they have going on around them. So, that's our [organization's] role, is to provide education for them'.

In addition to this ongoing dialogue to educate and advocate for education-related bills and priorities, community leaders went beyond talking about policy at the macro level and utilized their roles and organizations in other ways to impact and appropriate language policy in practice within local contexts across the state of Arizona. Community leaders described using their flexible and multifaceted roles to influence language policy across layers and players, such as listening to issues shared by schools and districts to widely share the challenges with macro-level stakeholders, educating parents to become advocates for their children, starting and leading charter schools that emphasize multilingualism and partnering with federal entities to bring legal actions against the state to impact EL education.

Chris emphasized his efforts to include EL families in advocacy efforts around language policy mandates directly impacting their children. Whereas one facet of his job included lobbying at the State Capitol, he recognized his agency to influence language policy in practice through his work in local educational settings with low-income parents, many of whom had children labeled as ELs. He explained,

> A lot of it is just about engaging those parents [of ELs] in the conversation. Our organizers speak Spanish because that's the [primary] language. We meet parents where they're at. We help them understand their rights as citizens or as parents in the education system, [such as] that they can have translation at school board meetings. They can be [advocates], regardless of [if they are a] citizen or non-citizen, that it's important and it's necessary for them to be involved in their child's education.

Within the organization's focus on parental rights and advocacy within state and national education, Chris appropriated policy through open and honest communication with parents. Arizona language policy has stipulated that parents have the right to opt children out of ELD; however, per ADE mandate, schools and districts are not allowed to inform parents of that option. Chris recognized the opportunity of his organization to inform parents as a third party:

> School districts aren't allowed to communicate that [waiver] information to the parents, from what I understand, so where else are they going to get that information without an organization that's focused on telling people that? In our experience, schools are trying to comply with the law, not just the ELD, but just laws overall. There's a compliance culture within education. They're not necessarily being as innovative as they could, and this is an obscenity. It's difficult to innovate the way the law is structured.

Although Chris felt the obligation to inform parents of their rights, he struggled with the possibility that ELs might receive little to no language-specific support in general education classroom settings. In the future, he hoped to form innovative EL-focused partnerships with districts where his organization informed parents of their rights and local school districts offered strong research-based programs as alternatives to ELD.

Hector, the leader of a community group focused on the rights of Latinos, described his organization's use of charter schools to appropriate educational and language policies in practice. From his experience as a community advocate, Hector found that 'charter schools are not as regulated' by the ADE, allowing space and agency for the appropriation of policy in practice. In his case, he described finding the *implementational space* (Johnson & Freeman, 2010) for culturally and linguistically responsive curriculum, despite the policy restrictions at the state level. Speaking specifically to the controversial ban on ethnic studies, Hector explained his schools' appropriation to maintain culturally specific coursework:

> There was a bill that was passed to eliminate any ethnic studies, although it was really initially targeted at Chicano studies but obviously it carried forward into affecting other communities as well. But those regulations really never cascaded down to charter schools in the same format. For us, we never framed it as Chicano studies. We've kind of framed it more from a cultural relevancy [curriculum], and so we were able to incorporate cultural competency, if you will, more into our teaching and learning.

Taking advantage of his small network of charter schools, in contrast to the large public school district in the center of the ethnic studies debate, Hector framed the curriculum with more nebulous and less political discourse. Specific to language policy, Hector recognized the central role of parents in choosing appropriate programs for their children. He asserted,

For us, it's a one size *doesn't* fit all. Our approach is always about giving people choices. At the end of the day, if parents are informed, if parents believe that they have choices, they'll make the best choice for them and their kids. That's really what we advocate.

Similar to Chris, Hector engaged in collaborative efforts with parents to maintain and share agency within restrictive language policy mandates at charter schools.

Unlike Chris and Hector's work with families and schools at the local level, and Esther and Bill's collaboration with stakeholders at the state level, Louis appropriated policy through federal measures. He was not bashful in explaining why he utilized federal avenues to challenge language policy, describing his continuous frustration and lack of patience for the dysfunctional state legislature and hopeless EL Task Force and ADE. In addition to critiques of state layers of language policy, Louis specifically targeted the inefficacy of the task force in their design and monitoring of the ELD model. He explained,

They [task force members] were repeatedly asked to look at different models, [and] they refused to do so throughout the term of the task force while it was in existence. I think much of it was politically motivated. They knew what was going on, they knew that what the evidence was showing [regarding EL education]. They never demanded any kind of analysis, rigorous analysis, about whether it [ELD model] was working or not. They didn't want to know and then, I do a lot of this kind of litigation, and that's typical. They don't want to know facts, [because] that gets in the way of ideology.

From the perspectives and experiences of Louis, a seasoned attorney regularly focused on litigation involving Arizona EL education, task force members made language policy decisions as driven by conservative political influences and corresponding monolingual and assimilative ideologies in contrast to the common claim that policies and practices came from 'what's best for kids'. Recognizing the political and ideological nature of these policy decisions within both state government and state education layers, Louis partnered with federal agencies to bring suit against the state of Arizona for various facets of the language policy. He asserted,

We took that occasion to challenge the 4-hour model on two grounds. First, that the 4-hour model denied students access to the academic curriculum in violation of the EEOA [Equal Educational Opportunities Act] and second, that it unduly segregated students without a compelling reason in as much as the 4-hour model has not been demonstrated to be any more effective at teaching kids English.

Whereas this legal effort targeting the 4-hour block failed, the other suit regarding the Home Language Survey (HLS) and the Arizona English Language Learner Assessment (AZELLA), described in Chapter 3, found in favor of Louis and the federal government, thus shifting the state's practice in identifying ELs.

In addition to finding the space to appropriate language policy in practice during the first five years of implementation, community leaders and state legislators alike looked toward more opportunities in the future. The passage of House Bill 2425 in 2013, brought to the floor by the Education Committee chairperson in the House of Representatives, led to the dissolving of the EL Task Force and shifted responsibility for the ELD model to the Board of Education. With the task force previously maintaining power over macro-level language policy regulations, which they did little to nothing to change over the course of the first five years of implementation, state government players seemed optimistic about the possibility of changes in language policy due to this important shift. Chris explained,

> The timeliness of the State Board's review [of the ELD model] is important so we can engage in that conversation and present a parent perspective, present a perspective of students who've been in the [ELD] model for a long time, with having things [policy in practice] assessed and engage parents in that kind of advocacy effort.

As Chris considered the upcoming review of the ELD model and recognized his organization's commitment to involving parents in the political process to advocate for their children, Senator Ray hoped that the State Board would do what the task force failed to do over five years – allow flexibility for local school districts. He expressed,

> If they're [the State Board] going to look at revamping [EL education], I would certainly be in favor of turning the districts loose and letting them come up with their own [EL] program that fits their area, because I don't believe there is ever one-size-fits-all districts. Everybody has different demographics, different things they need to deal with... To me, the more I can let the school districts come up with plans that meet the guidelines, and the students are progressing, then why should I, as a state legislator, have anything to worry about?

After multiple years of having scant control over official language policy due to the power of the task force, this former educator and Republican lawmaker still utilized conditional discourse despite the shift of power to a new institutional entity. Whereas state government players seemed somewhat optimistic about the shift of power away from the task force, the future of EL education remained in the hands of another small and politically connected group of individuals, as the governor appointed all Board of Education members.

Discussion: Language Policy (P)layers in State Government

In this chapter, I shared findings from the final layer and players explored in this study on Arizona language policy in practice. Previous chapters probed the layers of the language policy onion (Ricento & Hornberger, 1996) in Arizona, starting with teachers at the center and moving out to describe school and district leaders at the local education layer and task force members, state administrators and teacher educators at the state education layer. Previously backgrounded in the chapters focused on local and state education layers, this chapter foregrounded the perspectives and experiences of state legislators and community leaders engaged in policy work at the macro level of state government. Situated in the external layer of language policy, state government players engaged in multi-faceted social, economic and educational policy work that both implicitly and explicitly influenced the education of ELs in Arizona. This more broad focus at the macro level of state policy was one emergent distinction with local and state education players in the study.

Demonstrating the divide between micro-level practice in ELD classrooms and macro-level policy work at the State Capitol, findings indicated distinct perspectives and experiences between state government players and those in Greenwood. State players described different educational priorities than local educators, such as their convergence on issues such as educational funding and the CCS influencing the education of all students across the state of Arizona. In contrast, ELD teachers and leaders shared perspectives and experiences that honed in on the day-to-day work of teaching ELs and the resulting challenges from language policy restrictions in the local context of Greenwood. Whereas local and state players agreed upon the pedagogical issues related to student segregation within the ELD model, the primary challenge within the JESD – teacher placement, preparation and attrition – remained completely unnoticed by state lawmakers and community leaders. Among this small, collaborative and powerful circle of predominantly White, English-dominant men, state government players seemed unaware of the isolation and struggles faced by ELD teachers in local settings.

When considering findings at the state education and state government layers of language policy in practice, an interesting question emerges: who has the power, influence and agency to make changes in policy and practice for ELs in Arizona? Whether situated in elected or non-elected positions in state governance, players on both sides of the political aisle shared in their disapproval of the restrictive language policy and the resulting ELD model utilized with ELs in educational practice. Nevertheless, the unchecked and unprecedented power of the EL Task Force resulted in scant change to the official policy regulations across five years of implementation in schools. At the same time, despite recognizing their extraordinary influence over language policy in practice, task force members Alex and Pat consistently deflected agency over policy design and implementation, citing the related legislation (i.e. House Bill 2064) drafted and passed by state lawmakers. Similarly, ADE administrators redirected responsibility for the ELD model, referencing their compliance to state legislation and the resulting task force model. All the while, ELD teachers in local contexts such as Greenwood – as well as school leaders, district administrators, teacher educators and community advocates – embraced their agency as policy players to negotiate and appropriate language policy in practice to best reach and teach students in Arizona classrooms.

Part 3

Discussion

8 Rationalizing the Education of English Learners in Arizona: The Complexities of Language Policy in Practice

Just a few short miles from central Phoenix, where lawmakers, lobbyists and administrators conducted educational and language policy work from their legislative and executive offices, local educators engaged in daily practice with English learners (ELs) in classrooms and schools. While predominantly upper-middle-class, White, native English-speaking individuals legislated, lobbied and led statewide efforts to enforce the EL Task Force's prescriptive English Language Development (ELD) model of instruction, Greenwood teachers and leaders worked to implement a restrictive language policy while simultaneously supporting the learning of culturally and linguistically diverse children and adolescents. Originally Mexican territory turned Arizona ranching and farming community, this 21st-century suburban school district welcomed students and families from predominantly low-income households, including immigrant and refugee families speaking Spanish, Vietnamese, French, Arabic, Farsi, Somali, Karen and 30 other languages. Parents enrolled their children in the Jackson Elementary School District (JESD), surely with hopeful aspirations for an excellent American education. For the almost 2000 students who did not pass the Arizona English Language Learner Assessment (AZELLA) standardized test of English proficiency and subsequently received the label of EL, district and school officials placed their children in ELD classrooms for four hours of skill-based English instruction.

For students, the EL label meant separation from their English-proficient peers, resulting in the stigmatization of ELD as the 'stupid class' where children received low-level skill-driven instruction. Due to the passage of House Bill 2064 by state legislators and the corresponding ELD model designed by the EL Task Force, students no longer engaged in content-based learning side-by-side with their peers but rather learned grammar, vocabulary, reading, writing and conversation skills in hourly blocks of time with ELs at similar levels of English proficiency. In addition to English-medium instruction mandated by Proposition 203, district-level decisions further restricted students' language use. EL coaches instructed teachers to *punish* children with negative consequences when native language use was overheard in classrooms in attempt to deter native languages, maximize English usage and safeguard compliance with state policy. Despite the dearth of academic content instruction as mandated in the ELD model, state policy required ELs to take standardized tests of content, including mathematics and science, which school and district leaders used to measure student achievement and teacher efficacy. Regardless of students' progress, report cards consistently reflected performing *beneath grade level*, as district leaders indicated to teachers that ELs could not be considered *at grade level* due to placement in ELD classrooms.

These multiple policy mandates from state and district players resulted in challenging contexts for the predominantly novice teachers in ELD classrooms. Despite macro-level players' attempts to homogenize classrooms based on AZELLA scores, teachers encountered ample diversity in language background, English proficiency level, grade level, learning needs, circumstances of immigration and acculturation and time in the ELD program. Notwithstanding these multiple variables, the task force's model prescribed teachers with rigid mandates for teaching grammar and linguistic skills and unreasonably expected all students to test out of the EL label in one year.

In addition to these challenges, teachers entered ELD classrooms with scant knowledge and skills to negotiate the unknown context of teaching four hours of content-devoid language instruction. Taking advantage of the limited qualifications required by the Arizona Department of Education (ADE) to be considered *highly qualified* to teach ELD, Teach for America (TFA) ensured corps members could be placed in ELD classrooms after a 5-week introduction to teaching and 15-hour online course on Structured English Immersion (SEI) methods. With these underprepared teachers bearing the *highly qualified* label, district leaders hired and school leaders placed corps members in ELD classrooms due to a shortage of certified teachers willing to teach in this complex setting. After completing the TFA summer institute, corps members received ongoing supervision by Phoenix regional office staff members, who paired ELD-trained teachers with special education or English language arts experts without EL-specific knowledge or skills. Through TFA's university partnership, corps members enrolled in SEI endorsement courses, which utilized the ADE-mandated curriculum to prepare teachers for sheltered content instruction in general education settings rather than the skill-based approach in ELD classrooms. Exacerbating the need for novice ELD teachers, the federal lawsuit against the state resulted in a 40% increase in ELs as hundreds of students were returned to ELD from mainstream classrooms.

While attempting to implement a restrictive language policy in practice in effective ways to meet the needs of their heterogeneous groups of EL students, novice teachers simultaneously sought to mediate the multiple forms and functions of professional development and support. Specifically, ELD teachers met with competing recommendations, advice and orders to comply or not comply with language policy mandates. Voices emphasizing compliance came at the district level: Targeted training and coaching came from the English Language Learner (ELL) department at the JESD, focused primarily on compliance mandates in response to top-down pressures from ADE administrators. Other voices at the school level advised non-compliance in favor of upping overall school performance numbers; meanwhile, with ELD teachers isolated from general education teachers in and across grade levels, school leaders often encouraged teachers to ignore compliance and plan for content instruction. Despite the ample opportunities and great need for targeted professional support, the lack of alignment to the realities and demands of the ELD instructional setting left teachers overwhelmed and underprepared as they grappled with the challenges of the restrictive language policy in practice.

Arizona Language Policy in Practice: Considering the Layers and Players

As illustrated throughout this text, various layers and players influenced the daily educational experiences of ELs in Arizona. Teachers worked to make meaning of policy demands in daily classroom practice in increasingly diverse and complex classroom settings – whether those policy demands came from state legislation passed by Senate and House lawmakers, the instructional mandates outlined in the task force's ELD model, the compliance demands enforced by ADE administrators or district leaders' decisions regarding language use and policy implementation. With this study, I aimed to provide a holistic picture of the complex, multilayered language policy context in Arizona using the perspectives and experiences of those engaged in policy work every day. Via exploration and inclusion of the multiple layers and players engaged in Arizona language policy in practice, findings demonstrated how various policy players influenced the education of ELs by decisions made in classrooms, schools, districts, community colleges and universities, as well as at the ADE, state legislature, community advocacy meetings and EL Task Force sessions (Hornberger & Johnson, 2007; Levinson & Sutton, 2001; Ricento & Hornberger, 1996).

Three novice TFA teachers of ELD classrooms in Greenwood, Arizona engaged in daily practice with ELs spanning from first grade to middle school. Participants described ample challenges in the complex classroom setting, including that they were asked to use prescriptive methods for skill-based teaching to a heterogeneous group of students who differed in terms of native language, English proficiency level, age, country of origin, immigration status, learning needs and beyond. With limited EL-specific preparation from TFA prior to entering the classroom (Heineke & Cameron, 2011, 2013; Hopkins & Heineke, 2013), teachers recalled embracing the compliance-based training provided by the JESD, particularly in their first year, when the prescriptive structures served as the sole guidance in implementing ELD mandates in daily practice (Lillie *et al.*, 2012; Lillie & Markos, 2014). Teachers reflected on the inefficacy of other professional supports and learning opportunities, including the misaligned SEI endorsement coursework that emphasized content teaching in general education classrooms (de Jong *et al.*, 2010; Hopkins, 2012; Lillie *et al.*, 2012; Murri *et al.*, 2012; Rios-Aguilar, 2012a).

As evidenced by differences across experiences of the first-, second- and third-year teachers in this study, more time in ELD classrooms led to additional agency and policy appropriation as teachers' competencies as EL educators developed over time (Brat & Cain, 2013; Heineke & Cameron, 2013; Mackinney & Rios-Aguilar, 2012). Teachers actively made decisions in instructional planning and implementation to skirt policy regulations, such as writing two sets of lesson plans; and to better meet students' learning needs and goals, such as merging the ELD blocks for integrated literacy instruction. Nonetheless, ELD teacher attrition, fueled partially by the 2-year commitment of TFA corps members, led to a continuous cycle of novice teachers in these high-need and challenging settings (Gándara & Maxwell-Jolly, 2006; Heineke *et al.*, 2014). Whereas third-year teacher Annie persisted as the 'veteran' ELD teacher beyond her TFA commitment, Tammie returned home to Boston and Paula shifted into the role of district-level EL instructional coach after two years of teaching in ELD classrooms.

In the JESD, to maximize compliance with state language policy regulations, district administrators maintained direct oversight of the ELD teachers across the district. Four district administrators in various roles in the ELL department participated in this study; unique from other layers, all district-level players were bilingual, with three of four self-identifying as Spanish-dominant bilingual Latinas. Employed by the department serving as the direct link to state administrators, JESD leaders prided themselves in being 100% in compliance with language policy. On the one hand, district administrators insisted on compliance within teacher training and support, specifically due to the large number of novice teachers in ELD classrooms each year. On the other hand, these players embraced the implementational space to negotiate policy demands, including the focus on biliteracy with parents and content integration with teachers (Johnson & Freeman, 2010). Unlike previous studies that demonstrated the dearth in content instruction for ELs in schools, including limited time for mathematics and no time for science and social studies (Lillie *et al.*, 2012; Lillie & Markos, 2014), district administrators partnered with classroom- and school-level players to appropriate policy by integrating academic content into the 4-hour ELD block. Nonetheless, district players in the ELL department still tacitly accepted many policy mandates, including the insistence on teaching grammar and discrete language skills (Clark, 2009).

Despite the formal structure that placed the responsibilities for training and supporting ELD teachers in the hands of ELL department administrators, individual ELD classrooms remained situated within larger schools. In this way, on-site school leaders influenced the daily practice of EL students and teachers. Four school leaders participated in this study – all White, native English speakers with extensive experience in Arizona education who espoused an overall dislike for the restrictive language policy and its resultant impacts on classroom- and school-level practice. Charged to manage whole school buildings, within which EL education was only one facet of the larger institutional entirety, school leaders described challenges including the organization of students in classrooms across grades and proficiency levels, the staffing of ELD classrooms with veteran teachers largely unwilling to take on the challenging context, the supporting of teachers to engage in effective practice simultaneous to top-down mandates, the balancing of multiple and often contrasting initiatives such as Common Core Standards (CCS), the evaluation of teachers using content-based measures and ultimately the retention of high-quality teachers due to the revolving door of ELD classrooms.

Additionally, school leaders described pressures to comply and related their fears of ramifications for non-compliance (Grijavla & Jiménez-Silva, 2014); however, they maintained agency to appropriate policy when possible. At public schools in particular, leaders recognized the social isolation of both students and teachers in ELD classrooms, resulting in challenging and complex contexts for teaching and learning (Lillie *et al.*, 2012; Lillie & Markos, 2014); despite district-level supervision of ELD teachers, school leaders admitted to coaching teachers to creatively lesson plan to circumvent the ELD mandates in daily classroom practice. Whereas JESD leaders disliked the compliance-focused teacher training provided by the district, the charter school leader required a direct line to the ADE for these supports, which he perceived as highly prescriptive and largely unhelpful.

Spanning out from the local context, state education players from the ADE and higher education, who engaged with macro-level language policy through compliance monitoring and teacher training, offered insightful perspectives. The ADE, specifically the Office of English Language Acquisition Services (OELAS), maintained responsibility for monitoring school districts and charter schools for compliance with language policy implementation (HB 2064, 2006). Two ADE and OELAS administrators participated in this study – both White, native English-speaking women who previously worked in Phoenix-area public schools. In addition to supervising schools and districts, the ADE connected to teacher education programs offering SEI endorsement coursework (Moore, 2012). Next, EL teacher education faculty from White, native English-speaking backgrounds represented one community college and one 4-year university, both with campuses located in Greenwood. With decades of combined experience dating back to the epoch of bilingual education in Arizona, these four players drew upon prior involvement with ELs to make meaning of language policy, rationalizing changes with what they perceived as failures of previous policies (e.g. poor quality of bilingual teachers, student submersion in SEI classrooms).

Despite similar rationalization, state education players appropriated policy distinctly. ADE administrators tacitly accepted and deferred agency to the task force, conceptualizing the ELD instructional model, discrete-skill focus and corresponding tools as simplifying practice for teachers (ADE, 2007, 2008). Conversely, teacher educators actively critiqued and negotiated the ADE curricular framework guiding SEI coursework, discerning the lack of alignment with language policy and appropriating course content in line with what they recognized as good pedagogy, including sheltered content teaching, native language support and policy negotiation (Arias, 2012; Markos & Arias, 2014).

Distinct from players engaged in everyday practice with language policy, such as ELD classroom teachers, district ELL leaders, OELAS administrators and EL teacher educators, state lawmakers and community organizers collaborated more broadly on educational policy. Four state lawmakers serving on their respective education committees in the Senate and House, as well as five community leaders working on a variety of education-related issues, participated in this study – six of these nine were from White native English-speaking backgrounds. In contrast to prototypical educational policymakers from non-education backgrounds, four legislators and three community organizers had teaching backgrounds in Arizona, providing pertinent lenses and experiences that guided decision-making. Responsible for multiple facets of social and educational policy, these players discussed broader issues influencing Arizona education, such as school finance and the CCS. When specifically considering language policy, all players disagreed with the ELD model, with both sides of the political aisle merging around issues related to student segregation (Faltis & Arias, 2012; Gándara & Orfield, 2012; García, 2011). Community leaders described implementational space to educate parents to build policy knowledge and advocacy, to creatively appropriate policy in less-regulated charter schools and to bring federal litigation against the ADE (Hogan, 2014; Johnson & Freeman, 2010). On the other hand, state legislators discerned limited agency to influence language policy, primarily due to the unprecedented power espoused by the EL Task Force.

Two participants provided perspectives and experiences as EL Task Force members, the layer of the onion influencing all layers and players involved in EL education. Created by House Bill 2064 and charged to design and monitor program models for ELs, the task force welcomed nine appointed members who wielded unprecedented power over EL education (HB 2064, 2006; Lawton, 2012). In this study, Pat and Alex recognized their dual legislative and executive roles yet deferred responsibility and displaced blame to requirements stipulated in House Bill 2064. In the design phase, the task force utilized agency beyond the formal policy document to create top-down mandates extending the 4-hour block of skill-based instruction for all ELs, amplifying the impact of policy appropriation and affecting ELs across the state. In the monitoring phase, these players described the ongoing politics plaguing the task force, in which members refused to change the model despite the pleas of local educators (Haver, 2013; Lawton, 2012). Conceptual critiques of Arizona language policy have centered around the task force, specifically on the legality of the ELD instructional model based on precedents for EL programs established in *Castañeda v. Pickard* (August et al., 2010; Combs, 2012; Faltis & Arias, 2012; García, 2011; Krashen et al., 2007, 2012; Long & Adamson, 2012; Martínez-Wenzl et al., 2012). Nevertheless, official language policy regulations have remained unchanged since its original implementation in 2008. The recent power shift from the task force to the State Board of Education has reunited hope in change in EL education (HB 2425, 2013).

Overall, study findings merged to demonstrate the holistic picture of language policy in practice, including the complexity across layers and players and the experiences and perspectives from various institutional roles. Previous empirical studies have focused on teachers (Brat & Cain, 2013; Heineke, 2015; Heineke & Cameron, 2011, 2013; Mackinney & Rios-Aguilar, 2012; Rios-Aguilar et al., 2012a), school leaders (Grijalva & Jiménez-Silva, 2014), individual school implementation (Lillie et al., 2012; Lillie & Markos, 2014) and teacher education (de Jong et al., 2010; Hopkins, 2012; Murri et al., 2012), along with broader conceptual pieces critiquing macro-level policy (Arias, 2012; August et al., 2010; Combs, 2012; Faltis & Arias, 2012; García, 2011; Hogan, 2014; Krashen et al., 2007, 2012; Long & Adamson, 2012; Martínez-Wenzl et al., 2012). A significant contribution of this study was the extension beyond local implementation to consider the cross-layer interaction, interplay and implementation of language policy in practice, recognizing the dynamic system of layers and players who influence EL education inside and outside the classroom (Hornberger & Johnson, 2007; Levinson & Sutton, 2001; Menken & García, 2010; Ricento, 2000; Ricento & Hornberger, 1996).

Nevertheless, I aimed to maintain a central focus on teachers, exploring how various layers and players intersected and interacted to influence how teachers negotiated and enacted language policy in their daily practice, on the ground within the classroom, actually working with the ELs about whom so many at the upper layers spoke and wrote distally. Moving beyond the concentric layers of the 'language policy onion', findings indicated the importance of 'growing the onion' to consider the historical nature of the contemporary context, 'peeling the onion' to uncover ideologies guiding players' perspectives, 'slicing the onion' to consider vertical issues crossing language policy and 'stirring the onion' to explore ways players collaborated across layers to appropriate language policy in practice (Hornberger & Johnson, 2007; Menken & García, 2010; Ricento & Hornberger, 1996). I now span out to discuss the findings in the broader sociocultural and sociohistorical context of language policy in practice.

Educational Reform and the Education of English Learners in Arizona

Lessons learned in this study are most meaningful when contextualized within the broader educational policy agenda in Arizona, situated in the southwestern US, and within the larger culture of American educational reform. Jal Mehta (2013: 5), a nationally recognized Harvard professor of education, has described 'the allure of order' in the repetitive cycles of top-down policy efforts to 'fix' education in the US over the past century. Using a cultural approach to analyze the history of educational reforms, he characterized American educational reformers as utilizing *organizational rationalization* in the name of efficiency to push change in classrooms and schools across the nation. Disregarding both scholarly research and practical experience, policymakers have treated teaching like factory work, seeking to provide order in the system with prescriptions and procedures rather than professional knowledge, skills and discretion. In this way, teaching has become institutionalized as a 'semi-profession' (Mehta, 2013: 6). Mehta (2013) contends that reformers have imposed scientific rationality on schooling, focusing on the measurable in place of the meaningful and relying on top-down policy in place of bottom-up professionalization.

Similar to federal-level educational reforms, Arizona policymakers have attempted to centralize and standardize education from the state level. To fully appreciate the findings of this study grounded in the sociocultural context of Arizona, one must consider the deeper assumptions behind these efforts to rationalize schools. Mehta (2013: 248) described it this way: 'Choices we make about how to reform schools reflect a broader set of values about what we want for our students, how we regard our teachers, and what our vision of educational improvement is'. To explore these values and assumptions driving the organizational rationalization behind official language policy, I discuss the findings with four interconnected lenses: (a) an historical lens on the cycles of rationalizing the education of ELs, (b) an ideological lens on the prevalence of monolingualism and language-as-problem, (c) a pedagogical lens on the failure to prepare and professionalize classroom teachers and (d) a political lens on the institutional vantage and leverage points in language policy.

The historical lens: Cycles of rationalizing the education of English learners

Pendulum shifts are frequent and common among historical education trends in Arizona and the broader US, with ongoing cycles of reforms to subsequent reforms (e.g. Honig, 2006; Mehta, 2013; Mitchell, 2011). In the past century, the power of educational decision-making in schools has shifted from local control to increasing district, state and federal regulation over local practice (Mehta, 2013). Each leading to increasing prescription and supervision from above, American reform movements historically followed similar trajectories. Following the declaration of a crisis in quality destabilizing the educational institution, powerful external stakeholders have elevated and backed an external logic in hopes of controlling and improving failing schools, despite teachers' and others' attempts to resist these movements (Mehta, 2013). Just as Mehta's historical analysis uncovered cycles of rationalization in broad educational policy at the federal level, the larger culture of American educational reform has pervaded the institution in state and local settings. Following similar trajectories from national reform movements, various cycles of rationalization have driven language policy regulations over the past century in the southwestern state of Arizona. Evident from the findings from this study, veteran policy players utilized these cycles of rationalization to make meaning of language policy in practice (Figure 8.1).

Dating back to education in Arizona's early statehood, the first cycle of rationalization centered on the concession of local control for state-mandated English-only instruction for ELs. Arizona has long embraced local control over education, which characterized broader US policy a century ago (Mehta, 2013; Pickering, 1966). Situated on land that was formerly Mexico, Arizona's territorial schools originated around networks of community stakeholders who maintained ample local control over most facets of education but deferred to the state for decisions regarding EL education (Pickering, 1966). In a young state inhabited by many Latino and Native American residents, educators implemented the state-mandated '1C classes' for all non-native English speakers, looking to assimilate residents to create an 'imagined community' bounded by the English language (Anderson, 1983; Rolstad et al., 2005; Sheridan, 1986). Responding to the crisis to 'incorporate "foreign" students into the mainstream of U.S. society' (Sheridan, 1986: 224), official language policy elevated the logic that the linguistically diverse population required abandonment of local control for state-mandated courses focused on discrete English skills. This

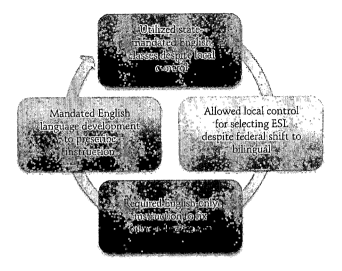

Figure 8.1 Cycles of rationalization of Arizona language policy

relinquishment of power to the state continued across Arizona education, as evidenced by micro and meso-level players in this study.

Shifting the stance on local control, the second cycle of rationalization sought to skirt federal efforts around bilingual education in favor of English-medium instruction. After decades of skill-based English instruction for Arizona ELs, bilingual education emerged as a federal priority following the civil rights movement and Bilingual Education Act of 1968 (Pickering, 1966; Sheridan, 1986). These shifts in federal educational policy required and provided funding, training and resources for appropriate instruction and equal educational opportunities for ELs (EEOA, 1974). To remain in compliance with federal legislation, Arizona language policy regulations shifted to incorporate bilingual education, despite contrasting conservative ideologies of monolingualism and assimilation prevalent across the state (Crawford, 2000; Valdéz, 2001). Nevertheless, after elevating the logic of local control in educational decision-making, the same reasoning that was dispelled for decades to allow state-mandated English classes, policymakers rallied behind the need for English-medium instruction for ELs. Behind the efforts of powerful external players and state legislators, Senate Bill 1160 passed in 1984 only after significant revisions, the most notable being local control for districts to opt for English as a Second Language (ESL) in place of bilingual education (Sacken & Medina, 1990). Despite the opposition of local educators and bilingual education advocates who resisted this shift, official language policy was revised, making bilingual education optional as well as limiting teacher credentialing standards, funding and grade ranges for bilingual services (Sacken & Medina, 1990).

Bilingual education lost additional ground with the third cycle of rationalization, known widely as the *English-only movement*, which conceded the shift from bilingual to English-medium instruction in Arizona classrooms (Crawford, 2000; Valdéz, 2001). Despite evidence of the efficacy of certain bilingual programs (McCarty, 2002; Rolstad *et al.*, 2005), bilingual education in Arizona has never had the opportunity to yield its full potential, as tied to previous policy decisions to remove bilingual teaching certification standards and limit funding for bilingual program implementation (Sacken & Medina, 1990). Citing what they purported as the failures of bilingual education, English-only advocates declared a crisis of quality in native language instruction in supporting students' English acquisition (Haver, 2013). Backed by millionaire Ron Unz and his California-based movement, English for the Children supporters elevated their logic of monolingual instruction to meet the goal of English proficiency for non-native speakers of English (Combs, 2012; Haver, 2013). As evidenced by the findings from this study, ideologically diverse individuals supported efforts to improve EL education, rationalizing the policy shift with perceptions of the ineffectiveness of bilingual education due to lack of teacher preparation and program articulation. Despite the efforts of local educators and university faculty in resisting the English-only movement, Proposition 203 successfully passed, mandating English-medium instruction for ELs (Combs, 2012; Combs *et al.*, 2011).

Situated most recently in the historical trajectory of Arizona language policy, the fourth cycle of rationalization pushed beyond monolingual mandates to further prescribe instruction for ELs, thus shifting from the nebulous SEI model to the more restrictive ELD model. Initiated by the declaration of a crisis of quality in EL education, with a specific emphasis on the widespread interpretation and implementation of SEI in classrooms across the state following the passage of Proposition 203, state administrators and lawmakers pushed for restrictions and prescriptions to EL instruction (Combs, 2012; Hogan, 2014). Backed by core members of the original English-only movement, stakeholders elevated their logic that ELs required more time-on-task in English language skills prior to learning academic content, resulting in the 4 hours of mandated skill-based ELD instruction (Clark, 1999, 2009; Haver, 2013). As demonstrated by the findings in this study, by reforming the reform with which many did not agree – the SEI approach to teaching ELs in content-based, general education classrooms – players rationalized the shift in hopes of control and improvement to varied implementation that often mirrored submersion. Despite local educators' and university faculty members' attempts to resist these formal policy shifts, the unilateral power of the EL Task Force, guided by English-only ideologies and prescriptive mindsets, led to the successful passage of House Bill 2064 in 2006 (Combs, 2012; Hogan, 2014).

Alongside wider educational reform movements across the US (Honig, 2006; Mehta, 2013; Mitchell, 2011), Arizona underwent similar, state-level cycles of rationalization in educational policy, including specific shifts in language policy that influenced the education of ELs. Arizona language policy represents a cycle of reforming reforms, including the rationalization of the new reform due to the failures of the previous one – whether deferring local control to implement skill-based, English-only classes, maintaining local control to prioritize ESL over bilingual education, purporting the failures of optional bilingual education in favor of mandated monolingual instruction or pushing the need for increased prescriptions to return to skill-based English classes. As veteran policy players in this study asserted, these cycles of rationalization became the default across layers, as both monolingual and bilingual advocates alike rationalized the historical trajectory of language policy shifts from bilingual to SEI to ELD. In other words, whereas players across layers engaged in agentive language policy work, their perspectives, decisions and rationales connected to previous experiences in EL education across the bilingual, SEI and ELD epochs in Arizona.

The ideological lens: The prevalence of monolingualism and language-as-problem

Assimilative and monolingual ideologies have run beneath these historical cycles of rationalization in EL education, particularly targeting immigrants and non-native English speakers in Arizona (Crawford, 2000; Kohut et al., 2006; Schmidt, 2000; Valdéz, 2001). Whereas scholars have considered language ideologies as driving language policies (e.g. Crawford, 2000; Ricento, 2000; Shohamy, 2006), Mehta (2013) argued that between policy and ideology is the *policy paradigm*, or the problem definition driving the reform; in this way, the *language policy paradigm* is the critical unit of analysis to understand the cycles of rationalization in EL education. During the conflict stage of any given cycle of rationalization, problem definitions in the form of political arguments frame the types of policy solutions that are desirable. After a problem definition triumphs and thus becomes the dominant narrative that precludes dissent, the result is a policy paradigm (Mehta, 2013). Despite the monolingual ideology and language-as-problem definition that has always pervaded discourse in Arizona (Crawford, 2000; Ruiz, 1984), findings from this study indicated that the shifting language policy paradigm in the mid-2000s drove state policy change.

With the passage of House Bill 2064 in 2006 and the subsequent change to policy regulations for the school-based instruction of ELs, the language policy paradigm shifted in Arizona. Running beneath the cycles of rationalization for decades, the policy paradigm and associated political debate centered on the medium of instruction in classrooms with the English-only movement in the 1990s. The passage of Proposition 203 solidified the master narrative of English as the *medium* for learning (Crawford, 2000). Grounded in Arizona's ever-present monolingual ideology, this previous paradigm resulted in SEI as the resultant language policy in practice (ADE, 2000). After six years of SEI, where ELs learned English and other academic content in classrooms with mainstream peers, the Superintendent and Deputy Superintendent of Instruction leading the ADE declared the nebulous requirements and varied implementation of the language policy as a problem (Hogan, 2014). State players framed their argument with the assertion that ELs need English proficiency prior to learning academic content, and this argument triumphed as the policy paradigm with the passage of House Bill 2064 in 2006. In this way, *English as the prerequisite for learning* became the master narrative by which the debate was now framed, bringing various consequences and functions. See Table 8.1 for a graphic representation of language policy paradigms in Arizona.

The paradigm shift changed the constellation of players directly engaged in macro-level discussion and decisions regarding language policy in practice with the formation of the EL Task Force. Considering broader educational policy, Mehta (2013) explained,

> When new problem definitions come to the fore, new actors become involved, and new cleavages are created. New paradigms can motivate the formation of new groups, which in turn can have a significant effect on subsequent debate. Precisely because these new groups accept the dominant conception of the problem, they are welcomed by the broader political environment and can play a critical role in shaping policy alternatives. (Mehta, 2013: 19)

In this case of Arizona, the new *English as prerequisite for learning* paradigm led to the formation of the nine-member EL Task Force, which had a significant impact on the subsequent debate regarding the appropriate approach to educating ELs. Elected state officials appointed the task force members, with appointees allotted to the Governor, Senate President, Speaker of the House and State Superintendent of Public Instruction (HB 2064, 2006). In this way, the resulting membership reflected the politics and ideologies of those in elected positions in the given sociocultural and

Table 8.1 Arizona language policy paradigms

	Prior to 2006	After 2006
Ideology	English monolingualism	English monolingualism
Policy paradigm	English as *medium* of learning	English as *prerequisite* for learning
Policy regulation	Structured English Immersion	English Language Development
Policy practices	Varied by local context	Varies by local context

sociohistorical context, including individuals who had aligned themselves with the conservative party or English-only movement, as evidenced in this study by Alex and Pat, respectively (Combs, 2012; Haver, 2013; Hogan, 2014; Lawton, 2012). Not only were these nine task force members welcomed to the discussion, but findings also indicated the critical role and unprecedented power of these politically connected few in shaping both official policy regulations and the education of ELs in local settings.

Succeeding the influence on the constellation of players at the table, the new paradigm then influenced whose voices and perspectives were allowed in the larger policy dialogue, specifically during the task force design process of the ELD model. Mehta (2013) described the role of policy paradigms in changing the overall nature of the debate:

> A dominant problem definition serves to bound the potential possibilities of what can be advocated, thus acquiring a powerful agenda-setting function. Policy entrepreneurs who offer solutions that are consistent with the broader agenda are elevated, while those whose solutions do not fit the master narrative are marginalized. In this way, not only does the new problem definition provide a template for its proponents; it also can constrain the positions its opponents take. (Mehta, 2013: 19)

As the task force embarked on the design process, the policy paradigm inherently included particularly individuals in, or excluded particular individuals from, influencing the ongoing discussion and consequent decision-making. As indicated in this study by task force members and university faculty, multiple perspectives were considered in the design process, yet the viewpoints of only a select few emerged to directly influence policy alternatives. University-based scholars' feedback, emphasizing second language acquisition theory and research and arguing for native language instruction, did not align with the master narrative and were therefore dismissed by task force members (Haver, 2013).

Instead, consultant Kevin Clark put forth solutions aligned with the *English as prerequisite for learning* paradigm by introducing the language star, discrete language skills and the specific time-on-task breakdown of the 4-hour ELD model (Clark, 1999, 2009; Haver, 2013). Regardless of his lack of qualifications in comparison with the esteemed university scholars, Clark connected ideologically with the broader task force agenda, thus elevating his status in the official policy negotiations (Combs, 2012; Hogan, 2014). This debate has continued since the inception of the ELD model, as scholars have argued the illegality of the model due to the lack of expertise and research supporting the skill-based framework (August *et al.*, 2010; Combs, 2012; Faltis & Arias, 2012; García, 2011; Krashen *et al.*, 2007, 2012; Long & Adamson, 2012; Martínez-Wenzl *et al.*, 2012); however, efforts have resulted in little to no change in official regulations, demonstrating the strength of the policy paradigm.

Following shifts in the relevant players and perspectives, the policy paradigm of *English as prerequisite for learning* took on various functions in practice across layers, including strategic, constitutive and regulative functions. Shortly after the shift in paradigm, players utilized the *strategic* function to advance their roles in the policy discussion. Mehta (2013: 21) defined the strategic function: 'When a new way of defining a problem becomes central, actors can promote their existing positions by linking them to the new paradigm'. As demonstrated by study findings, players working within state education and district layers promoted their positions by linking them to the new paradigm. Employed by the ADE at the discretion of State Superintendent Tom Horne, who originally pushed for ELD policy prescriptions (Hogan, 2014), Gayle and Gabby strategically affiliated with the *English as prerequisite for learning* paradigm, connecting existing positions at the ADE and prior experiences as a reading interventionist and foreign language learner. In Greenwood, Cynthia and Peter reserved their value of bilingualism and aligned with the paradigm to strategically position the district in compliance with state policy. In addition to those who affiliated themselves with the new language policy paradigm, players also perceived other individuals' strategic advancement using *English as prerequisite for learning*. Contributing to what Louis defined as his 'little empire', JESD leaders, ADE administrators and task force members described how Kevin Clark advanced his business and financial interests as the ELD consultant across Arizona (Clark, 1999, 2009; Combs, 2012; Haver, 2013; Hogan, 2014; Lawton, 2012).

Whereas certain policy players linked themselves to the paradigm for personal or professional reasons, such as employment or compliance, findings demonstrated that all participants used the language policy paradigm to make meaning of practice, which is pertinent in understanding the agentive decisions and appropriation made by various players across layers. Reflecting the *constitutive* function, the policy paradigm directly influenced 'how people interpret or understand the world' (Mehta, 2013: 21). Similar to ideologies that function best when invisible (Fairclough, 2003; Gee, 2002) or the powerful influence on individuals who do not consciously recognize the ideological nature of their thoughts, words and actions, players' discourse indicated the constitutive function of the paradigm without individuals explicitly recognizing its role in their meaning and decision-making in practice.

Perhaps the most poignant demonstration of the constitutive function was the lack of discussion of native language instruction by participants, particularly those who described themselves as former bilingual educators and current EL advocates, including Cynthia in district administration, Wendy at the community college and Esther at the community organization. Policy decisions and proposed solutions instead centered on monolingual instruction, particularly within the paradigm of *English as prerequisite for learning*, such as the rationalization of its use as an intervention to learn English and teach English skills prior to content learning. Although players indeed had the agency to individually make meaning of policy (Brat & Cain, 2013; Combs *et al.*, 2005; Heineke, 2015), the language policy paradigm established the norm guiding interpretation, resulting in players' use of the construct of ELD to shape decisions that did not include bilingual programs or supports.

Similar to the constitutive function that shaped players' policy perceptions and interpretations, the regulative function was evidenced in how participants then carried out language policy in practice. After over five years of strategically aligning and constitutively interpreting language policy in practice, the *English as prerequisite for learning* paradigm has become a significant regulator in the possibilities for EL education in Arizona. Mehta (2013: 21) described the *regulative* function of policy paradigms that in turn 'limit the range of positions that are possible'. Confirming previous research in restrictive Arizona EL classroom settings, findings from this study demonstrated players' negotiation and appropriation of policy in practice (Brat & Cain, 2013; Heineke, 2009, 2015; Heineke & Cameron, 2011, 2013; Mackinney & Rios-Aguilar, 2012). Nonetheless, the *English as prerequisite for learning* paradigm and ELD policy regulated the manifestations of both micro and macro-level players' appropriation. In Greenwood, teachers integrated hourly ELD blocks, such as connecting vocabulary with reading, and leaders encouraged the use of content materials to teach language skills. In state education, players discussed optimism with the shift in policy oversight from the task force to the Board of Education (HB 2425, 2013) and proposed policy changes, such as reducing the 4-hour ELD block to 2 hours. Whereas players indeed appropriated language policy in practice, the *English as prerequisite for learning* paradigm and corresponding ELD policy regulated what they perceived as possible, demonstrating the need to shift the paradigm to influence change in policy (Mehta, 2013).

The pedagogical lens: The failure to prepare and professionalize classroom teachers

Operating within cycles of rationalization driven by ideologies and policy paradigms, macro-level policy players have continuously enacted top-down policies in attempt to prescribe teaching practice, stemming from the lack of teacher professionalism in American education. Educational policymakers have long viewed teachers as 'less than capable actors on the bottom of the policy chain' and teaching as a 'semi-profession' requiring reform efforts that script practice in classrooms and schools (Mehta, 2013: 6). Despite policy scholars' situation of teachers at the center of policy in practice (Datnow *et al.*, 2006; Hornberger & Johnson, 2007; Levinson &

Sutton, 2001; Menken & García, 2010; Ricento & Hornberger, 1996), the perpetuating progressions of reforming reforms in the US imply that teachers are the problem in need of fixing (Duncan, 2011; Mehta, 2013). This historical trend of de-professionalizing teaching has recently manifested in the debate on US and international teacher preparation, fueled by the 5-week teacher training model used by TFA and their global counterparts affiliated with Teach for All (TFA, 2014a; Teach For All, 2015).

Current language policy regulations in Arizona have only exacerbated the conceptualization of teaching as a semi-profession, as evidenced in this study by task force and ADE players' perceptions that ELD teachers needed significantly less knowledge, training and skills than general education teachers. Guided by the *English as prerequisite for learning* paradigm, macro-level players espoused the belief that ELD teachers needed a basic knowledge of the English language, paired with top-down standards and tools to teach discrete language skills to homogenous groups of labeled EL students. Tied to the assumed simplified knowledge base for ELD settings, in contrast to what players described as more complex settings in which teachers taught various academic content areas to heterogeneous groups of students, state leaders set low qualifications for *highly qualified* ELD teachers. Because of this, micro-level players like school and district leaders were able to hire and place underprepared novice teachers, like the TFA corps members in this study, in classroom contexts that in reality were highly complex and challenging – and therefore, undesirable contexts to veteran teachers in the school and district who might instead be precisely those best suited in terms of training and experience for such classrooms.

Indicative of respected professions, the notion of *social closure* must first define who can and cannot become a certified practitioner in the field (Mehta, 2013). The federal government attempted to socially close the profession of teaching with the 'highly qualified' provision of No Child Left Behind (NCLB), which aimed to improve the overall quality of teachers and reduce teachers with emergency credentials, as well as requiring states to set specific guidelines for entry into the profession (NCLB, 2001: 1473). Pursuant to federal requirements, the ADE defined guidelines regarding who received 'highly qualified' status, including specific requirements for those eligible to teach in ELD classroom settings: (a) bachelor's degree; (b) intern, provisional or standard teaching certificate; (c) bilingual, ESL or SEI endorsement; and (d) passing score on subject-specific assessment (ADE, 2014). Despite the attempt to provide social closure and define the eligibility for a certified practitioner of ELs, the qualifications resulted in a wide hodgepodge of actual qualifications on the ground (Arias, 2012; de Jong *et al.*, 2010; Hopkins, 2012; Hopkins & Heineke, 2013; Lillie *et al.*, 2012; Lillie & Markos, 2012). In this study, teacher participants earned *highly qualified* status as TFA corps members because they had attained bachelor's degrees in non-education-related fields, intern teaching certificates after five weeks of training and provisional SEI endorsements after a 15-hour online course.

Social closure to professional practice also includes licensing those individuals and institutions that provide pre-service training to ensure that entry-level practitioners meet certain initial standards of quality (Mehta, 2013). Considering the preparation of teachers more broadly in Arizona, the lack of standardization between institutions, organizations and programs that train teachers problematize this notion of social closure, particularly exacerbated by the large presence of online universities (e.g. University of Phoenix) and alternative certification programs (e.g. TFA), in addition to traditional programs at community colleges and universities (Moore, 2012, 2014). Specific to EL education, the ADE attempted to regulate teacher training through SEI endorsement requirements for institutions of higher education, which has resulted in staunch misalignment between the ADE curricular framework and ELD settings as well as the classes carried out in practice (Arias, 2012; Moore, 2012, 2014). In a pointed illustration of the problematic nature of the state's attempt to socially close the profession of EL teaching through the SEI endorsement, participating teachers in this study received initial training from TFA and received a portion of the SEI endorsement via an online course. Teachers Paula, Tammie and Annie each recounted initially entering Greenwood classrooms without knowing the meaning of the 'ELD' acronym, as well as recalling no specific preparation or knowledge to work with ELs.

With the wide array of qualifications falling within Arizona's label of *highly qualified* teachers (ADE, 2008, 2014), prepared through a variety of approaches and ideologies of teacher preparation, no consensus has emerged across layers and players regarding *what practitioners need to know* to teach in ELD settings. In contrast to teaching as a semi-profession, Mehta (2013: 24) contended, 'Stronger professions possess... a well-developed knowledge base the practitioners are required to possess'. In fact, across the history of American education, stakeholders have lacked consensus on the substantive knowledge about subjects being taught, pedagogical knowledge about how to teach and pedagogical content knowledge about how students learn (Mehta, 2013; Shulman, 1986).

In EL education in Arizona, findings from this study indicated the differing and often contradictory perceptions of players involved in teacher training regarding pertinent knowledge and skills for EL teachers. For example, whereas state and district administrators described teacher training focused on the English language, specifically knowledge of grammar and discrete language skills, teacher educators emphasized pedagogical content knowledge on how to support language development in content instruction. For teachers in this study who moved through various teacher-training layers (e.g. TFA, district trainings guided by ADE priorities, university coursework), their self-described unpreparedness for the ELD classroom context connected to the lack of consensus on the needed knowledge base for teaching ELs. See Table 8.2 for an overview of study findings related to teacher knowledge for ELs.

As previously described, TFA has operated in the US as an alternative path to teaching certification, targeting non-education majors from top colleges and universities, providing them with five weeks of summer training and placing them in high-need urban and rural settings (TFA, 2014a). For the teachers in this study, along with others in the JESD, TFA provided initial preparation prior to entering ELD classrooms. The 5-week summer institute for corps members placed in Phoenix and 51 other regions centered on pedagogical knowledge about how to teach by setting high expectations and planning five-step lessons to demonstrate significant gains for all students (Farr, 2010; TFA, 2014b). Despite the direct correlation between TFA regions and school districts with high populations of ELs, the nature and needs of instruction for this sub-group remain consistently outside the organization's preparatory curriculum (Heineke & Cameron, 2013; Hopkins & Heineke, 2013). Absent from the TFA summer institute have been both substantive knowledge about ELD and pedagogical content knowledge on how students learn language. Consistent with previous research (Heineke & Cameron, 2011, 2013), corps members in the present study entered classrooms as native English speakers but had no other prerequisite knowledge of ELD, as evidenced by teachers' unfamiliarity with the ELD acronym. Similarly, participants did not recall preparation related to ELs, perhaps because the 90-minute, scripted EL-focused summer session (a) allotted only six minutes to second language acquisition and (b) focused heavily on teaching strategies with

Table 8.2 Players' perceptions of pertinent practitioner knowledge

Practitioner knowledge	Teach for America	Public instruction	Higher education
Substantive content knowledge of subject being taught (ELD)	n/a	Emphasis on teachers' knowledge of grammar and language skills	n/a
Pedagogical knowledge about how to teach English learners	High expectations and five-step lesson plan to teach all students	Compliance with instructional blocks by discrete language skill	Sheltered instructional strategies for teaching academic content
Pedagogical content knowledge of how students learn language	n/a	n/a	Second language acquisition theories

the erroneous equation of ELs to students with special needs (Hopkins & Heineke, 2013).

After initial teacher preparation (e.g. TFA), the next point of contact was often with the ADE's approach and ideology to preparing teachers for ELD settings. Players working at public school districts and charter schools received training directly from OELAS administrators, and district-level administrators then used similar training techniques to prepare teachers for ELD instruction within the mandated model. In both the state- and district-level trainings described by participants in this study – including the perspectives of both the providers and receivers of the trainings at the ADE, charter schools, school districts and classrooms – the focus of teacher knowledge relied heavily on substantive content knowledge of ELD, specifically targeting teachers' knowledge of grammar and discrete language skills (ADE, 2008, n.d.; Clark, 1999, 2009). With the staunch focus on building teachers' knowledge of discrete language skills, these trainings included minimal pedagogical knowledge, stating instead implicitly and directly that teaching ELs strictly required compliance with state policy, such as the use of ELP standards and the required blocks of skill-based instruction. ADE-guided trainings also left out pedagogical content knowledge specific to how students learn language, as Kevin Clark's time-on-task philosophy appeared to answer any questions related to how students learned via ELD instruction (ADE, 2007; Clark, 2009; Krashen et al., 2007).

For teachers and teacher preparation, building practitioners' knowledge includes a variety of programs and tracks through institutions of higher education in Arizona, including 4-year universities, community colleges and for-profit universities. For the teacher participants in this study, university coursework to satisfy the state-required SEI endorsement followed their initial teacher preparation and preliminary training on the ELD model. Unlike TFA and ADE teacher training that equated ELs to students with special needs (Hopkins & Heineke, 2013) or learning English through time on task (ADE, 2007; Clark, 2009), respectively, findings from this study indicated that university-based teacher educators provided the sole focus on pedagogical content knowledge on how students learn language, drawing from second language acquisition theory and research. As teacher educators Frank and Wendy described in this study, their preparation of teachers was aligned to and drew from EL and bilingual education scholarship, particularly how students learned a second language as connected to their first and the need to embed ELs with mainstream peers to scaffold language development in content area instruction. Extant literature by Arizona scholars and teacher educators has confirmed this focus on second language acquisition theory and research as central to preparing quality educators of ELs (Arias, 2012; Markos & Arias, 2014), yet current practice in teacher preparation omits this foundational knowledge.

In addition to preparing teachers for pedagogical content knowledge on how students learn language, institutions of higher education also emphasize pedagogical knowledge about how to teach ELs and substantive content knowledge of ELD; however, these often contrasted with those bodies of knowledge presented by other layers and players involved in teacher training (Moore, 2012, 2014). Guided by the ADE curricular framework for SEI endorsement coursework (ADE, 2005, 2011), paired with the content-based EL teaching strategies that participants in this study considered to be good practice, teacher educators focused the bulk of teacher training on sheltered instructional strategies for how to provide ELs access to academic content instruction (Arias, 2012; Markos & Arias, 2014). Despite following the policy regulations and curricular requirements written by the ADE, this focus on content-based language learning represented staunch misalignment between teacher education and the ADE's approach to pedagogical knowledge about how to teach ELs. By emphasizing sheltered teaching in content areas rather than skill-based blocks of language instruction, this also led to differing approaches to substantive content knowledge, in that SEI coursework did not require any content related to grammar and other discrete language skills (ADE, 2005, 2011).

Limited qualifications to teach in ELD classrooms, in conjunction with conflicting messages across stakeholders and misaligned bodies of knowledge related to EL teaching and learning, resulted in a lack of common norms and standards of good practice (Mehta, 2013). In Greenwood, district and school leaders hired and placed underprepared novices in ELD classrooms, where they remained professionally isolated from their colleagues in general education settings due to the unique nature of the instructional mandates. Additionally, teachers described having to answer to multiple mentors and to different organizations with conflicting conceptions of language policy in practice. For example, TFA insisted upon significant gains as measured by standardized tests of academic content, whereas the ADE and district monitored for compliance with policies and use of ELP standards (ADE, 2008, n.d.; Farr, 2012). Exacerbated by other issues, such as poor teacher pay and the limited temporal commitments of TFA (i.e. a 2-year service commitment), professional isolation has resulted in consistent ELD teacher attrition (Heineke & Cameron, 2011, 2013; Heineke *et al.*, 2014). The low and declining levels of teacher professionalism in Arizona may also connect to the limited role of teachers' unions in this right-to-work state, as educators lack the collective bargaining rights to insist on higher pay and improved work conditions.

Despite the proliferation of ELD teaching as a semi-profession in contemporary language policy in practice with the shift to the *English as prerequisite for learning* paradigm, the lack of teacher professionalization both nationally and locally has fueled the cycles of rationalization across the history of EL education in Arizona. Mehta (2013) asserted,

In the absence of a respected knowledge base, clear standards for how to do the work, extensive training of new practitioners, and consistency in outcomes, education has left itself exceedingly vulnerable to external movements that seek to shape and control schooling and teachers' work. In a nutshell, failed professionalization breeds external rationalization. (Mehta, 2013: 28)

Across the US, macro-level policymakers and their network of strategically aligned external stakeholders have maintained power over official policy regulations, rationalizing the need for top-down reforms over the bottom-up professionalization of teaching and teachers. In Arizona, macro-level players have utilized official language policies to decrease the qualifications and corresponding knowledge base to teach ELs, including the purposive redaction of bilingual teacher certification standards to pass Senate Bill 1160 in 1984 (Sacken & Medina, 1990) or the significant reduction of required teacher credentials from the 18-credit-hour ESL endorsement to the 6-credit-hour SEI endorsement following Proposition 203 in 2000 (de Jong *et al.*, 2010; Hopkins, 2012; Lillie *et al.*, 2012; Murri *et al.*, 2012; Rios-Aguilar *et al.*, 2012a). By failing to professionalize teaching through high standards and a well-developed knowledge base rather than prepare and empower the central players in language policy in practice, the rationalization merry-go-round of EL education continues.

The political lens: Institutional vantage and leverage points in language policy

Within the broad conceptualization of teaching as a semi-profession (Mehta, 2013) – and particularly ELD teaching – Arizona language policy values and prioritizes macro-level players' viewpoints over those of micro-level educators engaged in daily practice with ELs. Heedless of the requests and pleas from teachers and leaders in local communities, task force members and others who strategically aligned themselves to the policy paradigm espoused the power to influence EL education in Arizona (Haver, 2013; Lawton, 2012). As opposed to conceptualizing and involving local players as part of the solution, a powerful few implemented top-down restrictions to 'fix' classroom instruction for students labeled as ELs. Despite this exclusive network maintaining power via top-down decision-making at the macro level, local educators indeed have voices and roles in educational policy in practice, as evidenced by the findings in this study. Recognizing and aiming to obliterate this agency, Arizona politicians attempted to silence public school teachers and leaders and prevent them from entering into any political or policy-focused dialogue; in this unsuccessful legislation, state lawmakers wanted to restrict educators' voices on statewide educational issues, which typically run counter to the conservative viewpoints of those in power (SB 1172, 2015).

Previous scholarship in the field has consistently demonstrated that individuals with political authority and power attempt to influence language use by guiding and orchestrating language policy and planning (e.g. Ricento, 2000; Ricento & Hornberger, 1996; Schmidt, 2000; Shohamy, 2006; Spolsky, 2004). In Arizona language policy, scholars have specifically tied power to money (i.e. the citizens' initiative of Proposition 203 funded by Ron Unz; Combs, 2012) or position (i.e. educational and political elite guiding legislation; Lawton, 2012), but beneath the political funds and networks driving educational policy, culture has constructed and shaped power. In other words, specific individuals connected to the language ideology and policy paradigm within a particular context appear to hold all the cards (Mehta, 2013). In Arizona language policy in practice, unfalteringly grounded in the English monolingual ideology (Crawford, 2000; Valdéz, 2001), present study findings indicated a dichotomized power structure based on English proficiency. When considering the players making macro-level decisions in state education and government, one can see the prioritization of White, native English speakers – particularly those who have aligned themselves with the policy paradigm and corresponding skill-based ELD instructional policy.

Despite the powerful network of macro-level players who utilized policy paradigms and regulations in attempt to prescribe language use in Arizona classrooms, findings indicated the agency of local educators who made policy decisions in daily practice to foster the learning of ELs. Overall, this study sought to understand the holistic landscape of language policy in practice by exploring the perspectives and experiences of various layers and players engaged in the daily work of EL education (Hornberger & Johnson, 2007; Levinson & Sutton, 2001; Menken & García, 2010; Ricento & Hornberger, 1996). All demonstrating agency, players utilized distinct *policy vantage points*, as reflected in their perceptions of EL education; and *policy leverage points*, described through individual and collaborative experiences with appropriating language policy in practice. Mehta (2013: 31) explained, 'Fights over policy are due not only to differences in interest or values but also to the different institutional vantage points at which the contesting actors sit'. Similar to Mehta's exposition of distinct vantage points between policymakers and local educators within federal educational policy, present findings indicated that different institutional vantage points led to varying understandings of the issues and challenges of ELD policy in practice. Whereas vantage points provided an important lens to consider perspectives from various layers, leverage points described by policy players emphasized on-the-ground experiences in carrying out and shaping language policy in practice in the complex sociocultural context of Arizona.

When considering policy vantage points, distinction has emerged between the perspectives of (a) those engaged in daily educational practice within a local community, such as Greenwood; and (b) those engaged in statewide efforts impacting multiple districts and schools. Mehta (2013) described the historical pattern of differing perspectives between macro-level policymakers and micro-level educators with this insight:

> Whether one sits on the right or left of the aisle is less important that whether one spends one's days in the schoolhouse or the statehouse.... Policymakers are, by definition, responsible for many schools and sit at a considerable distance from them. Teachers and principals are responsible for a single school and sit inside it. The result is that the two groups have different ways of seeing. Policymakers see general properties of schools, things that can be counted and measured from afar. School people see the particulars; they may know little to nothing about the school landscape as a whole, but they know much, including much that is not easily measured, about the schools in which they sit. (Mehta, 2013: 31)

Findings from this study indicated the differing problem definitions between players, such as the macro-level focus on student segregation as a conceptual critique of ELD model versus the micro-level focus on teacher attrition as a practical challenge occurring in schools. Additionally, state legislators and community leaders approached educational policies broadly, whereas local players emphasized the immediate impact on daily practice in ELD classrooms. Even those macro-level players who were once teachers, including Esther, Chris, Senator Ray and Representatives Dua and Rex, utilized macro-level policy vantage points, demonstrating lengthy temporal and conceptual separation from their former positions.

As evidenced by macro-level players' lack of knowledge around significant policy issues occurring on the ground, such as ELD teacher attrition as well as the prioritization of seemingly inconsequential educational policies in content-devoid ELD classrooms (i.e. the CCS), these broadest-level individuals' institutional vantage points often remained detached from the daily realities of language policy in practice. Nevertheless, these state education and government players guided the top-down rationalization and implementation of Arizona language policy through their far-reaching policy leverage points, privileging the decontextualized perspectives from the statehouse over the schoolhouse (Mehta, 2013: 31).

This study's findings demonstrated that all players across layers made active decisions about the implementation of language policy in practice, including classroom teachers, school leaders and district administrators. Nevertheless, EL Task Force members and state administrators maintained control over the formal policy regulations and guidelines that aimed to manage teachers' and students' language use in schools across the state. In this way, the overall prioritization of the perspectives of a small and powerful network of politically powerful individuals demonstrated the amplification of appropriation, where decisions of macro-level players influenced the broader scope of EL education (Johnson & Freeman, 2010; Levinson & Sutton, 2001; Menken, 2008). The prioritization of decontextualized perspectives did not come without cost, as demonstrated by what task force member Pat described in retrospect as the 'unintended consequences' of macro-level policy decisions, such as the state mandate resulting in long-term ELs in homogenously grouped classrooms devoid of content (ADE, 2008) or the federal litigation that resulted in vast increases in labeled ELs placed in and returned to ELD classrooms (OCR, 2012).

Despite official policy regulations prioritizing the decontextualized perspectives far removed from ELD classrooms, local players utilized their own leverage points to implement policy in practice to support the learning of ELs. Some of these are evident in teachers working to integrate language skills across the 4-hour block, school leaders coaching teachers to design separate sets of lesson plans or district administrators finding space to train parents to maintain students' bilingualism; in cases like these, the individual actions of local policy players interrupted the top-down mandates for discrete skill instruction. Additionally, local educators collaborated across layers to provide what they perceived as appropriate education of ELs, such as the integration of academic content topics into language blocks.

Overall, findings indicated that classroom teachers, school leaders and district administrators utilized their unique local policy vantage and leverage points to interpret and appropriate language policy in daily practice in their specific educational context to promote and foster the education of ELs. With this current study and previous research demonstrating the central and active role of local players in language policy (Brat & Cain, 2012; Combs et al., 2005; Heineke, 2015; Heineke & Cameron, 2011, 2013; Hornberger & Johnson, 2007; Menken, 2008; Menken & García, 2010), it begs the questions: Why not embrace the role of the local educator in language policy in practice? Why not focus efforts to prepare teachers and leaders to make informed decisions, grounded in a strong knowledge base on EL teaching and learning?

Macro-level attempts to design static and restrictive policies to prescribe practice for local educators notwithstanding, paired with efforts to implement these policies through threats and fears regarding non-compliance, players in this study utilized distinct vantage points and leverage points to make meaning and appropriate policy in practice. Mehta (2013: 270) has asserted the failure of American education is partly due to unremitting efforts 'to solve a problem of professional practice by bureaucratic means'. Indeed, the ways in which players visualized educational improvement have varied across layers, typically dichotomized between those who envision solutions from the top down as compared with the bottom up: Should daily educational practices be guided by macro-level control over local settings or by the commitment of those working with children and adolescents in classrooms and schools? Does meaningful reform and change in education happen when teachers comply with top-down policy or when they focus on supporting unique and diverse students learning in classrooms? As stakeholders look to positively influence the education of ELs, the agency of players across layers must be recognized, particularly the policy practices occurring at the center of the language policy onion (Hornberger & Johnson, 2007; Ricento & Hornberger, 1996). Through a shared commitment to the professionalization of teaching rather than continued attempts to restrict language use through official regulations, policy players can embrace the complexity of language policy in practice and improve EL education.

Discussion: Language Policy Across (P)layers

Drawing from the perspectives and experiences of those engaged in language policy work from classrooms to the Capitol, findings indicated that the decisions made across layers and players interacted and influenced EL education in daily practice. Whereas macro-level stakeholders attempted to prescribe EL instruction through top-down mandates and insistence on statewide compliance, micro-level educators actively made decisions when implementing language policy in daily practice in diverse and complex classroom settings. In this latest cycle of rationalization of Arizona language policy, state players continued the historical trend of reforming reforms or attempting to compensate for past bad policies with worse policies. The current *one-size-fits-all* language policy conveys an 'allure of order' (Mehta, 2013: 1), where macro-level players perceive restrictive mandates as the magic potion to fix EL education in Arizona. Nonetheless, this study has demonstrated the complexity of language policy in practice within presumed restrictive contexts, which has implications for the instruction of EL students as well as the related preparation of teachers. To stop the cycles of rationalization, policymakers, educators and other stakeholders must embrace the complexity of language policy layers and players and therefore recognize the detriments of unilateral policy regulations when attempting to positively affect educational change for ELs.

Using historical, ideological, pedagogical and political lenses on the findings, in this chapter, I argued for the need to shift the policy paradigm in EL education in Arizona. A focus on enriching and empowering those at the center of language policy – *the professionalization of the classroom teacher of ELs* – is warranted and long overdue (Hornberger & Johnson, 2007; Mehta, 2013; Ricento & Hornberger, 1996). The trend of enacting sweeping, across-the-board, top-down education reforms to try and resolve problems cannot continue; stakeholders must focus resources on *teacher professionalization* to positively influence education and move beyond rationalization. That is, to improve the education of ELs in a meaningful way, we must move away from top-down policies and pressures and instead focus on the bottom-up professionalization of the teachers who engage in daily work with ELs, aiming toward recruiting those with deep knowledge and commitment to the field of teaching culturally and linguistically diverse students. Describing this issue in the larger context of educational reform in the US, Mehta (2013) explained,

> The people we draw into teaching are *less than our most talented*; we give them short or nonexistent training and equip them with little relevant knowledge; we send many of them to schools afflicted by high levels of poverty and segregation; and when they don't deliver the results we seek, we increase external pressure and accountability, hoping that we can do on the back end *what we failed to create on the front end*. (Mehta, 2013: 7) (emphasis added)

9 Looking Forward: Recommendations for English Learner Education

Eight years removed from the initial implementation of English Language Development (ELD) instruction in Arizona classrooms, the political and policy context has shifted with the election of a new governor and State Superintendent of Public Instruction as well as the shift in responsibility of the ELD model from the task force to the State Board of Education (HB 2425, 2013). Sworn into office in January 2015, new Arizona governor Doug Ducey promptly cut public education funding to yield one of the lowest states for per-pupil funding in the nation (Cochran, 2015) and increased the budget for private organizations, including Teach for America (TFA). Educators have left Arizona by the thousands (Strauss, 2015) – not least because of conservative attempts through state legislation to prevent educators from publicly sharing political viewpoints, paired with the lowest teacher salaries in the US – leaving a dire teacher shortage across the state. After the former State Superintendent did not re-run for office amid racist online blog comments targeting Spanish-speaking Latinos (Hendley, 2014; Longo, 2014), the new official, who ran on the platform of eliminating the Common Core Standards (CCS) from Arizona schools, took the reins.

Meanwhile, the Board of Education approved preliminary 'refinements to the SEI [Structured English Immersion] models', which school districts and charter schools can begin to implement in the 2015–2016 school year (State of Arizona, 2014). In elementary settings, English learners (ELs) must still receive four hours of skill-based instruction, but teachers can integrate the hourly blocks of writing and grammar as well as those for reading, oral conversation and vocabulary. Once ELs reach intermediate proficiency on the Arizona English Language Learner Assessment (AZELLA), the 4-hour block can be reduced to three hours. In secondary settings, EL coordinators may decide to reduce the 4-hour requirements by two hours for ELs testing at intermediate proficiency when deemed appropriate for the individual student. Unfortunately, overarching problems with the language policy in practice – including student segregation and stigmatization, limited content instruction and native language supports, misaligned and compliance-focused teacher training and consistent ELD teacher attrition – remain off the radar for those in power at the current language policy table.

Shift Policy Paradigm	Strengthen the Profession
☐ Go beyond tweaking policy	☐ Raise teaching qualifications
☐ Start with interests of students	☐ Define knowledge and skills
☐ Integrate language & content	☐ Prepare responsive teachers
☐ Consider role of native language	☐ Foster support & collaboration
☐ Prioritize local policy lenses	☐ Prioritize teacher retention

Figure 9.1 Recommendations for English learner education

Situated in both the historical and contemporary context of Arizona education, the findings of this study can support the discussion as policy players look to solve the state's educational woes, specifically focused on changes to language policy and the education of ELs. Drawing from the holistic picture of language policy in practice, players' perspectives and experiences can inform the policy dialogue and spotlight the practical realities and challenges, particularly in the daily work of educating ELs in local communities. In addition to informing the next shift in language policy in Arizona, educational stakeholders from the US and around the world might also use the findings and recommendations to critically consider the education of ELs in their specific context.

Maintaining a stance on the critical importance of the perspectives and experiences of teachers in the classroom with ELs, I close with recommendations. These are organized through overarching principles to shift language policy in practice in Arizona and other contexts, including needed ideological shifts and actionable recommendations for how various players might contribute to change. Envisioning meaningful change to EL education as occurring across layers and players, I emphasize the involvement of and collaboration between all language policy players in two primary areas: Collectively, players must *shift the policy paradigm* and *strengthen the teaching profession*. See Figure 9.1 for an outline of recommendations for EL education described in this chapter.

Recommendation Area # 1: Shift the Language Policy Paradigm

To improve the education of ELs in Arizona and elsewhere, stakeholders must push beyond the language policy paradigms that have historically guided US policy-related discussions and decisions (Mehta, 2013). As evidenced by the recent dialogue in Arizona focused on changing mandates from 4 to 3 hours of ELD instruction, the *English as prerequisite for learning* paradigm continues to drive the policy discussion and restricts the range of possible solutions. In this section, I set forth recommendations for policy players in Arizona and other educational contexts to critically consider the paradigms implicitly informing and driving official language policies to open opportunity for decisive changes to EL education. A paradigm shift is called for: Players must go beyond tweaking policy, consistently act with students' interests first, integrate language and academic content in EL instruction, consider the roles of native languages in development and academic achievement and prioritize *local* – as opposed to state – policy perspectives.

Shift the language policy paradigm: Go beyond tweaking language policy

Meaningful change in the education of ELs must come from collaborative and creative deliberation grounded in educational theory and research rather than patchwork efforts that tweak or dust off and repackage previously unsuccessful reforms. Findings from this study indicate that policy players negotiated and appropriated policy within the monolingual ideology and *English as prerequisite for learning* paradigm, using the 4-hour skill-based block to mediate and regulate decisions in practice. Often unbeknown to the players themselves, language ideologies and paradigms shape the decisions and actions of policy in practice (Crawford, 2000; Fairclough, 2003; Gee, 2000; Mehta, 2013; Ricento, 2000; Shohamy, 2006; Spolsky, 2004). Perhaps during the Arizona Board of Education's review of the ELD program model, representatives across layers must come to the table to share perspectives, experiences and solutions. After recognizing and discussing the implications of language policy in practice, stakeholders must return to established educational theory and practice to move beyond tweaking the existing policy. In addition to state and local educators engaging in policy dialogue, state legislators should reclaim their agency in the educational policy process, drafting and passing legislation that does not limit the possibilities for practitioners to provide effective education for ELs. When stakeholders critically consider and shift the language policy paradigm, purposeful and positive transformation of EL education can result.

Shift the language policy paradigm: Act for students' best interests

Every child deserves equal access to an excellent education that celebrates, targets and incorporates his or her unique strengths and needs to foster learning (EEOA, 1974). In this study, players experienced myriad challenges in practice caused by official policy regulations that segregated students labeled as ELs in ELD classrooms, including social stigma and isolation, negative self-image, long-term placement in skill-based settings and lack of content knowledge and learning. Extant literature confirms these negative social, emotional, linguistic and academic implications of separating ELs from English-proficient peers (Faltis & Arias, 2012; Gándara & Orfield, 2012; García, 2011). In contrast, when ELs' funds of knowledge are valued and incorporated into classroom curricula and instruction, EL and non-EL students engage and achieve at greater levels (González *et al.*, 2005; Moll, 1990; Moll *et al.*, 1992; Moll & González, 1997). Language policy dialogue must maintain students' best interests at the center, heeding what research and practice indicate is integral to positive social, emotional, linguistic and academic development and achievement (Heineke *et al.*, 2012; Herrera, 2010; Wrigley, 2000). Central to their commitment to education, all players must question the motivations behind top-down policy demands, using their agency and positions to instead consider and advocate for the needs of students. To improve the education of ELs, policy players across layers must prioritize the interests of this large and growing population rather than those powerful few who stand to benefit politically or financially.

Shift the language policy paradigm: Integrate content and language instruction

All ELs must have equitable access to academic content learning across their educational experiences, regardless of school setting or program model. As evidenced in Greenwood, local educators consistently toil with the consequences of extensive learning time devoid of content, particularly long-term ELs who spend multiple years in ELD classrooms receiving only skill-based English instruction. Previous theory and research substantiate that ELs learn content and language simultaneously when engaged in meaningful academic tasks that promote both cognitive and linguistic development while maximizing students' engagement and motivation to learn (Cummins, 1981, 2000; Faltis, 2006; Fillmore, 1991; Krashen, 1999; Mackey, 2007). Despite continued debate in Arizona and across the US, the New Standards may be a leverage point to insist on providing ELs with access to academic content concurrent to language development (Heritage *et al.*, 2014; Walqui & Heritage, 2012; VanLier & Walqui, 2012). Although individuals can accomplish this integration through policy appropriation, collaborative efforts across layers are needed to promote student achievement. In local schools and districts, vertical planning can ensure consistent effort to integrate rigorous content instruction across grade levels and content areas. In state education and government, players must consider changes to the program model to merge content with language development. By ensuring all students have access to rigorous content curriculum and instruction, educators and other policy players set ELs up for long-term success in school and in life.

Shift the language policy paradigm: Consider the role of students' native languages

Students enter schools with ample funds of knowledge and resources for learning, perhaps the largest of which is their native language (Edelsky, 1986; Hudelson, 1987; Moll & González, 1997; Ruiz, 1984). Arizona language policy specifies that native language support can be used in Arizona classrooms and schools, although participants in this study interpreted the policy in distinct ways. Whereas a handful of participants in the classroom, district, and university utilized agency to incorporate native language in their practice, others – even former bilingual teachers and supporters – dismissed native language as an option. Nonetheless, decades of educational scholarship verify that tapping into students' native languages is of utmost importance in fostering English and content learning (e.g. Cummins, 2000; Edelsky, 1986; Escamilla, 1999; Hudelson, 1987; Jiménez et al., 1996). Further, bilingualism leads to various social, cultural, educational cognitive, linguistic, economic and political benefits (see de Jong, 2011). Because of the monolingual ideology that pervades both Arizonan and American society, stakeholders must first deconstruct the language-as-problem mindset that frames ELs with a deficit-based lens (Ruiz, 1984). Then, whether in bilingual or monolingual settings, educators must be familiar with the language of the policy itself – not others' interpretations of policy – to define the role and use of native language in EL teaching and learning (Combs et al., 2005; Heineke, 2015). Pushing beyond work within the confines of extant policy, legislators can re-write laws to better reflect the 21st-century multilingual world and allow opportunity for high-quality and effective education for ELs. When policy and practice embrace and build on students' assets, educators and other policy players create productive and inclusive learning environments for all children.

Shift the language policy paradigm: Prioritize local language policy in practice

Any changes in language policy must prioritize the perspectives and experiences of those it most immediately affects, including students, parents and teachers. Findings from this study indicate distinct disconnected policy perceptions of macro- and micro-level layers, with the decontextualized perspectives of macro-level players influencing official language policy as well as repercussions in local practice. Extant literature confirms that classroom teachers play active roles in language policy in practice, directly mediating and influencing the educational experiences of ELs (Hornberger & Johnson, 2007; Ricento & Hornberger, 1996). Additionally, parents and families of ELs must be integrated in meaningful ways to support and advocate for their children's education (Ramírez et al., 1991). When engaged in any educational policy conversation, local educators, students, parents and families must be brought to the table, and their perspectives and experiences should be prioritized and incorporated into the decision-making process. In this way, macro-level stakeholders must recognize and negotiate how prevailing ideologies and paradigms shape the nature of the debate, ensuring local voices are not – unintentionally or intentionally – silenced or marginalized (Mehta, 2013). See Table 9.1 for possible leverage points for various policy players. By conceptualizing students, parents and teachers as active participants in language policy rather than passive policy targets, all stakeholders maintain a voice in transforming EL education.

Table 9.1 Possible leverage points by policy players

Policy players	Possible leverage points
Classroom teachers	• Know federal and state laws to purposefully appropriate policy in practice to advocate for and support student learning. • Seek out professional development opportunities beyond minimum requirements of states, districts or organizations, such as national conferences (e.g. National Association of Bilingual Education).
School leaders	○ Foster school culture and environment that celebrates language diversity and learning and demonstrates value and inclusive practice for EL students, families and teachers. • Build opportunities for collaboration into the school schedule and calendar and provide teachers with the needed structures and materials to engage in professional learning communities.
District administrators	• Prioritize the hiring of teachers with extensive EL-specific knowledge and skills, followed by appropriate compensation and support. • Partner with school leaders, teacher educators and community organizers to serve as a clearinghouse for resources and supports for teachers, parents and families of ELs.

(Continued)

Teach For America	• Extend teacher preparation for ELs in initial training and ongoing support, both targeting and integrating EL-related knowledge and skills into the organization's curriculum. • Delay placement of corps members in complex EL settings until they have demonstrated the necessary knowledge, skills and mindsets to positively impact EL student achievement.
Teacher educators	• Prepare linguistically responsive teachers who are knowledgeable about policy and their active roles in language policy in practice. • Extend teacher education for ELs beyond state-mandated requirements, considering ways to target and integrate EL-related content throughout teacher education programs.
State administrators	• Facilitate cross-layer discussions with teachers, leaders, students, parents and teacher educators to collaboratively craft policy that builds on research and responds to local practice. • Lead efforts to develop professional teaching standards to outline the core knowledge and skills needed for teachers to effectively meet the needs of linguistically diverse students.
State legislators	• Make regular visits to schools within constituencies, dialoging with teachers, leaders, students and parents regarding local-level successes and challenges in EL education. • Draft, support and advocate for legislation that serves the best interests of students, families and teachers.
Community leaders	• Engage parent and families in the policy discussion, preparing them as actors and advocates for effective EL education. • Serve as external partners that bring together networks of local educators and other stakeholders with the goal to share best practices and resources for EL education.
Students and families	• Ask school and district personnel about the rights of students, parents and families per federal and state laws regarding EL education. • Attend forums and events at the state and local level to advocate for equal access to educational opportunities and experiences.

Recommendation Area # 2: Strengthen the Teaching Profession

To improve EL education, a paradigm shift in language policy must be paired with prioritizing and strengthening the professionalism of EL teachers specifically and teaching generally (Mehta, 2013). Although the de-professionalization of teachers has plagued the broader US in recent years, Arizona has exacerbated the issue with all teachers and specifically teachers in ELD classrooms. To build teacher professionalism, we must move past the use of top-down policy mandates to prescribe classroom practice, recognizing teachers as policy *actors* rather than *targets* (Hornberger & Johnson, 2007; Levinson & Sutton, 2001; Ricento & Hornberger, 1996). This can be accomplished by raising the bar for teaching qualifications and what is considered truly *highly qualified* to teach ELs, defining a more standardized and consistent knowledge and skill base for teachers, responsibly preparing responsive teachers, ensuring that teachers feel supported and have a voice in collaboration and making EL teacher retention a priority – such that ELD classrooms no longer have a revolving door. In so doing, we can begin to deconstruct the deficit-based view of teachers and conceptualize the teacher as an invaluable expert professional.

Strengthen the teaching profession: Raise the qualifications for teachers of English learners

ELs require and deserve well-prepared, knowledgeable, effective teachers who can meet their unique and diverse needs and foster their learning and development. In this study, teachers entered the ELD classroom unprepared or underprepared, without the basic knowledge and skills to teach ELs despite being deemed *highly qualified* by state qualifications (ADE, 2014). Scholars highlight the classroom teacher as the primary in-school factor to foster or inhibit student achievement (Darling-Hammond, 2000; Haycock, 1998; Sanders & Rivers, 1996), particularly with marginalized sub-groups such as ELs (Gándara & Maxwell-Jolly, 2006). Further, teaching ELs is more than just good teaching: There is a very real need for additional knowledge and skills beyond general qualifications for general education settings specific to the developmental and academic needs of ELs (de Jong & Harper, 2005; Villegas & Lucas, 2002; Lucas *et al.*, 2008). In Arizona, the most effective teachers of ELs enter classrooms with extensive teacher preparation in ESL or bilingual education rather than the limited knowledge gleaned via a few hours of SEI coursework (de Jong *et al.*, 2010; Hopkins, 2012; Lillie *et al.*, 2012; Murri *et al.*, 2012; Rios-Aguilar *et al.*, 2012a). Stakeholders must insist on higher criteria for teachers of ELs. At the federal and state levels, policy players should raise the minimum requirements for teachers in EL settings, such as removing the intern certificate option and increasing EL-specific knowledge and skills, including specific training in second language acquisition (Hopkins & Heineke, 2013). In local schools and districts, leaders can set standards for EL teacher placement, looking beyond the *highly qualified* label to ensure appropriate preparation to meet the learning needs of students. These acts of social closure can raise the status of EL teaching at both the macro and micro levels, recognizing teachers as experts in supporting the learning and development of this large, growing and important sub-group of students (Mehta, 2013).

Strengthen the teaching profession: Define the knowledge and skills of an effective teacher

Learning a second language is a lengthy and complex process – particularly the English language, with its many irregularities and idiosyncrasies. *Mastering* such a language necessitates 4–10 years for learners to achieve proficiency and 7–9 years to catch up to native English-speaking peers on measures of academic achievement (Collier, 1989; Cummins, 2000; Hakuta *et al.*, 2000). *Teaching* those students who are engaged in acquiring a second language, as well as simultaneously adjusting to American schools and broader mainstream culture and learning academic content like mathematics, science and social studies, is equally as complex (de Jong, 2011; de Jong & Harper, 2005). Add on the myriad policies and demands on classroom teachers, including CCS and other policies, emphasis on standardized testing and high-stakes teacher evaluations, and we begin to see the deep and extensive knowledge base needed to negotiate policy in practice to effectively support the learning and development of a diverse array of students. This study evidenced the limited and misaligned knowledge base across policy players, particularly those engaged in teacher training and preparation – limited to the two-page curricular outline dictating the content of 90 hours of required EL teacher preparation (ADE, 2005, 2014) and misaligned in their disagreement over needed knowledge for effective EL teaching.

In the past two decades, educational and linguistic scholars have reiterated the need for teachers to possess core knowledge to support the teaching and learning of ELs, including language and linguistics, second language acquisition theory and EL-specific pedagogy (Lucas *et al.*, 2008; Valdés *et al.*, 2005; Villegas & Lucas, 2002). Drawing from national efforts to define a core knowledge base for EL teachers (Fenner & Kuhlman, 2012), states and communities must engage in collaborative efforts to outline the needed knowledge, skills, and mindsets possessed by effective and well-rounded teachers of ELs in specific educational contexts.

Tapping into the rich resources available across the layers and players in state-level education, administrators must bring teachers, leaders and teacher educators to the table to have active voices and roles to support this important dialogue and work toward identifying a set of mutually agreed upon skills and competencies that characterize master EL teachers. After shifting the language policy paradigm to allow a wider array of stakeholders at the table, local educators and scholars can contribute their vast knowledge, expertise and experience to push forward the profession of EL teaching (Arias, 2012; Combs *et al.*, 2005, 2012; Faltis & Arias, 2012; García, 2011; Lillie *et al.*, 2010, 2012; Lillie & Markos, 2011; Markos & Arias, 2014).

Strengthen the teaching profession: Prepare effective and responsive teachers for diverse contexts

In addition to a well-developed knowledge base, teachers must be adequately prepared to apply understandings in complex practical settings to support student learning, development and achievement. Novice ELD teachers in this study, who had undergone limited training and preparation, struggled to use prescriptive mandates and standardized tools in meaningful ways in diverse classroom contexts. Extant research has confirmed the ample diversity and heterogeneity of students with the EL label, such as native language, country of origin, circumstances of immigration, educational background and language and literacy abilities (see de Jong, 2011). Nonetheless, traditional approaches to teacher preparation and training tend to silo ELs into a homogenized group to provide teachers with one-size-fits-all strategies for the classroom (Heineke, 2014). In what Lucas and colleagues have termed *linguistically responsive practice*, teachers must be trained to apply the core knowledge base for EL teaching and learning to respond to students' specific abilities and needs within the complex realities of today's classrooms (Lucas *et al.*, 2008: 361; Villegas & Lucas, 2002: 20). When teachers recognize the diverse and unique assets, abilities and needs that individual students bring to the classroom, they can respond to provide targeted and rigorous instruction (Moll & González, 1997).

This shift away from the perception of unilateral implementation of prescriptive language policy in practice begins with the recognition of the diversity within the label of EL, followed by multifaceted efforts in teacher preparation and training across schools, districts, institutions of higher education and state education. Just as extant literature has demonstrated the harmful nature of segregating ELs from English-proficient peers in K-12 classrooms (Faltis & Arias, 2012; Gándara & Orfield, 2012; García, 2011), the explicit separation of 'EL' and 'mainstream' teaching methods in professional preparation and training exacerbates the silos and labels erroneously guiding practice in schools (Heineke, 2014). Teacher preparation efforts across layers must not uphold this dichotomy, whereby school professional development targets general education teachers while the district facilitates the EL-specific training. All players charged with educating teachers must consider how to prepare linguistically responsive educators, highly capable of applying their deep knowledge and skills in complex settings with students from diverse backgrounds within and beyond the EL label (Lucas *et al.*, 2008; Villegas & Lucas, 2002). When preparation provides a strong knowledge base for EL teaching and learning, paired with the skills and mindsets to implement effective instruction in practice in varied contexts with diverse learners, teachers can purposefully implement policy in practice by responding to students' unique strengths and needs.

Strengthen the teaching profession: Foster dynamic support and professional collaboration

Expert teachers' personal and professional development must continue after initial preparation, across careers and contexts, inclusive of site-specific support for teaching, ongoing opportunities for professional learning and collaboration that taps into the experiences and expertise of local policy players. As evidenced within and across schools in Greenwood, ELD teachers were typically isolated from their grade-level and school-site colleagues without consistent and targeted support from mentors, coaches and leaders. Working within the sociocultural paradigm, scholars recognize the pertinence of social interaction among teachers within the unique cultural contexts of schools and communities (Cochran-Smith & Lytle, 1999; McLaughlin & Talbert, 2006; Rogoff, 1994, 2003; Vygotsky, 1978; Wertsch, 1991). Moreover, there is efficacy in providing collaborative structures and supports for EL teacher learning, often broadly referred to as *professional learning communities* (PLCs; McLaughlin & Talbert, 2006), including teacher study groups (Clair, 1998; Heineke, 2009, 2015; Musanti & Pence, 2010), book clubs (Florio-Ruane, 2001; Rodgers & Mosely, 2008) and literature circles (Heineke, 2014; Martínez-Roldán & Heineke, 2011; Monroe-Baillargeon & Shema, 2010). In addition to these varied approaches to PLCs, collaborative action research promises to engage teachers and researchers in classroom-based inquiry focused on ELs (Burns, 2010; Cochran-Smith & Lytle, 1999).

Various layers and players must commit to the creative design and meaningful implementation of formal structures to sustain the dynamic support and professional collaboration for teachers of ELs. Within schools and districts, leaders must build the needed time, opportunity and structure for teachers to come together with colleagues, mentors and researchers to collaboratively learn and support one another (McLaughlin & Talbert, 2006). Across schools and districts, community organizers, state administrators and teacher educators can facilitate the sharing of best practices with a wider network of educators (Mehta, 2013). Above all, stakeholders must maintain that teachers' and students' needs are of central focus, constantly negotiating the top-down pressures and corresponding tendencies to focus on policy compliance or tie efforts to teacher evaluation (Heineke, 2015). To accomplish this, support and collaboration must hone in on student learning: whether engaged in PLCs, peer observation and coaching, collaborative instructional planning or classroom-based action research, educators must set goals and apply learning to positively influence the learning, development and achievement of students in classrooms (Cochran-Smith & Lytle, 1999; Little, 2002). When teachers engage in collaborative learning experiences that prioritize the local context and expertise, they continue to develop as high-quality teaching professionals and experts in supporting the students in their classrooms.

Strengthen the teaching profession: Prioritize the retention of master teachers of English learners

Finally, effective teachers must stay in classrooms serving ELs to positively influence the education of ELs over the long term. In the case of Greenwood, ELD teacher attrition emerged as the primary challenge on the ground in local schools and districts. The voluminous research base on teacher retention and attrition indicates this as a central problem across the US but particularly in schools with low-income and minority populations (e.g. Haberman, 2004; Hunt & Carroll, 2003; Leland & Murtadha, 2011). Teachers improve effectiveness with experience, most notably after two years of classroom experience; teacher attrition is detrimental to student achievement and has financial implications on local school districts (Barnes et al., 2007; Hawkins et al., 1998). EL teacher retention will no doubt be supported by implementing the above recommendations, including raising the qualifications and status of EL teachers; defining professional knowledge, responsive skills and asset-based mindsets for EL teaching; and building dynamic supports and collaboration for ongoing professional development. In addition, to demonstrate respect for and the status of EL teaching professionals, state and local players must consider increasing salaries and providing financial incentives to stay in classrooms, schools, districts and states. As a result, effective teachers remain in classrooms with the students who need and deserve their deep knowledge, expertise and experience.

Table 9.2 Guiding questions for collaborative policy conversations

Shift the policy paradigm	• What are our shared, long-term goals for the education of ELs? • How do current language policies contribute or deter from these long-term goals for the learning and development of ELs? • How do current language policies connect to and serve the best interests of EL students, parents and families? • How do other educational policies intersect and impact language policy (e.g. Common Core Standards)? • How do we provide ELs with equal educational opportunities and outcomes, including access to rigorous academic content? • What are the successes and challenges with local schools, districts and communities with regard to language policy in practice? • How can changes to language policy build upon successes and reduce the challenges to improve EL education? • How can theory and research inform changes to language policy to improve the education of ELs?
Strengthen the teaching profession	• How do we perceive the role of teachers in EL education? • Who are the teachers providing the education of ELs in classrooms and schools? • What are the qualifications that allow them to work with this important group of students? • How do we determine if teachers are successful in support EL student learning, development and achievement? • What are the needed knowledge, skills, and dispositions that teachers must possess to positively impact EL student learning? • How can we prepare and support teachers in a way that aligns with the theory and research for EL teaching and learning?

Conclusion

Lessons learned from this study have implications for all contexts and policy players with an interest in improving the education of ELs. As continued globalization and migration continues to diversify the linguistic landscape in every corner of the US, the situation in Arizona can serve as a place for others to begin conversations about language policy and EL education (Suárez-Orozco & Suárez-Orozco, 2001). The epicenter of the immigration debate in the US (Sandoval & Tambini, 2014), as well as the civil rights struggle for students to study their own cultural background and ethnicity (Cabrera *et al.*, 2014), Arizona's restrictive language policy and resulting skill-based content-devoid approach to the education of ELs must now take center stage in the public policy discussion (Gándara & Hopkins, 2010). Originally Mexican territory with residents predominantly speaking

Spanish and indigenous languages, Arizona has been engaged in EL education on a large scale for over 150 years (Milem *et al.*, 2013; Pickering, 1966). As stakeholders in other contexts with growing EL populations consider official language education policies to guide programs and practices in classrooms and schools, the case of Arizona presented in this text can serve to initiate productive dialogue on EL education. Considering the current state of Arizona education, characterized by poor student performance and rampant teacher attrition (Ushomirsky, 2013), stakeholders in other contexts must consider the repercussions of these cycles of rationalization and language policy decisions grounded in the monolingual ideologies that pervade American society (Crawford, 2000; Mehta, 2013; Valdéz, 2001).

Meaningful change is possible. As emphasized throughout this chapter, all layers and players must be committed to and involved in a dynamic collaborative process to shift policy and teaching paradigms to improve EL education. Stakeholders from local schools and districts, institutions of higher education, education-related organizations and government entities must come together to critically consider their active, interactive and interrelated roles with a critical lens on the effectiveness of policies in practice (Hornberger & Johnson, 2007; Johnson & Freeman, 2010; Ricento & Hornberger, 1996). See Table 9.2 for questions to begin collaborative policy conversations.

Players must collaborate to conduct research that investigates the implications of language policy in practice; however, researchers must consider the role of the policy paradigm in excluding their perspectives regardless of the results. In the case of Arizona, despite ample scholarship focused on the shortcomings of ELD (e.g. Arias & Faltis, 2012; Moore, 2014), official regulations have remained largely unchanged, demonstrating the power of the paradigm at regulating whose voices are heard in the broader discussion (Mehta, 2013). Whereas conceptual critiques can be dismissed and quantitative comparisons misconstrued, qualitative research can probe, profile and reveal the everyday realities of language policy in practice (McCarty, 2011; Menken & García, 2010). Within this vein of scholarship, I recommend *collaborative action research*, which brings together teachers and academics to explore and expose the complexities of daily practice. In addition to prioritizing the school-based experiences of students and teachers, classroom-based inquiry holds the potential to raise the status of local educators while bringing their vantage points on EL teaching and learning into the public and policy discussion (Burns, 2010; Cochran-Smith & Lytle, 1999; Mehta, 2013).

All US classrooms and schools have more cultural and linguistic diversity today than ever before, including a large and growing population of students labeled as ELs (Gándara & Hopkins, 2010; Shin & Kominski, 2011; USDOE, 2010). Despite the consistent growth of this population, most recently numbered at over 5.3 million across the country (National

References

Adebi, J. and Gándara, P. (2006) Performance of English language learners as a subgroup in large-scale assessment: Interaction of research and policy. *Educational Measurement: Issues and Practices 26*, 36–46.

Anderson, B. (1983) *Imagined Communities: Reflections on the Origin and Spread of Nationalism*: New York: Verso.

Aportela, A. and Laczko-Kerr, I. (2013). Oh, the places they'll go! Arizona public school choice and its impact on students. Phoenix, AZ: Center for Student Achievement. See http://azcharters.org/wp-content/uploads/2015/11/Revised-OhThePlacesTheyllGo_AZ-School-Choice-FNL.pdf (retrieved on 13 January 2015).

Arias, M.B. (2012) Language policy and teacher preparation: The implications of a restrictive language policy on teacher preparation. In M. Beatriz Arias and C. Faltis (eds) *Implementing Educational Language Policy in Arizona: Legal, Historical and Current Practices in SEI* (pp. 3–20). Bristol: Multilingual Matters.

Arizona Charter Schools Association (2015) *20 Years of Charters*. Phoenix, AZ: Author.

Arizona Charter Schools Association (2014) *Arizona Charter Schools: Support, Advocate, Lead*. Phoenix, AZ: Author.

Arizona Department of Education (2000) *Proposition 203*. See https://www.azed.gov/wp-content/uploads/PDF/PROPOSITION203.pdf (accessed 18 June 2009).

Arizona Department of Education (2005) Curricular framework for full Structured English Immersion (SEI) endorsement training. See http://www.azed.gov/english-language-learners/files/2011/10/seicurricularframework-completion.pdf (accessed 22 September 2015.)

Arizona Department of Education (2007) Arizona English Language Learners Task Force: Research summary and bibliography for Structured English Immersion program models. See https://cms.azed.gov/home/GetDocumentFile?id=55257a851130c008a0c55c0b (accessed 22 September 2015)

Arizona Department of Education (2008) Structured English Immersion frequently asked questions. See http://www.ade.state.az.us/oelas/sei/SEIModelsFAQs.doc (accessed 21 June 2009).

Arizona Department of Education (2011) Individualized language learner plan. See http://www.azed.gov/english-language-learners/files/2012/10/illp-guidance-document-complete-revised.pdf (accessed 7 October 2014).

Arizona Department of Education (2012) English language proficiency standards. See http://www.azed.gov/english-language-learners/files/2012/02/guidance-doc-finalized.pdf (accessed 7 October 2014).

Arizona Department of Education (2013) Procedure for identifying English language learners. See http://www.azed.gov/english-language-learners/files/2013/08/procedures-for-identifying-ell-studentsupdatejune2013-2.pdf (accessed 22 September 2015).

Arizona Department of Education (2014) Arizona highly qualified attestation form: Structured English Immersion classroom. See http://www.azed.gov/highly-qualified-professionals/files/2014/04/14-15-structured-english-immersion-teacher-attestation.pdf (accessed 7 October 2014).

Arizona Department of Education (2015a) State Board of Education. See http://www.azed.gov/state-board-education/ (accessed 22 September 2015).

Arizona Department of Education (2015b) State Superintendent of Education. See http://www.azed.gov/superintendent/ (accessed 22 September 2015).

Arizona Department of Education (2015c) About Arizona Department of Education. See http://www.azed.gov/about-ade/ (accessed 22 September 2015).

Arizona Department of Education (n.d.) Discrete skills inventory. See http://www.azed.gov/english-language-learners/files/2013/02/dsialllevels.pdf (accessed 7 October 2014).

Arizona Revised Statutes §§15-203 to 15-251

Arizona Revised Statutes §§ 15-751 to 15-754

August, D., Goldenberg, C. and Rueda, R. (2010) Restrictive state language policies: Are they scientifically based? In P. Gándara and M. Hopkins (eds) *Forbidden Language: English Learners and Restrictive Language Policies* (pp. 139–158). New York: Teachers College.

Baker, K. and de Kanter, A. (1983) Federal policy and the effectiveness of bilingual education. In K. Baker and A. de Kanter (eds) *Bilingual Education: A Reappraisal of Federal Policy* (pp. 33–86). Lexington, MA: Lexington Books.

Barnes, G., Crowe, E. and Schaefer, B. (2007) *The Cost of Teacher Turnover in Five School Districts: A Pilot Study*. Washington, DC: National Commission on Teaching and America's Future.

Bartlett, L. and Vavrus, F. (2014) Transversing the vertical case study: A methodological approach to studies of educational policy as practice. *Anthropology and Education Quarterly* 45, 131–147.

Bomer, R. and Maloch, B. (2011) Relating policy to research and practice: The Common Core Standards. *Language Arts* 89, 38–43.

Brat, K.R. and Cain, A.A. (2013) A delicate balance: The clandestine work of bilingual teachers of bilingual children in English-only borderlands classrooms. *Critical Inquiry in Language Studies* 10, 150–184.

Burns, A. (2010) *Doing Action Research in English Language Teaching: A Guide For Practitioners*. New York: Routledge.

Cabrera, N.L., Milem, J.F., Jaquette, O. and Marx, R.W. (2014) Missing the (student achievement) forest for all the (political) trees: Empiricism and the Mexican American studies controversy in Tucson. *American Educational Research Journal* 51, 1084–1118.

Cammarota, J. and Aguilera, M. (2012) 'By the time I get to Arizona': Race, language, and education in America's racist state. *Race, Ethnicity, and Education* 14, 485–500.

Carpenter, D., Ramírez, A. and Severn, L. (2006) Gap or gaps: Challenging the singular definition of the achievement gap. *Education and Urban Society* 39, 133–154.

Castañeda v. Pickard (1981) 648 F.2d 989, 1011. 5th Circuit.

Center for the Future of Arizona (2013) *The Arizona We Want 2.0*. Phoenix, AZ: Author.

Chimbutane, F. (2011) *Rethinking Bilingual Education in Postcolonial Contexts*. Bristol: Multilingual Matters.

City of Greenwood (2014) *Information for Tourists*.

Clair, N. (1998) Teacher study groups: Persistent questions in a promising approach. *TESOL Quarterly* 32, 465–492.

Clark, K. (1999) *From Primary Language Instruction to English Immersion: How Five California Districts Made the Switch*. Washington, DC: Research in English Acquisition and Development Institute.

Clark, K. (2009) The case for Structured English Immersion. *Educational Leadership* 66, 42–46.

Cobb, C.D. and Glass, G.V. (1999) Ethnic segregation in Arizona charter schools. *Education Policy Analysis Archives* 7, 1–39.

Cochran, J. (2015) Arizona school spending again near bottom of states. *The Arizona Republic*, 4 June.

Cochran-Smith, M. and Lytle, S.L. (1999) Relationships of knowledge and practice: Teacher learning in communities. *Review of Research in Education* 24, 249–305.

Collier, V.P. (1989) How long? A synthesis of research on academic achievement in a second language. *TESOL Quarterly* 23, 509–531.

Combs, M.C. (2012) Everything on its head: How Arizona's Structured English Immersion policy re-invents theory and practice. In M. Beatriz Arias and C. Faltis (eds) *Implementing Educational Language Policy in Arizona: Legal, Historical and Current Practices in SEI* (pp. 59–85). Bristol: Multilingual Matters.

Combs, M.C., Evans, C., Fletcher, T., Parra, E. and Jiménez, A. (2005) Bilingualism for the children: Implementing a dual-language program in an English-only state. *Educational Policy* 19, 701–728.

Combs, M.C., González, N. and Moll, L.C. (2011) US Latinos and the learning of English: The metonymy of language policy. In T.L. McCarty (ed.) *Ethnography and Language Policy* (pp. 185–203). New York: Routledge.

Crawford, J. (2000) *At War with Diversity: US Language Policy in an Age of Anxiety.* Clevedon: Multilingual Matters.

Crawford, J. and Krashen, S. (2007) *English Learners in American Classrooms: 101 Questions, 101 Answers.* New York: Scholastic.

Cummins, J. (1981) *Bilingualism and Minority-Language Children.* Toronto: OISE Press.

Cummins, J. (2000) *Language, Power, and Pedagogy: Bilingual Children in the Crossfire.* Clevedon: Multilingual Matters.

Darling-Hammond, L. (2000) Teacher quality and student achievement: A review of state policy evidence. *Education Policy Analysis Archives* 8 (1). See http://epaa.asu.edu/ojs/article/view/392/515 (accessed 9 March 2010).

Datnow, A. (2006) Connection in the policy chain: The "co-construction" of implementation in the comprehensive school reform. In M.I. Honig (ed.) *New Directions In Education Policy Implementation: Confronting Complexity* (pp. 105–124). Albany, NY: State of New York Press.

Datnow, A., Hubbard, L. and Mehan, H. (2002) *Extending Educational Reform: From One School to Many.* New York: Routledge.

Davis, K.A. (1994) *Language Planning in Multilingual Contexts: Policies, Communities, and Schools In Luxembourg.* Philadelphia, PA: John Benjamins.

de Jong, E.J. (2011) *Foundations for Multilingualism in Education: From Principles to Practice.* Philadelphia, PA: Caslon.

de Jong, E.J. and Harper, C.A. (2005) Preparing mainstream teachers for English language learners: Is being a good teacher good enough? *Teacher Education Quarterly* 32, 101–124.

de Jong, E.J., Arias, M.B. and Sánchez, M.T. (2010) Undermining teacher competencies: Another look at the impact of restrictive language policies. In P. Gándara and M. Hopkins (eds) *Forbidden Language: English Learners and Restrictive Language Policies* (pp. 118–138). New York: Teachers College.

Delisario, E.R. and Dunne, D.W. (2000) Ballot measures lead to heavy spending, lobbying. *Education World.* See http://www.education-world.com/a_issues/issues142.shtml (accessed 20 June 2009).

Duncan, A. (2011) A new approach to teacher education reform and improvement. Washington DC: Education Sector. See http://www.ed.gov/news/speeches/ (accessed 26 September 2009).

Echevarría, J., Short, K. and Vogt, S. (2013) *Making Content Comprehensible for English Learners: The SIOP Model.* Boston, MA: Allyn and Bacon.

Edelsky, C. (1986) *Writing in a Bilingual Program: Había Una Vez.* Norwood, NJ: Ablex.

EEOA (1974) *Equal Educational Opportunities Act.* 20 United States Code Section 1703.

Elfers, A.M. and Stritikus, T. (2014) How leaders build systems of support for classroom teachers working with English language learners. *Educational Administration Quarterly* 50, 305–344.

Erickson, F. (1986) Qualitative methods in research on teaching. In M. Wittrock (ed.) *Handbook of Research on Teaching* (3rd edn; pp. 119–161). New York: MacMillan.

Escamilla, K. (1999) Teaching literacy in Spanish. In R. De Veillar and J. Tinajero (eds) *The Power of Two Languages* (pp. 126–141). New York: Macmillan.

Fairclough, N. (2003) *Analysing Discourse: Textual Analysis for Social Research.* London: Routledge.

Faltis, C. (2006) *Teaching English Language Learners in Elementary School Communities: A Joinfostering Approach.* Upper Saddle River, NJ: Pearson.

Faltis, C. and Arias, M.B. (2012) Research-based reform in Arizona: Whose evidence counts for applying the Castenada test to structured English immersion models? In M. Beatriz Arias and C. Faltis (eds) *Implementing Educational Language Policy In Arizona: Legal, Historical and Current Practices in SEI* (pp. 21–38). Bristol: Multilingual Matters.

Farr, S. (2010) *Teaching as Leadership: The Highly Effective Teacher's Guide to Closing the Achievement Gap.* San Francisco, CA: Jossey-Bass.

Fenner, D. S. and Kuhlman, N. (2012) Preparing teachers of English language learners: Practical applications of the preK-12 TESOL professional standards. Annapolis Junction, MD: TESOL Press.

Fillmore, L.W. (1991) When learning a second language means losing the first. *Early Childhood Research Quarterly* 6, 323–346.

Fishman, J.A. (1979) Bilingual education, language planning, and English. *English World-Wide* 1, 11–24.

Flores v. Arizona (2000) Consent order. CIV 92-596. D. Arizona, 1992.

Florez, I.R. (2010) *Do the AZELLA Cut Scores Meet the Standards? A Validation Review of Arizona English Language Learner Assessment.* Los Angeles, CA: Civil Rights Project, University of California–Los Angeles.

Florez, I.R. (2012) Examining the validity of the Arizona English Language Learners Assessment cut scores. *Language Policy* 11, 33–45.

Florio-Ruane, S. (2001) *Teacher Education and the Cultural Imagination.* Mahwah, NJ: Lawrence Erlbaum.

Freeman, R. (2004) *Building On Community Bilingualism.* Philadelphia, PA: Caslon.

Fry, R. (2007) *How Far Behind In Math and Reading Are English Language Learners?* Washington DC: Pew Hispanic Center.

Gándara, P. and Maxwell-Jolly, J. (2006) Critical issues in developing the teacher corps for English learners. In K. Téllez and H. C. Waxman (eds) *Preparing Quality Educators for English Language Learners: Research, Policies, And Practices* (pp. 99–120). Mahwah, NJ: Lawrence Erlbaum.

Gándara, P. and Hopkins, M. (2010) The changing linguistic landscape of the United States. In P. Gándara and M. Hopkins (eds) *Forbidden Language: English Learners and Restrictive Language Policies* (pp. 7–19). New York: Teachers College.

Gándara, P. and Orfield, G. (2012) Segregating Arizona's English learners: A return to the "Mexican room"? *Teachers College Record* 114, 2.

García, E.E. (2011) Ya basta: Challenging restrictions on English language learners. *Dissent* 58, 47–50.

García, E.E., Lawton, K. and De Figueiredo, E.H.D. (2012) The education of English language learners in Arizona: A history of underachievement. *Teachers College Record* 114, 1–18.

García, O. and Menken, K. (2010) Stirring the onion: Educators and the dynamic of language education policies. In K. Menken and O. García (eds) *Negotiating Language Policies in Schools: Educators as Policymakers* (pp. 249–261). New York: Routledge.

García-Nevárez, A.G., Stafford, M.E. and Arias, B. (2005) Arizona elementary teachers' attitudes toward English language learners and use of Spanish in classroom instruction. *Bilingual Research Journal* 29, 295–318.

Gau, R., Palmer, L.B., Melnick, R. and Heffernon, R. (2003) *Is There a Teacher Shortage? Demand and Supply in Arizona.* Tempe, AZ: Morrison Institute for Public Policy.

Gee, J.P. (2002) *Social Linguistics and Literacies: Ideology in Discourses.* Philadelphia, PA: Routledge.

Gee, J.P. (2005) *Introduction to Discourse Analysis: Theory and Method.* London: Routledge.

Genesee, F. (1987) *Learning through Two Languages: Studies of Immersion and Bilingual Education.* Cambridge, MA: Newbury House Publishers.

Goldenberg, C. and Rutherford-Quach, S. (2012) The Arizona home language survey: The under-identification of students for English language services. *Language Policy* 11, 21–30.

González, N., Moll, L.C. and Amanti, C. (2005) *Funds of Knowledge: Theorizing Practices in Households and Classroom.* Mahwah, NJ: Lawrence Erlbaum.

Greenwood Bureau (2014) *History of the Community.*

Grijalva, G. and Jiménez-Silva, M. (2014) Exploring principals' concerns regarding the implementation of Arizona's mandated SEI model. In S.C.K. Moore (ed.) *Language Policy Processes and Consequences: Arizona Case Studies* (pp. 108–132). Bristol: Multilingual Matters.

Haberman, M. (2004) *Teacher Burnout in Black and White.* Houston, TX: The Haberman Educational Foundation.

Hakuta, K., Butler, Y.G. and Witt, D. (2000) *How Long Does It Take English Learners to Attain Proficiency?* Santa Barbara, CA: Linguistic Minority Research Institute.

Hanna, P.L. and Allen, A. (2013) Educator assessment: Accent as a measure of fluency in Arizona. *Educational Policy* 27, 711–738.

Haugen, E. (1972) *Ecology of Language.* Palo Alto, CA: Stanford University Press.

Haver, J. (2013) *English for the Children: Mandated by the People, Skewed by Politicians and Special Interests.* Lanham, MD: Rowman and Littlefield.

Hawkins, E.F., Stancavage, F.B. and Dorsey, J.A. (1998) *School Policies Affecting Instruction in Mathematics.* Washington, D.C.: National Center for Education Statistics.

Haycock, K. (1998) Good teaching matters: How well-qualified teachers can close the gap. *Thinking K-16* 3 (2), 1–8.

Haycock, K. (2011) *Edwatch State Reports: Arizona.* New York: The Education Trust.

Heineke, A.J. (2009) Teachers' discourse on English language learners: Cultural models of language and learning. Unpublished dissertation.

Heineke, A.J. (2014) Dialoging about English learners: Preparing teachers through culturally relevant literature circles. *Action in Teacher Education* 36, 117–140.

Heineke, A.J. (2015) Negotiating language policy and practice: Teachers of English learners in an Arizona study group. *Educational Policy.* Advance online publication. DOI: 10.1177/ 0895904813518101.

Heineke, A.J. and Cameron, Q. (2011) Closing the classroom door and the achievement gap: Teach for America alumni teachers' appropriation of Arizona language policy. *Education and Urban Society* 45, 483–505.

Heineke, A.J., Coleman, E., Ferrell, E. and Kersemeier, C. (2012) Opening doors for bilingual students: Recommendations for building linguistically responsive schools. *Improving Schools* 15, 130–147.

Heineke, A.J. and Cameron, Q. (2013) Teacher preparation and language policy appropriation: A qualitative investigation of Teach for America teachers in Arizona. *Education Policy Analysis Archives* 21, 1–25.

Heineke, A.J., Mazza, B.S. and Tichnor, A. (2014) After the two-year commitment: A quantitative and qualitative inquiry of Teach for America teacher retention and attrition. *Urban Education* 49, 750–782.

Hendley, M. (2014) More John Huppenthal comments surface, including his proposed ban on Spanish. *Phoenix New Times*, 24 June.

Heritage, M., Walqui, A. and Linquanti, R. (2014) *English Language Learners and the New Standards: Developing Language, Content Knowledge, and Analytical Practices in the Classroom*. Cambridge, MA: Harvard Education Press.

Hernández-Chávez, E. (1984) The inadequacy of English immersion education as an educational approach for language minority students in the United States. In California State Department of Education (ed.) *Studies on Immersion Education* (pp. 144–181). Sacramento, CA: California State Department of Education.

Herrera, S. (2010) *Biography-Driven Culturally Responsive Teaching*. New York: Teachers College Press.

Hoffman, D. and Rex, T.R. (2009) *Education Funding in Arizona: Constitutional Requirement and the Empirical Record*. Tempe, AZ: Center for Competitiveness and Prosperity Research.

Hogan, T. (2014) Flores v. Arizona. In S.C.K. Moore (ed.) *Language Policy Processes and Consequences: Arizona Case Studies* (pp. 1–27). Bristol: Multilingual Matters.

Honig, M.I. (2006) Complexity and policy implementation: Challenges and opportunities for the field. In M.I. Honig (ed.) *New Directions in Education Policy Implementation: Confronting Complexity* (pp. 1–24). Albany, NY: State of New York Press.

Hopkins, M. (2012) Arizona's teacher policies and their relationship with English learner instructional practice. *Language Policy* 11, 81–99.

Hopkins, M. and Heineke, A.J. (2013) Teach For America's preparation for English language learners: Shortcomings of the organization's teacher training model. *Critical Education* 4, 18–36.

Hornberger, N.H. (1988) *Bilingual Education and Language Maintenance: A Southern Peruvian Quechua Case*. Berlin: Mouton de Gruyter.

Hornberger, N.H. and Johnson, D.C. (2007) Slicing the onion ethnographically: Layers and spaces in multilingual language education policy and practice. *TESOL Quarterly* 41, 509–532.

House Bill 2064 (2006) 47th legislature, 2nd regular session. Phoenix, AZ.

House Bill 2425 (2013) 51st legislature, 1st regular session. Phoenix, AZ.

Hudelson, S. (1987) The role of native language literacy in the education of language minority children. *Language Arts* 64, 827–841.

Hunt, J.B. and Carroll, T.G. (2003) *No Dream Denied: A Pledge to America's Children*. Washington, DC: National Commission on Teaching and America's Future.

Iddings, A.C.D., Combs, M.C. and Moll, L. (2012) In the arid zone: Drying out educational resources for English language learners through policy and practice. *Urban Education* 47, 495–514.

Jackson Elementary School District (2014a) District snapshot.

Jackson Elementary School District (2014b) Home languages.

Jackson Elementary School District (2014c) SEI program descriptions.

Jackson Elementary School District (2014d) Compliance quick check.

Jackson Elementary School District (2014e) Weekly planning template.

Jackson Elementary School District (2014f) ELL Department duties and responsibilities.

Jackson Elementary School District (2014g) ELD course description.

Jackson Elementary School District (2014h) ILLP compliance monitoring.

Jiménez, R.T., García, G.E. and Pearson, P.D. (1996) The reading strategies of bilingual Latina/o students who are successful English readers: Opportunities and obstacles. *Reading Research Quarterly* 21, 90–112.

Jiménez-Castellanos, O., Combs, M.C., Martínez, D. and Gómez, L. (2013) *English Language Learners: What's at Stake For Arizona?* Phoenix, AZ: Morrison Institute for Public Policy.

Johnson, E.J. (2012) Arbitrating repression: Language policy and education in Arizona. *Language and Education* 26, 53–76.

Johnson, E. (2005) Proposition 203: A critical metaphor analysis. *Bilingual Research Journal* 29, 69–84.

Johnson, D.C. (2013) *Language Policy*. London: Palgrave MacMillan.

Johnson, D.C. and Freeman, R. (2010) Appropriating language policy on the local level: Working the spaces for bilingual education. In K. Menken and O. García (eds) *Negotiating Language Policies in Schools: Educators as Policymakers* (pp. 13–31). New York: Routledge.

Johnson, R.K. and Swain, M. (1997) *Immersion Education: International Perspectives*. New York: Cambridge University Press.

Jordan, M. (2010) Arizona grades teachers on fluency. *The Wall Street Journal*, 30 April.

Kohut, A., Keeter, S., Doherty, C., Suro, R. and Escobar, G. (2006) *America's Immigration Quandary*. Washington, DC: Pew Research Center for the People and the Press and Pew Hispanic Center.

Krashen, S. (1999) Sheltered subject matters teaching. *Cross Currents* 18, 183–188.

Krashen, S. (2001) Are children ready for the mainstream after one year of Structured English Immersion? See http://www.school.vis.ac.at/esl/.../11%20Krashen_Unz%201%20year%20Eng.doc (accessed 2 September 2009).

Krashen, S. (2004) Did immersion triumph in Arizona? See http://www.sdkrashen.com/content/articles/arizona.pdf (accessed 2 September 2009).

Krashen, S., Rolstad, K. and MacSwan, J. (2007) *Review of 'Research Summary and Bibliography for Structured English Immersion Programs' of the Arizona English Language Learners Task Force*. Takoma Park, MD: Institute for Language Education and Policy.

Krashen, S., MacSwan, J. and Rolstad, K. (2012) Review of 'Research summary and bibliography for Structure English Immersion programs' of the Arizona English language learners task force. In M.B. Arias and C. Faltis (eds) *Implementing Educational Language Policy in Arizona: Legal, Historical and Current Practices in Structured English Immersion* (pp. 107–120). Bristol: Multilingual Matters.

Language Policy (2012). See http://link.springer.com/journal/10993/11/1/page/1.

Lapkin, S. (1998) *French Second Language Education in Canada: Empirical Studies*. Toronto: University of Toronto Press.

Lau v. Nichols (1974) 414 U.S. 563.

Lawton, S.B. (2012) State education policy formation: The case of Arizona's English language learner legislation. *American Journal of Education* 118, 455–487.

Leckie, A.G., Kaplan, S.E. and Rubinstein-Avila, E. (2013) The need for speed: A critical discourse analysis of the reclassification of English language learners in Arizona. *Language Policy* 12, 159–176.

Leeman, J. (2012) Illegal accents: Qualifications, discrimination, and distraction in Arizona's monitoring of teachers. In O. Santa Ana and C. González de Bustamante (eds) *Arizona Firestorm: Global Immigration Realities, National Media, and Provincial Politics* (pp. 145–166). New York: Rowman & Littlefield.

Leland, C.H. and Murtadha, K. (2011) Cultural discourse on the frontline: Preparing and retaining urban teachers. *Urban Education* 46 (5), 895–912.

Levinson, B.A.U. and Sutton, M. (2001) Introduction: Policy as/in practice – A sociocultural approach to the study of educational policy. In M. Sutton (ed.) *Policy as Practice: Toward a Comparative Sociocultural Analysis of Educational Policy* (pp. 1–22). Westport, CT: Ablex.

Lillie, K.E., Markos, A., Arias, M.B. and Wiley, T.G. (2012) Separate and not equal: The implementation of structured English immersion in Arizona's classroom. *Teachers College Record* 114, 1–33.

Lillie, K.E. and Markos, A. (2014) The four-hour block: SEI in classrooms. In S.C.K. Moore (ed.) *Language Policy Processes and Consequences: Arizona Case Studies* (pp. 133–155). Bristol: Multilingual Matters.

Lillie, K.E. and Moore, S.C.K. (2014) SEI in Arizona: Bastion for states' rights. In S.C.K. Moore (ed.) *Language Policy Processes and Consequences: Arizona Case Studies* (pp. 1–27). Bristol: Multilingual Matters.

Linquanti, R. and Cook, H.G. (2013) *Toward a Common Definition of English Learner: A Brief Defining Policy and Technical Issues and Opportunities for State Assessment Consortia.* Washington, DC: Council of Chief State School Officers.

Little, J.W. (2002) Locating learning in teachers' communities of practice: Opening up problems of analysis in records of everyday work. *Teaching and Teacher Education* 18, 917–946.

Long, M.H. and Adamson, H.D. (2012) SLA research and Arizona's Structured English Immersion policies. In M.B. Arias and C. Faltis (eds) *Implementing Educational Language Policy in Arizona: Legal, Historical and Current Practices in Structured English Immersion* (pp. 39–57). Bristol: Multilingual Matters.

Longo, A. (2014) AZ schools superintendent outed as anonymous blogger. *Phoenix NBC News,* 18 June.

Lucas, T., Villegas, A.M. and Freedson-González, M. (2008) Linguistically responsive teacher education: Preparing classroom teachers to teach English language learners. *Journal of Teacher Education* 59, 361–373.

Mackey, A. (2007) *Conversational Interaction in Second Language Acquisition: A Series of Empirical Studies.* Oxford: Oxford University Press.

Mackinney, E. and Rios-Aguilar, C. (2012) Negotiating between restrictive language policies and complex teaching conditions: A case study of Arizona's teachers of English learners. *Bilingual Research Journal* 35, 350–367.

MacSwan, J. (2004) Bad data poison language study. *Arizona Republic,* 13 August.

Mahoney, K., Thompson, M. and MacSwan, J. (2004) The condition of English Language Learners in Arizona, 2004. In A. Molnar (ed.) *The Condition of PreK-12 Education in Arizona, 2004* (pp. 1–27). Tempe, AZ: Education Policy Research Laboratory, Arizona State University.

Mahoney, K., MacSwan, J. and Thompson, M. (2005) The condition of English Language Learners in Arizona, 2005. In D. García and A. Molnar (eds) *The Condition of PreK-12 Education in Arizona, 2005* (pp. 1–24). Tempe, AZ: Education Policy Research Laboratory, Arizona State University.

Mahoney, K., MacSwan, J., Haladyna, T. and García, D. (2010) Castañeda's third prong: Evaluating the achievement of Arizona's English learners under restrictive language policy. In P. Gándara and M. Hopkins (eds) *Forbidden Language: English Learners and Restrictive Language Policies* (pp. 50–64). New York: Teachers College.

Markos, A. and Arias, M.B. (2014) (Mis)aligned curricula: The case of new course content. In S.C.K. Moore (ed.) *Language Policy Processes and Consequences: Arizona Case Studies* (pp. 89–107). Bristol: Multilingual Matters.

Martínez-Roldán, C. and Heineke, A.J. (2011) Latino literature mediating teacher learning. *Journal of Latinos and Education* 10, 245–260.

Martínez-Wenzl, M., Pérez, K. and Gándara, P. (2012) Is Arizona's approach to educating its ELs superior to other forms of instruction? *Teachers College Record* 114 (9), 7.

McCarty, T. (2002) *A Place to be Navajo: Rough Rock and the Struggle for Self-Determination in Indigenous Schooling.* Mahwah, NJ: Lawrence Erlbaum.

McCarty, T. (2011) *Ethnography and Language Policy.* New York: Routledge.

McLaughlin, M. and Talbert, J.E. (2006) *Building School-Based Teacher Learning Communities: Professional Strategies to Improve Student Achievement.* New York: Teachers College Press.

Meece, J.L. and Kurtz-Costes, B. (2001) Introduction: The schooling of ethnic minority children and youth. *Educational Psychologist* 36, 1–7.

Mehta, J. (2013) *The Allure of Order: High Hopes, Dashed Expectations, and the Troubled Quest to Remake American Schooling.* New York: Oxford.

Menken, K. (2008) *English Learners Left Behind: Standardized Testing as Language Policy.* Clevedon: Multilingual Matters.

Menken, K. and García, O. (2010) Introduction. In K. Menken and O. García (eds) *Negotiating Language Policies in Schools: Educators as Policymakers* (pp. 1–10). New York: Routledge.

Milem, J.F., Bryan, W.P., Sesate, D.B. and Montaño, S. (2013) *Arizona Minority Student Progress Report: Arizona in Transformation.* Tucson, AZ: Arizona Minority Education Policy Analysis Center.

Mishler, E.G. (1986) *Research Interviewing: Context and Narrative.* Cambridge, MA: Harvard University Press.

Mitchell, D.E. (2011) The surprising history of education policy 1950 to 2010. In D.E. Mitchell, R.L. Crowson and D. Shipps (eds) *Shaping Education Policy: Power and Processes* (pp. 3–22). New York: Routledge.

Moll, L. (1990) *Vygotsky and Education: Instructional Implications and Applications of Socio-Historical Psychology.* New York: Cambridge University Press.

Moll, L.C., Amanti, C., Neff, D. and González, N. (1992) Funds of knowledge for teaching: Using a qualitative approach to connect homes and classrooms. *Theory into Practice* 31, 132–141.

Moll, L.C. and González, N. (1997) Teachers as social scientists: Learning about culture from household research. In P. Hall (ed.) *Race, Ethnicity, and Multiculturalism: Volume 1.* (pp. 89–114). New York: Garland.

Monroe-Baillargeon, A. and Shema, A.L. (2010) Time to talk: An urban school's use of literature circles to create a professional learning community. *Education and Urban Society* 42, 651–673.

Moore, S.C.K. (2012) 'They're just confused': SEI as policy into practice. In M.B. Arias and C. Faltis (eds) *Implementing Educational Language Policy in Arizona: Legal, Historical and Current Practices in Structured English Immersion* (pp. 121–141). Bristol: Multilingual Matters.

Moore, S.C.K. (2014) Ensuring oversight: Statewide SEI teacher professional development. In S.C.K. Moore (ed.) *Language Policy Processes and Consequences: Arizona Case Studies* (pp. 73–88). Bristol: Multilingual Matters.

Murrell, P.C. (2007) *Race, Culture, and Schooling: Identities of Achievement in Multicultural Urban Schools.* New York: Lawrence Erlbaum.

Murri, N.J., Markos, A. and Estrella-Silva, A. (2012) Implementing structured English immersion in teacher preparation in Arizona. In M. Beatriz Arias and C. Faltis (eds) *Implementing Educational Language Policy in Arizona: Legal, Historical and Current Practices in SEI* (pp. 142–163). Bristol: Multilingual Matters.

Musanti, S.I. and Pence, L. (2010) Collaboration and teacher development: Unpacking resistance, constructing knowledge, and navigating identities. *Teacher Education Quarterly* 37, 73–89.

National Center for Education Statistics (2015) 2015 mathematics and reading assessments: National results overview. See http://www.nationsreportcard.gov/reading_math_2015/#reading (accessed 7 January 2016).

National Clearinghouse for English Language Acquisition (2010) *The Growing Number of English Learner Students 1998/99–2008/09.* Washington, DC: Author.

National Conference of State Legislatures (2005) *Arizona English Language Learner Cost Study.* Denver, CO: Author.

NCLB (2001) *No Child Left Behind Act.* Pub. L. No. 107–110.

Office of Civil Rights (2009) Resolution agreement with Arizona Department of Education, Case Number 08094026.

Office of Civil Rights (2012) Resolution agreement with Arizona Department of Education, Case Number 08064006.

Orozco, R.A. (2012) Racism and power: Arizona politicians' use of the discourse of anti-Americanism against Mexican American studies. *Hispanic Journal of Behavioral Sciences* 34, 43–60.

Pennycook, A. (2000) Language, ideology and hindsight: Lessons from colonial language policies. In T.K. Ricento (ed.) *Ideology, Politics, and Language Policies: Focus on English* (pp. 49–66). Philadelphia, PA: John Benjamins.

Pickering, R.L. (1966) *Some Significant Events in the History of Arizona Education*. Phoenix, AZ: Designing Education for the Future.

Porter, A., McMaken, J., Hwang, J. and Yang, R. (2011). Common Core Standards: The new U.S. intended curriculum. *Educational Researcher*, 40, 103–116.

Ramírez, J.D., Yuen, S.D. and Ramey, D.R. (1991) *Longitudinal Study of Structured English Immersion Strategy, Early-Exit and Late-Exit Transitional Bilingual Education Programs for Language-Minority Children*. San Mateo, CA: Aguirre International.

Ricento, T.K. (2000) Ideology, politics and language policies: Introduction. In T.K. Ricento (ed.) *Ideology, Politics, and Language Policies: Focus on English* (pp. 1–8). Philadelphia, PA: John Benjamins.

Ricento, T.K. and Hornberger, N.H. (1996) Unpeeling the onion: Language planning and policy and the ELT professional. *TESOL Quarterly* 30, 401–427.

Rios-Aguilar, C., González-Canche, M.S. and Moll, L.C. (2012a) A study of Arizona's teachers of English language learners. Education in Arizona. *Teachers College Record* 114, 1–33.

Rios-Aguilar, C., González-Canche, M.S. and Sabetghadam, S. (2012b) Evaluating the impact of restrictive language policies: The Arizona 4-hour English language development block. *Education Language Policy* 11, 47–80.

Rogoff, B. (1994) Developing understanding of the idea of communities of learners. *Mind, Culture, and Activity* 1, 209–229.

Rogoff, B. (1995). Observing sociocultural activity on three planes: Participatory appropriation, guided participation, and apprenticeship. In P. M. J. Goodnow and F. Kessel (eds) *Sociocultural studies of mind* (pp. 139–164). Cambridge: Cambridge University Press.

Rogoff, B. (2003) *The Cultural Nature of Human Development*. New York: Oxford University Press.

Rodgers, R. and Mosely, M. (2008) A critical discourse analysis of racial literacy in teacher education. *Linguistics and Education* 19, 107–131.

Rolstad, K., Mahoney, K.S. and Glass, G.V. (2005) Weighing the evidence: A meta-analysis of bilingual education in Arizona. *Bilingual Research Journal* 29, 43–67.

Ruiz, R. (1984) Orientations in language planning. *National Association of Bilingual Education Journal* 8, 15–34.

Rumberger, R.W. and Tran, L. (2010) State language policies, school language practices, and the English learner achievement gap. In P. Gándara and M. Hopkins (eds) *Forbidden Language: English Learners and Restrictive Language Policies* (pp. 86–101). New York: Teachers College.

Sacken, D.M. and Medina, J.M. (1990) Investigating the context of state-level policy formation: A case study of Arizona's bilingual education legislation. *Educational Evaluation and Policy Analysis* 12, 389–402.

Sanders, W.L. and Rivers, J.C. (1996) *Cumulative and Residual Effects of Teachers on Future Student Academic Achievement*. Knoxville, TN: University of Tennessee Value-Added Research and Assessment Center.

Sandoval, C. and Tambini, C. (2014) *The State of Arizona.* Independent Television Service. See http://www.pbs.org/independentlens/films/state-of-arizona/

Schmidt, R. (1998) The politics of language in Canada and the United States: Exploring the differences. In T. Ricento and B. Burnaby (eds) *Language and Politics in the United States and Canada: Myths and Realities* (pp. 37–70). Mahwah, NJ: Lawrence Erlbaum.

Schmidt, R. (2000) *Language Policy and Identity Politics in The United States.* Philadelphia, PA: Temple University Press.

Seidman, I. (2006) *Interviewing as Qualitative Research: A Guide for Researchers in Education and the Social Sciences.* New York: Teachers College Press.

Senate Bill 1070 (2010) 49th legislature, 2nd regular session. Phoenix, AZ.

Senate Bill 1172 (2015) 52nd legislature, 1st regular session. Phoenix, AZ.

Sheridan, T.E. (1986) *Los Tucsonenses: The Mexican Community in Tucson, 1854–1941.* Tucson, AZ: University of Arizona Press.

Shin, H.B. and Kominski, R.A. (2010) *Language Use in the United States: 2007,* American Community Survey Reports, ACS-12. US Census Bureau, Washington, DC.

Shohamy, E. (2006) *Language Policy: Hidden Agendas and New Approaches.* London: Routledge.

Shulman, L. (1986) Those who understand: Knowledge growth in teaching. *Educational Researcher* 15, 4–14.

Spolsky, B. (2004) *Language Policy.* New York: Cambridge.

Spolsky, B. (2007) Towards a theory of language policy. *Working Papers in Educational Linguistics* 22 (1), 1–14.

State of Arizona (2014, 8 December). Approved refinements to the SEI models. See http://www.azed.gov/english-language-learners/files/2015/01/approved-refinements-to-the-sei-models.pdf (accessed 29 September 2015).

Strauss, V. (2015) Why teachers are fleeing Arizona in droves. *The Washington Post,* 19 June.

Suárez-Orozco, M.M. and Suárez-Orozco, C. (2001) *Interdisciplinary Perspectives on the New Immigration.* New York: Routledge.

Teach for All (2015) *Our Approach.* See http://teachforall.org/en/our-approach (retrieved on 16 September 2015).

Teach for America (2014a) Our mission. See http://www.teachforamerica.org/our-mission (accessed 7 October 2014).

Teach for America (2014b) Where we work. See http://www.teachforamerica.org/where-we-work (accessed 7 October 2014).

Teachers College Record (2012) See https://www.tcrecord.org/library/Issue.asp?volyear=2012&number=9&volume=114.

Tharp, R.G. (1997) From at-risk to excellence: Research, theory, and principles for practice. Santa Cruz, CA: University of California at Santa Cruz, Center for Research on Education, Diversity, and Excellence. See http://www.cal.org/crede/pubs/research/rr1.htm (accessed 16 February 2007).

United States Census Bureau (2010) *Full Profile of Community Demographics: 2009 Estimates with 2014 Projections.* Chandler, AZ: Author.

United States Department of Education (2010) *The Condition of Education 2010* (National Center for Education Statistics 2010–028).

Ushomirsky, N. (2013) *Uneven at the Start: Differences in State Track Records Foreshadow Challenges And Opportunities For Common Core.* New York: The Education Trust.

Valdés, G., Bunch, G., Snow, C., Lee, C. and Matos, L. (2005) Enhancing the development of students' language. In L. Darling-Hammond and J. Bransford (eds) *Preparing Teachers for a Changing World: What Teachers Should Learn and Be Able To Do* (pp. 126–168). San Francisco, CA: Jossey-Bass.

Valdéz, E.O. (2001) Winning the battle, losing the war: Bilingual teachers and post-Proposition 227. *The Urban Review* 33, 237–253.

VanLier, L. and Walqui, A. (2012) Language and the Common Core State Standards. *Understanding Language: Language, Literacy, and Learning in The Content Areas.* Palo Alto, CA: Stanford University. See http://ell.stanford.edu/sites/default/files/pdf/academic-papers/04-Van%20Lier%20Walqui%20Language%20and%20CCSS%20FINAL.pdf

Villegas, A.M. and Lucas, T. (2002) Preparing culturally responsive teachers: Rethinking the curriculum. *Journal of Teacher Education* 53, 20–32.

Vygotsky, L.S. (1978) *Mind in Society: The Development of Higher Psychological Processes.* Cambridge, MA: Harvard University Press.

Walqui, A. and Heritage, M. (2012) Instruction for diverse groups of English language learners. *Understanding Language: Language, Literacy, and Learning in the Content Areas.* Palo Alto, CA: Stanford University. See http://ell.stanford.edu/sites/default/files/pdf/academic-papers/09-Walqui%20Heritage%20Instruction%20for%20Diverse%20Groups%20FINAL_0.pdf

Wertsch, J.V. (1991) *Voices of the Mind: A Sociocultural Approach to Mediated Action.* Cambridge, MA: Harvard University Press.

Wiley, T. (2012) Forward: From restrictive SEI to imagining better. In M.B. Arias and C. Faltis (eds) *Implementing Educational Language Policy in Arizona: Legal, Historical And Current Practices in Structured English Immersion* (pp. xiii–xxii). Bristol: Multilingual Matters.

Wiley, T. and Wright, W.E. (2004) Against the undertow: Language-minority education policy and politics in the 'age of accountability.' *Educational Policy* 18, 142–168.

Wright, W.E. (2005a) The political spectacle of Arizona's Proposition 203. *Educational Policy* 19, 662–700.

Wright, W.E. (2005b) English language learners left behind in Arizona: The nullification of accommodations in the intersection of federal and state language and assessment policies. *Bilingual Research Journal* 29, 1–30.

Wright, W.E. (2005c) *Evolution of Federal Policy and Implications of No Child Left Behind for Language Minority Students.* Tempe, AZ: Language Policy Research Unit.

Wright, W.E. (2014) Proposition 203 and Arizona's early school reform efforts: The nullification of accommodations. In S.C.K. Moore (ed.) *Language Policy Processes and Consequences: Arizona Case Studies* (pp. 45–72). Bristol: Multilingual Matters.

Wright, W.E. and Choi, D. (2006) The impact of language and high-stakes testing policies on elementary school English language learners in Arizona. *Education Policy Analysis Archives* 14, 1–17.

Wrigley, T. (2000) *The Power to Learn: Stories of Success in the Education of Asian and Other Bilingual Pupils.* Stoke on Trent: Trentham Books.

Zamora, P. (2007) Impact of No Child Left Behind on English language learners. Testimony before the House Education and Labor Committee, Early Childhood, Elementary and Secondary Education Subcommittee. Washington, DC. See http://www.spannj.org/032307PeterZamoratestimony.pdf (accessed 9 September 2014).

Zehr, M.A. (2010) Arizona ed officials weigh in on teachers' fluency issues. *Education Week,* 26 May.

Index

social closure 185–186
social studies 75, 89, 105–106, 160, 173
social-emotional 46–47, 95, 103, 129, 137, 199
sociocultural theory 8–12, 67, 87, 101–102, 206
Somali 79, 155, 169
Spanish 11–12, 21–23, 36, 70, 72, 84, 93–95, 102, 113, 116–120, 127, 135, 147, 155–156, 161, 209
Speaker of the House 31, 138, 181
special education 20, 27, 76–79, 82, 88, 133, 170, 188
standardized tests 3–4, 7, 13, 39–43, 63, 75, 81, 92–93, 118, 126, 141, 150, 154, 169–170, 189, 203–205
State Board of Education 17, 31, 35, 53–56, 109, 157, 164–165, 175, 184, 196, 198
State House of Representatives 17, 32, 138–140, 152–153, 171, 174
State Senate 17, 32, 138–140, 145, 152–153, 171, 174
State Superintendent of Public Instruction 16–18, 31–32, 39, 42, 110–111, 152, 181, 196
stigmatization 46, 51, 73, 79, 88, 169, 196, 199
strategic function 183
Structured English Immersion 7, 26–30, 121–125
submersion 7, 13, 27, 29, 53, 63, 121–122, 132, 174, 179
Supreme Court 34, 52, 141

Teach for All 185
Teach for America 58, 71–72, 75–79, 81–82, 85–88, 93, 97, 136, 141, 170–172, 185–189, 196
teacher certification 20–23, 29, 56, 70–71, 134–136, 154, 179, 184–187

teacher educator 54–55, 112–113, 131–136, 174, 186–189, 205, 207
teacher evaluation 93, 100–101, 173, 204, 207
teacher preparation 19–21, 53–58, 95–97, 112–113, 132–136, 154, 160, 179, 185–188, 203–206
teacher professionalism 184–190, 194–195, 203
teacher retention 99–101, 140, 173, 207
teacher shortage 20–21, 97, 196
territorial history 16–20, 31, 35, 110, 177
time-on-task principle 33, 48–50, 179, 182
Title III 24
Title VII 22
top-down policy 7, 9–12, 29, 52, 171, 175–176, 184–185, 190, 192, 194–195, 199, 203, 207
Treaty of Guadalupe Hidalgo 67
tribal communities 4, 145–146, 150
Tucson 20, 35

unintended consequences 14, 193
universities 17, 20–23, 32–33, 53–55, 60–61, 75, 77, 86, 88, 109, 111–116, 121–122, 134–136, 154, 170–171, 174, 186–188, 200
University of Arizona 20, 32
University of Phoenix 20, 186
Unz, Ron 7, 24–25, 179, 191

vantage points 177, 190–193, 209
vertical case study 59–64, 212
Vietnamese 70, 72, 169

waivers 26–27, 29, 161–162
workforce development 86, 140–144, 147

Yuma 20